Life in the Trinity

AN INTRODUCTION TO THEOLOGY WITH
THE HELP OF THE CHURCH FATHERS

Donald Fairbairn

For Harold & Darlene,
with thanks for your
friendship and the prayer
that this book will be
a blessing to you.

Don Fairbairn

Oct. 27, 2009

IVP Academic

An imprint of InterVarsity Press
Downers Grove, Illinois

InterVarsity Press
P.O. Box 1400, Downers Grove, IL 60515-1426
World Wide Web: www.ivpress.com
E-mail: email@ivpress.com

InterVarsity Press® is the book-publishing division of InterVarsity Christian Fellowship/USA®, a movement of students and faculty active on campus at hundreds of universities, colleges and schools of nursing in the United States of America, and a member movement of the International Fellowship of Evangelical Students. For information about local and regional activities, write Public Relations Dept., InterVarsity Christian Fellowship/USA, 6400 Schroeder Rd., P.O. Box 7895, Madison, WI 53707-7895, or visit the IVCF website at <www.intervarsity.org>.

Design: Cindy Kipple

Images: Trinity of Uglic, Russian Icon by Andrei Rublev at Ruliev Museum, Moscow, Russia. Scala/Art Resource, NY
 Saints Paraskeve, Gregory the Theologian, John Chrysostom and Basil the Great at the Tretyakov Gallery, Moscow, Russia. HIP/Art Resource, NY

ISBN 978-0-8308-3873-8

Printed in the United States of America ∞

Library of Congress Cataloging-in-Publication Data

Fairbairn, Donald.
 Life in the Trinity: an introduction to theology wih the help of
 the church fathers/ Donald Fairbairn.
   p. cm.
 Includes bibliographical references and index.
 ISBN 978-0-8308-3873-8 (pbk.: alk. paper)
 1. Trinity—History of doctrines—Early Church, ca. 30-600. I.
 Title.
 BT109.F35 2009
 230—dc22

                                                                      2009026597

P	19	18	17	16	15	14	13	12	11	10	9	8	7	6	5	4	3	2	1
Y	24	23	22	21	20	19	18	17	16	15	14	13	12	11	10	09				

To my beloved Jennifer

John 15:9

Contents

Preface

This book seeks to integrate the various truths of Christianity around a single theme that has been articulated clearly by some of the greatest theologians of the early church but that has often been underemphasized in modern Western theology books. This theme is the relationship between God the Father and God the Son, a relationship in which believers share as we are united to God by the Holy Spirit. The conviction of many of the church fathers[1] was that all of Christian life was meant to be a reflection of and a participation in that central relationship between the Father and the Son.

This book is designed as a textbook for courses in Christian theology, and I envision four major situations in which it can be most useful. First, for introductory-level, one-semester theology courses, this book can serve as a standalone textbook, or perhaps as the main textbook with a few other sources (ancient and modern) assigned for supplemental reading. Second, it can be useful for pastors, general Christian readers and lay study groups. Third, for more advanced, multisemester theology courses,

---

[1]The phrase "church fathers" refers to the Christians during the first several centuries after the end of the New Testament who profoundly shaped the church's interpretation of Scripture and its understanding of its theological and spiritual life. The period of the church fathers is called the "early church" or the "patristic" period (from the Latin word for "father"), and it is often considered to have extended from about 100 to 800.

this book can serve as a supplement to longer, more comprehensive theology books and can provide a perspective that such books may lack. And fourth, for courses in historical theology, this book can give an overall framework that should make primary sources from the early church more comprehensible. In order to make the book useful for these different audiences, I have arranged it with three levels of material, and I would like to explain this arrangement briefly.

For the benefit of pastors, general readers and students who have little background in formal theology, I have sought to keep the main argument in the text uncluttered by nonbiblical quotations, references to modern theological debates, and other similarly technical material. My argument throughout the book is based on my analysis of crucial biblical passages, especially from the Gospel of John, which occupies a vital place in the New Testament but which has been perhaps slightly underused in Protestant theological study because of Protestantism's profound focus on Paul's writings. We will read John's Gospel and the rest of Scripture as I have learned to read them from the church fathers, paying attention to the passages to which they have directed my attention. But in the text of the book itself, we will listen primarily to the biblical writers, not to later theologians commenting on Scripture.

In addition to the text, the book contains sidebars that offer brief quotations from the church fathers themselves. There is a fair bit of variety in the writings of the early church, but amid this variety, there is one strand of thought that I believe to be particularly biblical and fruitful. Of the church fathers who exemplify this strand of thought, there are four on whom I will focus the most. These are Irenaeus of Lyons (a second-century Greek speaker who lived in what is today southern France), Athanasius of Alexandria (a fourth-century Egyptian who ministered in Greek and Coptic), Augustine of Hippo (a Latin speaker who lived in North Africa in the fourth and fifth centuries) and Cyril of Alexandria (a Greek speaker who followed in Athanasius's footsteps in Egypt during the early fifth century). Accordingly, in the sidebars, I quote these theologians often and a number of others less frequently, thus enabling readers to gain some exposure to the way patristic writers expressed their ideas. There is also an appendix giving guidance for those who wish to read further in the writings of these four church fathers.

In keeping with the relatively nontechnical nature of the book, it contains few footnotes, and the footnotes that are included offer further biblical citations related to the ideas of the text or explain patristic treatments of those ideas. The footnotes do not compare the church fathers' ideas with today's theological debates or with current interpretations of the passages I am considering. Modern commentaries and theological textbooks are readily accessible and usually easy to navigate, so students and other readers who are interested in comparing patristic and modern interpretation should be able to find appropriate modern discussions of the issues without any guidance from me. Although the notes do not direct readers to those modern sources, comparing patristic and modern ideas can be quite fruitful for theological study. Teachers may wish to use this book and its notes as a jumping-off point by assigning students to compare what the church fathers write about particular topics with the way modern scholars articulate the same ideas, or how patristic and modern commentators interpret the same biblical passages.

The presentation of the material in three levels—text, sidebars and footnotes—is designed to keep the book as uncluttered as possible and make its main ideas accessible to all, while also giving students and other interested readers some additional material to consider. People with no prior knowledge of the early church should be able to understand and follow the argument of this book using only the text and a Bible to look up the passages discussed in the text. I hope that this relative simplicity will commend the book for use in introductory theology classes and even lay studies.

However, the very simplicity and brevity that make a book like this useful for beginning theologians might seem to make it superfluous for more advanced students. After all, if students are going to read a thick volume like Millard Erickson's *Christian Theology,* Wayne Grudem's *Systematic Theology* or Alister McGrath's *Christian Theology: An Introduction* (or even a multivolume work like Thomas Oden's *Systematic Theology* or Donald Bloesch's Christian Foundations), it might seem that a short book like this one would have little or nothing new to offer. However, I believe this book can complement more comprehensive theology textbooks in three important ways and thus can benefit more advanced students and the professors who teach them.

First, this book can enable readers to see the whole forest, not just a succession of individual trees. The more comprehensive and detailed a textbook is, the harder it is for readers to see how the many topics fit together. In spite of the intentions of the author, the reader of such a comprehensive book might be left with the impression that theology is a set of facts whose connection to each other and to ordinary Christian life is indecipherable. A very comprehensive book might leave students thinking only in terms of doctrines—individual teachings of the faith—when in fact one is supposed to recognize doctrine (singular), the unified teaching of Christianity. Because of this pitfall associated with longer systematic theology textbooks, there is also a need for books of more modest length that, because they do not go into as many details, are able to give readers a clearer picture of Christian doctrine as a whole. This is intended to be one such book, and as such, it can be valuable even to students who are already reading the longer theology textbooks.

A second way in which this book can complement more comprehensive Western systematic theology textbooks is that it listens to a different set of voices than those books usually do. This book will interact with Scripture and with the ways the early church understood it, without much reference to the way more recent Christian theologians have understood it.[2] Such lack of interaction with contemporary discussions is a weakness in some ways, but it may be a strength as well. Omitting direct references to current discussions can enable us to attend to voices from the early church. We need to hear those voices precisely because they are different from our own: they do not merely reinforce what we already think the Bible means but rather challenge

---

[2]I am by academic training a historical theologian, and particularly a specialist in the fourth through sixth centuries. My research does not ordinarily involve interaction with contemporary theological discussions. Instead, I speak to those contemporary discussions from the thought world of the early church.

us with another way of understanding it and with a different conception of what its central message is, of what lies at the heart of the Christian faith. I do not believe that these new voices contradict our own articulation of the faith, but rather they can complement our understanding of Scripture and make it more complete.

A third way this book can complement a longer, more comprehensive theology textbook is that it uses a different set of integrative themes than is typical in Western theology. If the sheer number of theological topics discussed in a comprehensive textbook can make it hard for the reader to see the forest through the trees, then it is obviously important for any textbook to help readers see the whole forest clearly by articulating a small number of themes around which it organizes the rest of the topics. These themes then become the scarlet thread that enables one to navigate the labyrinth of Christian theology and to hold the various truths of the faith together. For evangelical theologians, the integrating themes are usually the classic distinctives of the Reformation such as *sola Scriptura* (the Bible alone as the authority), *sola Christo* (salvation through Christ alone) and *sola fide* (justification by faith alone).

I fully affirm these and other Reformation distinctives, but nevertheless, this book does not use these as its integrating themes. I am convinced that we need to understand these Reformation ideas as part of a broader context of scriptural teaching, a context that we often underemphasize or even omit. To give an obvious example, the centerpiece of many evangelical systematic theologies is the doctrine of justification by faith. This is without a doubt one of the crucial truths of our faith, but is justification the very center of Christian faith, the be-all and end-all of theology? To answer this question affirmatively would be to imply that the heart of God's relation to humanity has to do with status, with whether a person is credited as being righteous or credited as being a sinner and thus under God's wrath. But if this were the very heart of God's relation to people, then what would we gain from being in right status before God? What would we be placed into such a status for? If one answers, "for heaven," then what is heaven? If one answers, "for a relationship with God," then what does such a relationship involve? These questions show that as crucial as justification is, it is not the heart of Christianity, but rather, it is a prerequisite and a means to something even more central. We are not justified just to be justified; we are justified in order to enjoy something else.

That "something else" has been best expressed (I believe) not by contemporary evangelicalism or even by the Reformers but by the church fathers. During the several centuries after the end of the New Testament, the church was able, through exhaustive study of Scripture and often excruciating discussion, to articulate the great doctrines of the Trinity and the person of Christ. And in articulating these doctrines, the church also expressed a unified vision of Christian life, an understanding of the "something else" in which we participate once we are justified. The Fathers expressed this "something else" by using the Greek word *theōsis* (a word that I will leave untranslated for now and will explain in some detail in chapter 1 of this book). The idea of *theōsis* has several different aspects to it, but I will argue that the primary aspect—at least in the thought of many church fathers—is that Christians share in the Son's relationship to the Father. This will be the integrating theme for this book, the scarlet thread that I will used to weave the tapestry of Christian doctrine as a unified whole. I hope that this atypical integrative theme will help readers to see and grasp that unified whole in a new way.

Therefore this book is not meant as a comprehensive systematic theology textbook arranged according to the traditional Western topics (called *loci*) of theology, emphasizing the classic distinctives of the Reformation, and written in dialogue with other theological books of a similar vein. It is by no means meant to supplant such books or to denigrate their value. Rather, it is meant to supplement them and perhaps to help students understand them more easily. It seeks to call evangelical readers back to an aspect of the Christian faith that I believe is even more central than, and indeed foundational to, our evangelical emphases on conversion, justification and a personal relationship with Christ. This aspect is the Son's relationship to the Father. Because of these ways in which this book can complement longer, more traditional Western theology textbooks, I believe it is valuable for students taking advanced theology courses in which they are required to read more comprehensive books.

Thus this is a book that I hope will prove useful to students and teachers, to beginners and more advanced theologians, to the academy and the church. I hope it succeeds in calling our attention to the church fathers' interpretations of the book they cherished and exalted above all others, the Bible. Most of all, I pray that this book may help to point us anew to the relationship that many church fathers recognized lies at the heart of the Bible and thus at the heart of Christian faith—the relationship between the Father and the Son.

Donald Fairbairn
Erskine Theological Seminary
Due West, South Carolina

Solis personis trinitatis gloria

Acknowledgments

I would like to thank some of the many people who have contributed to the writing of this book. First, my wife, Jennifer, and our children, Trey and Ella. From nearly the beginning of our acquaintance, Jennifer and I have regarded John 15:9 as a theme verse for our relationship, and in our marriage and our family we have sought to embody and reflect the love between the Father and the Son that lies at the heart of the Christian faith.

I would like to thank my students throughout Europe and North America, but especially at Donetsk Christian University (Ukraine), Evangelical Theological Faculty (Belgium) and Erskine Theological Seminary (South Carolina). Their attention and their many questions over the past seventeen years have been indispensable in the formulation and articulation of the ideas I present in this book.

I would like to thank Dr. Gary Deddo, senior editor at IVP Academic, and the two anonymous readers of this book's rough draft. The three of them provided me with invaluable feedback, and in particular, they alerted me to ways in which my assertions could easily be misinterpreted. The revisions that have grown out of their criticisms have made this, I hope, a much better book than it would have been otherwise.

It is sometimes said that Christian thinkers need to have a dead mentor, a major thinker from the history of the church at whose feet they can sit figuratively, just as they sit more literally at the feet of their living teachers. I have many dead mentors (my wife's description of my work is that I study "really old dead guys"), and foremost among them is Cyril of Alexandria. He was often maligned in his own time and has subsequently been vilified in the judgment of some historians, but he had the courage and the brilliance to articulate the heart of the Christian faith at a time when the church faced one of its greatest theological crises. I acknowledge my great debt to Cyril's writings.

It is customary in this space for the author to acknowledge that the deficiencies remaining in the book are his own. In my case, such an acknowledgment is far from being merely perfunctory. I feel keenly my inadequate familiarity with contemporary Christian theological discussions, and that unfamiliarity doubtless leaves this book with significant shortcomings. But I pray that what I offer from the early church and from my reflection on Scripture may contribute to the contemporary theological task of articulating the Christian faith clearly and comprehensively for our generation.

Explanation of
Patristic Citations

In this book's sidebars and footnotes, I cite patristic writings by abbreviations of their titles, followed by book, chapter and paragraph number. To make it easier for readers to find the writings, I also indicate the translation I am quoting and the page number. In some cases, these translations come from well-known series, and so I indicate the translation by the abbreviated title and volume of the series. In the case of standalone works or volumes from less well-known series, I indicate the translation by the name of the translator/editor. I have taken the liberty of normalizing the punctuation and capitalization of quotations in the public domain without noting these changes. In cases where I have made substantive changes to the printed translation, I indicate as much. The series which I cite by abbreviations are as follows:

ACW   Ancient Christian Writers. New York: Newman
           Press, 1946–.
ANF   Ante-Nicene Fathers. Ed. Alexander Roberts and
           James Donaldson. 10 vols. New York: Christian
           Literature Publishing Company, 1885-87. Reprint
           Peabody, Mass.: Hendrickson, 1995.
FC   The Fathers of the Church. Washington, D.C.: Cath-

olic University of America Press, 1947-.

NPNF[1]   Nicene and Post-Nicene Fathers, First Series. Ed.
                 Philip Schaff. 14 vols. New York: Christian Litera-
                 ture Publishing Company, 1886-1889. Reprint,
                 Peabody, Mass.: Hendrickson, 1995.

NPNF[2]   Nicene and Post-Nicene Fathers, Second Series. Ed.
                 Philip Schaff and Henry Wace. 14 vols. New York:
                 Christian Literature Publishing Company and
                 Charles Scribner's Sons, 1890-1900. Reprint, Pea-
                 body, Mass.: Hendrickson, 1995.

The following is a list of the abbreviated and full titles for the patristic writings I quote in the sidebars, as well as bibliographical details
about the translations I am using.

ATHANASIUS OF ALEXANDRIA (WROTE IN GREEK, LIVED CA. 296-373)

Ag. Arian.   *Against the Arians*
                  Athanasius. *Four Discourses Against the Arians.* Trans.
                  John H. Newman and A. Robertson. In NPNF[2],
                  vol. 4, 306-447.

On Incar.   *On the Incarnation of the Word*
                  Athanasius: Contra Gentes and De Incarnatione. Trans.
                  Robert W. Thomson, 134-277. Oxford Early
                  Christian Texts. Oxford: Clarendon, 1971.

On Syn.   *On the Synods*
                  Athanasius. *De Synodis.* In NPNF[2], vol. 4, 451-80.

AUGUSTINE OF HIPPO (WROTE IN LATIN, LIVED CA. 354-430)

City of God   *Concerning the City of God Against the Pagans*
                  Augustine. *Concerning the City of God Against the Pagans.*
                  Trans. Henry Bettenson. London: Penguin, 1972.

Conf.   *Confessions*
                  Augustine. *Confessions.* Trans. R. S. Pine-Coffin.
                  London: Penguin, 1961.

On Doc.   *On Christian Doctrine*

Augustine. *On Christian Doctrine.* Trans. D. W. Robertson Jr. The Library of Liberal Arts. New York: Macmillan, 1958.

On Trin.   *On the Trinity*

Augustine. *The Trinity.* Trans. Edmund Hill. The Works of Saint Augustine: A Translation for the Twenty-first Century, vol. 5. Brooklyn, N.Y.: New City Press, 1991.

BASIL THE GREAT (WROTE IN GREEK, LIVED CA. 330–379)

On HS   *On the Holy Spirit*

Basil the Great. *On the Holy Spirit.* Trans. David Anderson. Popular Patristics Series. Crestwood, N.Y.: St. Vladimir's Seminary Press, 1980.

CYRIL OF ALEXANDRIA (WROTE IN GREEK, LIVED CA. 375–444)

Ag. Nes.   *Five Books Against Nestorius*

Cyril, Archbishop of Alexandria. *Five Tomes Against Nestorius.* Trans. P. E. Pusey. Library of the Fathers of the Holy Catholic Church, vol. 47. Oxford: James Parker and Co., 1881.

Bearer of God   *Against Those Who Refuse to Call Mary the Bearer of God*

Cyril of Alexandria. *Against Those Who Are Unwilling to Confess That the Holy Virgin Is Theotokos.* Trans. George Dion Dragas. Patristic and Ecclesiastical Texts and Translations. Rollingsford, N.H.: Orthodox Research Institute, 2004.

Christ Is One   *That the Christ Is One*

Cyril of Alexandria. *On the Unity of Christ.* Trans. John A. McGuckin. Popular Patristics Series. Crestwood, N.Y.: St. Vladimir's Seminary Press, 1995.

Com. Jn.	Commentary on John

Cyril, Archbishop of Alexandria. *Commentary on the Gospel According to S. John.* Vol. 1: S. John 1-8. Trans. P. E. Pusey. Library of the Fathers of the Holy Catholic Church, vol. 43. Oxford: James Parker & Co., 1874.

Cyril, Archbishop of Alexandria. *Commentary on the Gospel According to S. John.* Vol. 2: S. John 9-21. Trans. Thomas Randell. Library of the Fathers of the Holy Catholic Church, vol. 48. London: Walter Smith, 1885.

Expl. Anath.   *Explanation of the Twelve Anathemas*

McGuckin, John A. *St. Cyril of Alexandria: The Christological Controversy.* Supplements to *Vigiliae Christianae* 23, 282-93. Leiden: E. J. Brill, 1994.

On Sol.   *On the Solutions to Dogmatic Questions*

Cyril of Alexandria: Select Letters. Trans. Lionel R. Wickham. Oxford Early Christian Texts, 180-213. Oxford: Oxford University Press, 1983.

Pasch. Let.   *Paschal Letters*

The selections presented in the book are my translations.

Schol.   *Scholia on the Incarnation*

The selections presented in the book are my translations.

Thes.   *Thesaurus on the Holy and Consubstantial Trinity*

The selections presented in the book are my translations.

CYRIL OF JERUSALEM (WROTE IN GREEK, LIVED CA. 315-387)

Cat.   *Catechetical Lectures*

Cyril of Jerusalem. Trans. Edward Yarnold. The Early Church Fathers, 79-168. London: Routledge, 2000.

Myst. Cat.   *Mystagogical Catecheses*

Cyril of Jerusalem. Trans. Edward Yarnold. The Early
Church Fathers, 169-87. London: Routledge, 2000.

DECREES OF THE ECUMENICAL COUNCILS

In the book I give my own translations of the Nicene Creed and the
Chalcedonian Definition, but the citation of the decrees from the Fifth
Ecumenical Council is from Leith, John H., ed. *Creeds of the Churches.*
3rd ed , 50-53. Atlanta: John Knox Press, 1982.

GREGORY OF NAZIANZUS (WROTE IN GREEK, LIVED CA. 330-390)

Or.   *Orations*

Gregory of Nazianzus. *On God and Christ: The Five
Theological Orations and Two Letters to Cledonius.*
Trans. Frederick Williams and Lionel Wickham.
Popular Patristics Series. Crestwood, N.Y.: St.
Vladimir's Seminary Press, 2002.

GREGORY OF NYSSA (WROTE IN GREEK, LIVED CA. 330-395)

Not Three Gods   *Letter to Ablabius Concerning the Fact That There Are
Not Three Gods*

Rusch, William G., trans. *The Trinitarian Controversy,*
149-61. Sources of Early Christian Thought. Phil-
adelphia: Fortress, 1980.

IGNATIUS OF ANTIOCH (WROTE IN GREEK, LIVED CA. 35-CA. 107)

Let. Rom.   *Letter to the Romans*

Holmes, Michael W., ed. *The Apostolic Fathers: Greek
Texts and English Translations.* Grand Rapids, Mich.:
Baker, 1999.

IRENAEUS OF LYONS (WROTE IN GREEK, LIVED CA. 140-CA. 200)

Ag. Her.   *Against Heresies*

Irenaeus. *Against Heresies*. In ANF, vol. 1, 315-567.

Preach.   *Demonstration of the Apostolic Preaching*
                      Irenaeus of Lyons. *On the Apostolic Preaching*. Trans.
                      John Behr. Popular Patristics Series. Crestwood,
                      N.Y.: St. Vladimir's Seminary Press, 1997.

JOHN CASSIAN (WROTE IN LATIN, LIVED CA. 360-CA. 430)

Confer.   *Conferences*
                      John Cassian: The Conferences. Trans. Boniface Ram-
                      sey. In ACW, vol. 57.

JOHN CHRYSOSTOM (WROTE IN GREEK, LIVED CA. 347-407)

Hom. Jn.   *Homlies on the Gospel of St. John*
                      John Chrysostom. *Homlies on the Gospel of St. John*.
                      Trans. Charles Marriott. In NPNF[1], vol. 14, 1-334.

JOHN OF DAMASCUS (WROTE IN GREEK, LIVED CA. 655-CA. 750)

Orth. Faith   *The Orthodox Faith*
                      Saint John of Damascus: Writings. Trans. Frederick R.
                      Chase. In FC, vol. 37, 165-406.

ORIGEN (WROTE IN GREEK, LIVED CA. 185-CA. 254)

On Princ.   *On First Principles*
                      Origen. *On First Principles*. Trans. G. W. Butterworth.
                      Gloucester, Mass.: Peter Smith, 1973.

TERTULLIAN (WROTE IN LATIN, LIVED CA. 160-CA. 225)

Ag. Prax.   *Against Praxeas*
                      Tertullian. *Against Praxeas*. Trans. A. Souter. Transla-
                      tions of Christian Literature. London: Society for
                      Promoting Christian Knowledge, 1919.

On Flesh   *On the Flesh of Christ*
                      Tertullian. *On the Flesh of Christ*. In ANF, vol. 3,
                      521-42.

Chapter 1

Introduction

GETTING STARTED
IN CHRISTIAN THEOLOGY

Western textbooks of systematic theology usually begin with the question of authority. Is the Bible alone authoritative, or is the Bible's authority supplemented or even replaced by the authority of certain people? In evangelical Protestant circles, this question invariably leads theologians to ascribe unique authority—and sometimes even exclusive authority—to the Bible. The Scriptures are the preeminent and perhaps even the only source of Christian doctrine. But as important as the question of the Bible's authority is, the church fathers provide us almost no help in articulating a doctrine of Scripture. Instead, if we are to do theology with the help of the church fathers, a better place to start is the question of the unintended rift that sometimes opens up between doctrine and life. In this introductory chapter, I would like briefly to explain why the Fathers gave so little apparent attention to biblical authority and then to turn our attention to the rift between doctrine and life that the Fathers focused on much more intensely.

THE CHURCH FATHERS AND BIBLICAL AUTHORITY

For the church fathers, the question of the Bible's authority was almost a nonissue. Virtually every page of any patristic writing includes quotation after quotation from the Bible, and there is never any hint of doubt about whether the Bible is true. The overriding concern of the Fathers is not whether to believe the Bible but how to interpret it, not whether the Scriptures are authoritative but what they mean. The Fathers assumed that the Bible is accurate and authoritative, and if one may judge by the frequency of their quotations and the reverence they ascribe to it, one may also conclude that they regarded it as uniquely authoritative.[1] In most cases, they felt no need to declare the truthfulness or authority of the Bible directly.

Of course, we now live in a different intellectual age than the Fathers did, an age in which skepticism rather than belief is the norm, and in our world questions about authority are central to any discussion of what we are to believe. But at the same time, we should recognize that there is something significant hiding beneath the Fathers' seemingly too-easy belief in the truthfulness of Scripture. Assuming the authority of Scripture is in many ways a greater act of submission to God than seeking to demonstrate the Bible's uniqueness and accuracy. To some degree, trying to convince others that the Bible is reliable represents an effort to get people to trust us, to believe that we have sufficient arguments in our arsenal to prove that they should take the Bible seriously. By contrast, using the Bible, with no prefatory remarks about whether it is worthy of such respect, is to assign it an even higher place. To state this point differently, much modern theology argues that we should trust the Bible because we can demonstrate that it is reliable. In contrast, the Fathers assumed that the Bible is trustworthy because it came from God, and they assumed this so implicitly and wholeheartedly that they rarely even mentioned the Bible's uniqueness directly. They simply acted on the uniqueness of Scripture by memorizing it, studying it, citing it, using it. Because of this the Fathers have relatively little to offer to our articulation of the doctrine of Scripture, but in their practice they have a great deal to tell us about what submission to the authority of Scripture looks like.

---

[1]See, e.g., Athanasius's exhaustive passage-by-passage refutation of Arius's biblical interpretation in *Against the Arians*. See also Augustine's clear statement of the unique authority of Scripture in *On Baptism, Against the Donatists,* bk. 2, par. 4 (NPNF[1], vol. 4, 427).

Following the church fathers, I would like in this book to assume that the Bible is the unique and final authority, the primary source of truth on all matters related to God, his actions in history and humanity's relationship to him. You as the reader might already share this assumption, but even if you do not, I ask you at least to grant that the Bible might be reliable and thus can be taken seriously. Instead of starting with the doctrine of Scripture, I would like to begin our discussion of Christian theology by examining a problem that contemporary Christianity often unintentionally creates for itself.

AN UNINTENDED PROBLEM: DOCTRINE AND CHRISTIAN LIFE IN CONTEMPORARY EVANGELICALISM

One of the significant problems in contemporary Christianity is that people unwittingly drive a wedge between theology and the living of Christian life. Current evangelical theology is well articulated, carefully argued, logical and systematic, but the people in our churches (and indeed many of our church leaders) are not always able to grasp the relation between that theology and Christian life. Theology is what we believe, and Christian life is what we do, but the intimate connection between these is often not clearly stated and sometimes not even understood.

This is a bold claim, and you may or may not agree with it, but consider a couple of questions with me. First, what do we say is the centerpiece of the Christian faith? And second, what do we hear week after week in sermons, Sunday school classes and Bible studies? We often say that Jesus is the heart of our message, but if one were to chart the main point of every sermon from every Christian pulpit over the course of a year, one might be surprised to find out that certain other topics tend to get a lot more attention than Jesus does. Preachers, teachers and Bible study leaders tend to focus on what Christians are supposed to do, on how God helps us to do it, on the need for forgiveness, on the importance of the church and (in some churches) on what will happen at the end of the world. Now, all of these are important things, but I am convinced that they lie not at the center but somewhat out toward the edges of Christianity. What we say the Christian faith is all about and

what one hears week after week in church are not quite the same. So
even if you have gone to church every Sunday of your life, you might
not have heard clearly what lies at the very center of Christianity. You
may know many Christian doctrines, many teachings derived from the
Bible that explain what is true. And you may know a great deal about
what Christian life is supposed to look like. But have you clearly heard
how these fit together? Have you clearly heard what lies at the heart of
the faith, what binds all the different aspects of belief and practice together? If you are like many contemporary evangelicals, perhaps you
have not.

Why has this unintended split between doctrine and Christian life
taken place? To grapple with that question, we need to return to two
words I have used several times above: *doctrine* and *doctrines*. *Doctrine*
comes from the Latin word for "teaching," and thus Christian doctrine
as a whole is the teaching of the Christian faith about topics that Christians believe to be significant. "Doctrines" are individual teachings on
specific issues. Part of the reason there is a divorce between doctrine
and Christian life is that contemporary evangelicals normally understand "doctrines" as concepts, teachings, true ideas (to which we often
give the word *propositions*), and we unwittingly see these doctrines as
the objects of our faith. So we ask questions such as, "Do you believe
in the doctrine of justification by faith?" This question is perfectly
well-intended, but it does not ask what it means to ask. When we ask
this question, we intend the correct answer to be yes, but it is not. The
correct answer to the question should be a qualified no, because Christians do not believe in the doctrine of justification by faith per se, but
rather in the God who has justified us through our faith. He, and he
alone, is properly the object of our faith, our trust, our submission.
Doctrines are statements designed to point us to God; they are not
meant as objects of faith themselves. To state this another way, we believe that the doctrine of justification by faith is true because we trust
in the God who has justified us.

Now you may want to accuse me of needless hairsplitting here. But
I am convinced that part of the reason we tend to regard theology,
doctrine, as being somewhat irrelevant to Christian life is that our

theological discussions focus on the doctrines rather than on the God to whom those doctrines point. Theologians have unintentionally given the impression that the doctrines, the ideas about God, are the subject of our study. As a result, students and others unwittingly substitute truths about God for God. Then the most spiritually sensitive Christians, the ones who sense that there must be more to Christianity than knowing things about God, begin to look elsewhere besides doctrines for their understanding of Christian life.

I should hasten to add that this situation is not intentional. I am not by any means accusing Christian theologians and preachers of intentionally trying to hide anything from us or to drive a wedge between what we believe and what we should do. Instead, the problem is that at the heart of Christianity lies something that is deeply mysterious and perhaps hard to explain. And Christians tend to describe this mysterious center using certain words and phrases that have a lot of emotional resonance for us, even though (I am convinced) we cannot articulate what they mean. For example, how many times have you heard people talk about "a personal relationship with Christ"? Lots of times, right? But how often have you heard anyone really explain what that means? Maybe not so often. Maybe never. It is the same way with words like *grace* and *glory*. The more Christians use these words and phrases, the less obvious it becomes that we do not know what they mean. So we are able to give the impression that we know what we are talking about, without even realizing ourselves that maybe we do not.

Unlike some of us, however, the church fathers did know what they meant when they used the words and phrases we so often use. Indeed, they had to know what they meant, because when Christianity was very young, they were talking and writing to people who had never heard these ideas before, people who would not simply nod when they used the buzzwords, but who spoke up, asked questions and forced the church's preachers and teachers to come up with good answers. As I studied the church fathers and compared them with what I knew of the Bible and of Christianity, I began more and more to realize that they were on to something that we have largely forgotten, that they were able to articulate the heart of the Christian message in a way that we often cannot. To say it differently, they were able to articulate the connection between the doctrines of the faith and the Christian life in a clearer and more persuasive way than we are usually able to do. And because of this, they can help provide a solution to a problem that I believe faces contemporary evangelicalism: the unintended divorce between the way we talk about doctrine and the way we talk about the Christian life.

AN ANCIENT SOLUTION: *Theōsis* AS THE LINK BETWEEN DIVINE LIFE AND HUMAN LIFE

In a nutshell, the way the early church avoided the problem of divorcing doctrine from Christian life was by understanding all of Christian life in direct connection to God's life. The fathers of the church did not first speak about God, then speak about salvation and then speak about

---

Athanasius on Humanity's Becoming Divine (ca. 315):

> If someone wishes to see God, who is invisible by nature and in no way visible, he understands and knows him from his works, so he who does not see Christ with his mind, let him learn of him from the works of his body. . . . Let him . . . wonder that through such simple means these divine things have been revealed to us, and that through death immortality has come to all, and through the incarnation of the Word the universal providence and its leader and creator the Word of God himself have been made known. For he became man that we might become divine; and he revealed himself through a body that we might receive an idea of the invisible Father; and he endured insults from men that we might inherit incorruption.

On Incar., par. 54 (Thomson, 269)

Christian life. Instead, the way they spoke about God constituted their discussion of salvation and Christian life. One could say that they did not have separate doctrines about God and about salvation but rather that their doctrine of God was their doctrine of salvation. In the sidebar on the previous page, notice the direct connection the fourth-century Egyptian theologian Athanasius makes between the incarnation of the Son and our salvation. But saying that they had a single doctrine rather than separate doctrines is still not adequate, because their focus was not so much on the doctrine itself as it was on the God in whose life they shared. Doctrine, as they understood it, pointed beyond itself to God, in whose divine life human beings are called to share.

In order to speak of this sharing in divine life, the fathers of the church used a Greek word, *theōsis,* which is at once both important and easy to misunderstand. The word comes from the word *theos,* meaning "God," and it refers to the process by which human beings are made, in some sense, divine. (Notice Athanasius's use of the phrase "become divine" in the sidebar above.) Because of this, the word *theōsis* was rendered *deificatio* in Latin and is normally translated "deification" in English, but one should immediately recognize that the Fathers did not understand deification to mean that we become divine in the same way God is divine. Virtually all of them rigidly maintained the divide between God the creator and everything that he created (including human beings), and they insisted that no one could move from the human side to the divine side of that divide. No one who began to exist in time can become eternal in the sense of having existed before time. No one who is finite can become infinite. No one can become divine in the sense of becoming a fourth person of the Trinity. No one can become a child of God in the same way that Jesus is God's Son. The church was adamant on all of these points. But if by *deification* the early church did not mean that we transcend the creator/creature distinction, what did it mean? And how can an idea labeled with such a suspicious word be of any possible use in helping contemporary evangelicals overcome our dichotomy between doctrine and Christian life?

Answering these questions requires us to dig a bit into the world of patristic thought, and such digging will help to explain why I believe that the relationship between the Father and the Son within the Trinity is the scarlet thread of the Christian faith. In the mind of the early church, there were many biblical passages that lent support to the idea of *theōsis* as the link between God and humanity, but the two passages they mentioned most frequently in their writings were Psalm 82:6-7 and 2 Peter 1:3-4. The first of these passages reads, "I said, 'You are "gods"; you are all sons of the Most High.' But you will die like mere men; you will fall like every other ruler." Western interpreters typically take the phrases "gods" and "sons of the Most High" to be honorary titles given to kings and other rulers, not as literal or even quasi-literal statements about people who are somehow divine.[2] However, the early church was united in affirming that the phrases refer to people in general and that to be gods means to be sons of God.

The other passage, 2 Peter 1:3-4, reads, "His divine power has given us everything we need for life and godliness through our knowledge of him who called us by his own glory and goodness. Through these he has given us his very great and precious promises, so that through them you may participate in the divine nature and escape the corruption in the world caused by evil desires." Here one should notice that participation in the divine nature is linked to overcoming corruption and death. Furthermore, Peter follows these words with a list of godly qualities that believers are to acquire and foster: goodness, knowledge, self-control, perseverance, godliness, brotherly kindness and love (2 Pet 1:5-7). On the basis of this passage, the early church affirmed that *theōsis,* or deification, involved overcoming our mortality and corruption by participating in God's immortality and sharing more and more in the godly qualities Peter lists.

From these passages and others, the fathers of the church recognized that there were various aspects of *theōsis,* or deification. God grants us to share in his qualities (what Western theologians would later call "communicable attributes of God"), grants us to share in his immortal life (not in the sense that we gain the power to live forever on our own but in the sense that God, who alone is immortal by nature, grants us to live unendingly) and causes us to become sons and daughters of God. The last of these ideas can be subdivided further when one asks what it means to be a child of God. Sonship or adoption (obviously a major

---

[2]Notice that the NIV places the word *gods* in quotation marks, indicating that the editors do not believe it is to be taken literally.

motif in the New Testament)[3] might imply simply that we gain the status of sons, or it could mean that we share somehow in the warmth of love that the Father and the Son have.

These different aspects of *theōsis* are by no means mutually exclusive, and many scholars of the early church argue that the Fathers' concept of deification embraced all of them, and others as well.[4] However, I suggest that in most cases, one or another aspect tended to predominate in the thought of a given church father. For some, especially in the Latin-speaking part of the Christian world, the idea of deification as our sharing in the status of divine children rose to the surface. These writers tended to focus on issues such as guilt and innocence and to see forgiveness of sins and a changed status before God as the primary aspects of salvation. This strand of thought eventually came to dominate in the Western church, which is part of why modern Protestantism has majored so strongly on justification as a right status before God. For others, especially in the Greek-speaking world, deification was primarily a matter of sharing in divine qualities, and occasionally this idea became so prominent that the writers in question ran the risk of blurring the line between God and human beings. For still others, including some in both Greek- and Latin-speaking regions, the concept of deification was primarily a way to focus on the relational aspects of sonship: Christ is the natural, only-begotten Son of God, and in a way that is both similar and different, Christians become adopted sons and daughters of God, thus sharing by grace in the fellowship the Son has with the Father by nature.

DIVINE LIFE AS TRINITARIAN LIFE

As I have studied the way the Fathers wrote of Christian life, I have become increasingly convinced that the third of these strands represents the best and most biblical way of articulating the idea of *theōsis*. It is of course true to speak of salvation as a change of status and to express

---

[3]See, e.g., Rom 8:14-23; 9:4, 26-27; 2 Cor 6:18; Gal 3:26–4:7; Eph 1:5; Heb 12:5-8.

[4]The most comprehensive recent treatment of the subject is found in Norman Russell, *The Doctrine of Deification in the Greek Patristic Tradition* (Oxford: Oxford University Press, 2004). Russell addresses a variety of facets of *theōsis*, but he does not seek to argue (as I do) that the Fathers should be grouped according to which aspect of *theōsis* is their primary emphasis.

salvation in the categories of guilt, forgiveness and justification. It is also true to speak of salvation (especially what Protestants call the process of sanctification) in terms of acquiring and developing the qualities of God, although most evangelicals would prefer to describe this process using the more directly biblical phrase "being conformed to the image of Christ" (see Rom 8:29). But I suggest that neither of these is the central aspect of Christian life. Instead, both forgiveness and becoming Christlike flow from our participation in a relationship, from our becoming sons and daughters by adoption so as to share in the communion that the natural Son has with God the Father. Furthermore, I believe that this way of understanding salvation and Christian life was widely represented in, and perhaps even the consensus of, the early church.[5] This is the strand of patristic thought that I believe has the most to teach contemporary evangelicalism and that can help to end the unintentional divorce between theology and Christian life that often plagues our churches, colleges and seminaries. This is the strand of thought to which I would like to direct our attention in the course of this book.

LIFE IN THE TRINITY: THE FORGOTTEN HEART OF CHRISTIAN FAITH

Accordingly, the scarlet thread around which this book seeks to organize the various truths of Christianity is the life of the Trinity, the relationship that the trinitarian persons share with one another. This book grows out of my conviction (forged as I have learned to read the Bible the way a certain strand of thought in the early church interpreted it) that all of Christian life, and indeed all of human life, is directly related to the central relationship that exists. This is a relationship that is shared among Father, Son and Spirit, but in Scripture it is particularly expressed in terms of the Father's relationship to his beloved Son. What many (perhaps most) within the early church meant by the disconcerting word *theōsis,* or deification, was believers' sharing

---

[5]For a fuller discussion of these three strands in the early church, see Donald Fairbairn, "Patristic Soteriology: Three Trajectories," *Journal of the Evangelical Theological Society* 50, no. 2 (2007): 289-310.

in the warm fellowship that has existed from all eternity between the persons of the Trinity, a fellowship that Scripture announces to us when it speaks of the Father's love for his Son. Because this concept is so central and so crucial, and yet the word used to describe it is so easy for contemporary Christians to misinterpret, I will normally not use the word *theōsis* or *deification* in this book. Instead, I will use phrases such as "participation in the Father-Son relationship," "sharing the love between the persons of the Trinity" and the like.

If I am right that this personal fellowship between the persons of the Trinity is the scarlet thread of Christianity, then why did the Protestant Reformers not emphasize it? Well, some of them did, and others of them assumed it without stating it so insistently. After all, they had to spend most of their energy writing about the issues on which they disagreed with Roman Catholicism, not the issues on which they agreed. But the longer we assume something without explicitly stating it, the more likely we are to forget it. And this, I fear, is what has happened in evangelicalism more recently. We have faithfully majored on the truths the Reformers stressed, but we have underemphasized the context in which they spoke those truths, to the point that we have forgotten what they knew and assumed. If we are to recover what the Reformers assumed, and thus to understand our own emphases (like justification by faith) in the context of the life of the Trinity in which those emphases make sense, we have to go back farther than the Reformation. We have to go back to the period of the church fathers, to remember their articulation of the heart of Christian faith as the Reformers themselves remembered it and made it the starting point for their own theology.

CONCLUSIONS

In this chapter, I have suggested that the early church succeeded better than we usually do at uniting doctrines and doctrine, theology and life, precisely because their integrating theological theme was one that spanned the gulf between the God on whom doctrine focuses and the believers who live out the Christian life. The concept of *theōsis*, understood correctly, provides a way of linking God's life to human life, and specifically to Christian life. We Christians are meant to live in a way that somehow participates in God's own life, so anything that we may say about God has direct applicability to the outworking of Christian life. Furthermore, I have argued that one common understanding of *theōsis* in the early church saw our participation in divine life primarily in terms of our sharing in the relationship between the Father and the Son. This strand was not the only one, and I do not intend to give the impression that the Fathers were completely monolithic in their understanding of Christianity. But it was a common strand, and even if I am not correct that it was the consensus, it was still a well-enough represented strand of thought that it deserves our attention today.

In this strand of thought, participation in divine life means primarily sharing in the life of the Trinity, sharing in the relationship that has characterized the Father, Son and Spirit from all eternity past. This understanding provides another appropriate place to begin the study of Christian theology besides the issue of authority, and I now turn to this understanding as I seek to probe the heart of the Christian faith with the help of the church fathers.

Chapter 2

The Heart of Christianity

THE SON'S RELATIONSHIP
TO THE FATHER

ONe could argue that the best way to start looking for the heart of Christian faith would be to ask what God has made us for, what his purpose in creating us was. That would then mean that we need to start with the book of Genesis and the account of God's creating human beings. Genesis would certainly be a good place to begin, but I believe that another appropriate place to start would be in the middle of history, indeed with an event close to the central point of human history, the death and resurrection of Christ.

A WINDOW INTO THE HEART OF THE FAITH: JESUS' WORDS IN JOHN 13–17

Jesus was crucified on a Friday in early April of the year 30 or 33, and the evening before he was crucified was one of the most emotionally charged, poignant evenings that anyone could possibly have lived through. He knew what was coming—his betrayal, arrest, trial and death by crucifixion—but his disciples did not. With those impending events in mind, he gathered his twelve disciples together for what they thought was simply a celebration of the Jewish Passover. Jesus' disciples did not know that when they came together, Jesus would do more than celebrate with them a past deliverance; he would also institute before them the representation of a future deliverance, a deliverance that he would bring about through his death and resurrection. The ceremony that Jesus instituted that evening is variously called the Lord's Supper, the Lord's Table, the Eucharist (which means "thanksgiving" in Greek) or simply Communion. But at the time, the disciples did not know that this would be the last meal they would share with Jesus before his death. They did not know that he was soon to die, although if they had been paying close enough attention to what he had said recently, they probably could have and should have known.[1]

Because of Jesus' knowledge of what would happen next and his disciples' ignorance of what was coming, the dynamic between them that evening was almost eerie. Every word he said, every action he performed, was pregnant with significance, but by and large, the disciples did not get it. Only looking back on that evening later did they recognize the full significance of what Jesus had said and done. We find the events of that evening described in several places in the New Testament. Matthew 26, Mark 14 and Luke 22 all give us the basic sequence of events—Jesus instituted the Lord's Supper in the upper room, left his disciples for a time while he prayed in the garden of Gethsemane, was arrested there and taken back into the city to be tried. Unlike the other three Gospels, John's Gospel gives us fewer of the things Jesus did (for example, John does not mention the prayer in the garden or even the institution of the Lord's Supper) but gives us much more detail about what Jesus said that evening. And these words of Jesus—words full of meaning as they came from one who knew he was about to die a premature death—give us a window into the heart and soul of the Christian faith. These words, recorded in John 13–17, were one of the key focal points of the early church's study and its articulation of the Christian message. These are the words I would like us to look at together in this chapter.

Keep in mind that the disciples were expecting Jesus' words to look backward, back to the Passover and the exodus, the great deliverance of God's people that had taken place so long before. To their surprise, Jesus

---

[1]See Mt 16:21-28 (and parallels Mk 8:31 and Lk 9:22-27); Mt 20:17-19 (and parallels Mk 10:32-34 and Lk 18:31-33).

spends a great deal of time looking forward, speaking of the future—the way the disciples will love and serve one another. And when he does look backward, he goes back not just to the Passover but all the way back to the "time" (one can hardly even use that word) before the world existed. They are expecting a look at what to them seems like the distant past, but Jesus gives them a look at the past before the past, before there was even a universe. And then from the past he takes them to the future, a future that he sees clearly but they, of course, do not. Jesus' words here are called the upper room discourse (Jn 13–16) and the high-priestly prayer (Jn 17). It should have been thrilling to listen to Jesus speak if the disciples had grasped what he was talking about. It must have been thrilling for them later to remember what he had said and recognize what he had meant. And it was thrilling for the church fathers to reflect on those words in the centuries that followed.

In this chapter I do not intend to go sentence by sentence through what Jesus says here. Instead, I would like to concentrate on a few key passages from John 13, 14, 15 and 17, and through these passages I would like to call your attention to the relation between God's love and the love believers are to have for one another.

CHRISTIAN LOVE: THE REFLECTION OF CHRIST'S LOVE

Israel in ancient times was a really dusty place. The scarcity of vegetation and the arid climate meant that for most of the year (except for the two rainy periods in October/November and March/April) the land was virtually a dust bowl, and the dust got onto everything that was outdoors. In addition, there was nothing like modern garbage collection or sewer systems; waste of all kinds was thrown out into the streets. And to top it all off, people generally wore open sandals when they were outside. So one of the urgent tasks was to keep all of that dust outside, rather than tracking it into the house. Since everyone's feet were dusty, the first order of business whenever one entered a house was to wash one's feet, and no one would ever want to do this for someone else, although sometimes a servant was forced to. One generally had to do it oneself.[2]

---

[2]Ancient Near Eastern social etiquette required the host to provide water for his guests to wash their feet, as mentioned in Gen 18:4; 19:2; 24:32; Judg 19:21. John the Baptist's statement that

In light of this background, the way Jesus begins this Passover celebration in John 13 is eye-popping to his disciples. He washes their feet. John tells us that this happened while the meal was being served (Jn 13:2-5), so at this point everyone's feet would already have been washed as they entered the upper room. But even if their feet are not dusty anymore, the mental associations raised in anyone's mind by foot washing are stunning. It is unthinkable to the disciples that anyone would voluntarily wash someone else's feet, and it is beyond unthinkable that Jesus, their master and teacher, would wash his disciples' feet. It would have been an act of breathtaking devotion for a student to wash his teacher's feet, but here is the teacher washing the students' feet! Jesus goes on to say that he has given them an example, that they are to serve each other with the same kind of humility he has shown his disciples through this unforgettable action. You can bet that this makes quite an impression on the twelve men gathered with him.

Then, not long after this, Jesus speaks the words that I would like to concentrate on. He says to the disciples:

> Now is the Son of Man glorified and God is glorified in him. If God is glorified in him, God will glorify the Son in himself, and will glorify him at once.
>
> My children, I will be with you only a little longer. You will look for me, and just as I told the Jews, so I tell you now: Where I am going, you cannot come.
>
> A new command I give you: Love one another. As I have loved you, so you must love one another. By this all men will know that you are my disciples, if you love one another. (Jn 13:31-35)

At first glance, this passage seems to be utterly preposterous. Jesus is about to die. Why would he speak of this moment as the moment when God is going to glorify him? How can Jesus say that God will be glorified in the Son, who is about to undergo the most humiliating, inglorious kind of death one can imagine? We might think that Jesus should complain that God is going to abandon him or that God should com-

---

he is not worthy even to untie the thongs of Jesus' sandals (Mk 1:7) is probably a reference to the task of removing a person's sandals before washing his feet as he comes into a house.

plain that he is going to be embarrassed in the Son. But instead Jesus speaks of glory. How can he say this? To understand this, we need to look fairly carefully at what "glory" means in the Bible.

Literally, the Hebrew word translated "glory" means "weight," and the Greek word means "praise." These words are starting from different ends of an idea, but the concept that both are heading toward is that God is the one who is massive, great, ponderous, magnificent and thus worthy to be praised. So when we "glorify God" or "give God glory," we are praising him because he is great and magnificent. This does not mean that we are giving him anything he does not already possess. He is majestic and spectacular whether anyone acknowledges this or not. Rather, for us to give God glory is to acknowledge that he is glorious, to state publicly that he is vastly greater than we are. This is why the Bible sometimes uses the phrase "ascribe to God the glory due his name" (see Ps 29:1-2) as a more precise version of the shorter phrase "glorify God."

However, one should recognize that majesty or greatness is not all that is conveyed by the word "glory." In addition, throughout the Old and New Testaments the glory of God is connected to his presence with his people. A brief look back through Israel's history will make this clear. Just after the exodus, as the people of Israel prepare to cross the Red Sea, God gives them a visible symbol of his presence with them—a pillar of cloud in the daytime and a pillar of fire at night (Ex 13:20-22). This pillar guides them during the upcoming forty years of wandering in the wilderness before they enter the land of Israel promised to them. Shortly after this, as the people are camped in the wilderness of the Sinai Peninsula, they begin to grumble against Moses and Aaron because they have no food. Moses and Aaron say to the people, "In the evening you will know that it was the LORD who brought you out of Egypt, and in the morning you will see the glory of the LORD, because he has heard your grumbling against him" (Ex 16:6-7). As promised, the next day, as Aaron is talking to the people, "they looked toward the desert, and there was the glory of the LORD appearing in the cloud" (Ex 16:10). Here the cloud that has previously signified God's presence is specifically called "the glory of the LORD," and furthermore, this event coincides with God's beginning to give the people manna to eat, another visible sign of his presence with them and provision for them (see all of Ex 16). Later, as the people camp at the foot of Mount Sinai and God begins to give them the Law, starting with the Ten Commandments (Ex 20), he calls Moses up to the top of the mountain. The text reads: "When Moses went up on the mountain, the cloud covered it, and the glory of the LORD settled on Mount Sinai. For six days the cloud covered the mountain, and on the seventh day the LORD called to Moses from within the cloud. To the Israelites the glory of the LORD looked like a consuming fire on top of the mountain" (Ex 24:15-17). Here, just after the breathtaking deliverance from Egypt that constituted Israel as a nation set apart for God, the Lord gives the people this constant reminder of his presence with them, his unique relationship to them. And the phrase Scripture uses for this presence is "the glory of the LORD."

For the rest of Israel's history, God's majestic greatness is linked to his unique presence with his own people through this cloud of "the glory of the LORD." After the tabernacle—the movable place of worship representing God's presence with his people—is completed, we read: "Then the cloud covered the Tent of Meeting, and the glory of the LORD filled the tabernacle. . . . So the cloud of the LORD was over the tabernacle by day, and fire was in the cloud by night, in the sight of all the house of Israel during all their travels" (Ex 40:34, 38). Similarly, once the temple—the stationary place of worship representing God's presence—is completed and the ark of the covenant is brought into its innermost room (the holy of holies), the text declares: "The cloud filled the temple of the LORD. And the priests could not perform their service because of the cloud, for the glory of the LORD filled his temple" (1 Kings 8:10-11). As he watches this event, King Solomon says, "The LORD has said that he would dwell in a dark cloud; I have indeed built a magnificent temple for you, a place for you to dwell forever" (1 Kings 8:12-13).

Of course the temple was not the final sign of God's presence with his people, nor was this earthly temple permanent. Instead the New Testament ties God's majestic presence with his people to the incarnation and life of Christ. As the angels appear to announce Jesus' birth to the shepherds, Luke writes, "The glory of the Lord shone around them" (Lk 2:9). When John describes the incarnation with the famous words, "The Word became flesh and made his dwelling among us," he explains by writing, "We have seen his glory, the glory of the One and Only, who came from the Father, full of grace and truth" (Jn 1:14). We shall look in detail at this passage later, but for now, the point is simply that the glory of God is connected to the presence of God with his people, and this presence is uniquely shown in the entrance of his one and only Son into the world. Finally, in the chapter just before the upper room discourse begins, Jesus speaks of his impending death by saying, "The hour has come for the Son of Man to be glorified" (Jn 12:23). This brings us up to where we are now, in the upper room, puzzling over Jesus' strange association of "death" with "glory." But now we can recognize that the idea of glory is not just that God is majestic and great. It is that this God, the only God, the God who is majestic, is with us and acting for us.[3]

With all this in mind, look at the first part of John 13:31-32 again: "Now is the Son of Man glorified and God is glorified in him. If God is glorified in him, God will glorify the Son in himself, and will glorify him at once." If God's glory is not just his greatness but his presence with us, then this passage must mean that the impending death of Jesus is the supreme way in which God is present with us. The God so vast that endless galaxies cannot contain him, so great that he could simply speak and cause the universe to burst into existence, so mighty that he could produce or circumvent the normal course of nature as he wished, is now about to show his glorious presence in the most unlikely way. If the teacher washing the disciples' feet was not unlikely enough, the Lord of the universe dying on the cross is surely the most unexpected demonstration of greatness. But this is what God is going to do. This is the very definition of what it means for God to be present with us. This is somehow going to be the most glorious moment in history. How that can be possible is something to which I will return later in this book, but for now we need to recognize that the Father is getting ready to

---

[3]For other uses of the word "glory" in connection with God's presence, see Ex 33:12-22; Lev 9:23-24; Deut 5:24; 1 Sam 4:21-22.

glorify both the Son and himself—by allowing the Son to die for us.

With this most improbable description of glory in place, Jesus then tells the disciples what he wants them—and all of us who follow Jesus today—to do. In the latter part of the passage we are considering, he says: "A new command I give you: Love one another. As I have loved you, so you must love one another. By this all men will know that you are my disciples, if you love one another" (Jn 13:34-35). It is hardly a surprise that Jesus wants Christians to love one another, and in fact the first sentence of this quotation is one of the most well-known sentences in the Bible. But notice two things about this passage. First, Jesus says that our love for one another is intimately connected to his love for us. As he has loved us, so we are to love one another. What is the nature of this connection? Does he mean because he has loved us, we should love one another? Surely he means at least this much. Does he mean we should love one another in the same way that he has loved us? Probably so, especially in light of the stunning demonstration of servant love he has given through washing the disciples' feet. I suggest that what Jesus means here includes both of those ideas but goes even further. He means we should love one another with the very same love with which he has loved us.

What Jesus means here becomes clearer later in the upper room discourse, but for now, we need to recognize that our love for one another is meant to be a mirror of the love Christ has shown us. And that leads directly to the second thing we should notice about the passage: that the way the world (that is, the broader society of people who do not yet follow Christ) will know we are Christ's disciples is by the way we love one another. Our love somehow grows out of Christ's love for us, and our love for one another reflects Christ's love for us. It is so much like his love that when people see us, they are reminded of the way Christ acted when he was on earth. If one asks what the heart of the Christian faith is, part of the answer is that a life reflecting the love Jesus has shown for us lies close to that heart. Notice that this is not the same as saying simply that we should love one another, that we are looking for some kind of community life in which people get along and are nice to each other. This is more than that, and a different kind of love than that. This is a love that is specifically connected to the life of one person who lived two thousand years ago, a person who is the Son of God. Near the heart of our faith, and thus near the heart of our theology, lies a love that reflects that love.

At this point, this is all pretty general, and (one might say) not particularly clear. We need to keep going, because as the upper room discourse progresses, Jesus gets increasingly specific about the kind of love he is talking about here.

OBEDIENCE: A MEANS OF LOVING

In the previous section of this chapter, you may have bristled at the fact that Jesus uses the word "command." You may not like the idea that religion (or life, for that matter) might involve commands. If so, then the title of this section may have really annoyed you. In fact, you may think that if one is focusing on obedience to commands, one cannot possibly have love as the underlying motivation. You may be thinking that "obedience" and "commands" belong in the sphere of duty, not in the sphere of love. If this is what you are thinking, then I ask you to set aside your annoyance temporarily, just long enough to listen to what Jesus tells his disciples a bit later in the upper room discourse. He says:

> If you love me, you will obey what I command. And I will ask the Father, and he will give you another Counselor to be with you forever—the Spirit of truth. The world cannot accept him, because it neither sees him nor knows him. But you know him, for he lives with you and will be in you. I will not leave you as orphans; I will come to you. Before long, the world will not see me anymore, but you will see me. Because I live, you also will live. On that day, you will realize that I am in my Father, and you are in me, and I am in you. Whoever has my commands and obeys them, he is the one who loves me. He who loves me will be loved by my Father, and I too will love him and show myself to him. (Jn 14:15-21)

Notice that at both the beginning and the end of this passage, Jesus connects love to obedience. If we love him, we will do what he commands. There are two things that we need to recognize about these statements.

First, Jesus directly contradicts the notion that love and obedience belong in different spheres, a notion that many people in contemporary society hold (whether consciously or subconsciously). We tend to think that something can be love only if it is between equals, and when we are talking about equals, obedience is out of place. We think that between equals, there is neither command nor obedience but that everything is worked out by consensus. Jesus' words here remind us that our relationship with him is not one of equals. Christianity affirms that Jesus is God, and an unbiased reading of the Gospels shows that Jesus understands himself that way. Yes, he is fully human too, just as we are. But first and foremost, he is God. At the time he says these words, he has been human for a bit more than thirty years, but he has been God from all eternity. We should not, cannot and do not relate to Jesus as equals. He is our God, our master, and we are his servants. (We will see shortly that we are more than merely his servants, but still, we are his servants.) Part of the reason we get annoyed whenever anyone speaks of obedience is that we do not like to admit that we are unequal to someone else. But when we are talking about Jesus, then the first thing we need to do in order to follow him is admit that we are not his equals. And since he is our master, he has every right to command us to do certain things and to expect our obedience. If that fact disturbs us emotionally, then perhaps the reason is that we are too proud to admit that we are not the highest beings in the universe. Once we clear our emotional baggage out of the way and recognize that Jesus does have the right to command us, we can see what he is saying here in a new light. By connecting love and obedience, Jesus is saying that for Christians, obedience is not a matter of mere duty. We, the servants, are called to obey our master, Jesus, out of love, not just out of duty. When Jesus commands us to do certain things, he is giving us the opportunity to love him by willingly keeping those commands rather than flatly disobeying them or keeping them merely grudgingly, merely out of a sense of duty. We can love him by obeying him joyfully and willingly.

The second thing we need to recognize about the link between love and obedience is that in the passage we looked at earlier, Jesus has also connected the two, but in a different way. There, the command was that we love one another. Here keeping the commands is part of the way we show that we love Jesus. Whether a person really loves Jesus will be evident from whether that person loves other people. In fact, our love for others is so reflective of our love for Jesus that John will later write in one of his own letters, "If anyone says, 'I love God,' yet hates his brother, he is a liar" (1 Jn 4:20). And we need to remember that our love for others reflects not only our love for Christ but also Christ's love for us. There is—or at least there should be—an intricate web of loving relationships that reflect each other; and willing, loving obedience plays a big part in these relationships.

It should already be clear that the picture of love and obedience that Jesus is instilling into his disciples here is very different from what we think of when we hear the word *love*. We probably think of love as an isolated, exclusive relationship between two people. We likely imagine it as a relationship that separates them from everyone else rather than bringing them closer to everyone else. We probably see it as a relation-ship on its own terms rather than a relationship that is meant to mirror something else. And of course, the concept of obedience is unlikely to enter into our picture of love. In contrast to all that, Jesus here calls us to obey as a reflection of our love for him, to love as an act of willing obedience, to love others because we love him, to love him as he has loved us. What Jesus calls us to is a very different kind of love from what we are familiar with.

If you look again at the passage we are considering (Jn 14:15-21), you see that so far I have discussed only the beginning and the end, the brackets if you will. What about the bracketed part, the middle of the paragraph? In between his opening and closing statements on obedi-ence, Jesus speaks of "another Counselor" whom he calls the "Spirit of truth," and whom we normally call the Holy Spirit. Jesus says of the Spirit: "The world cannot accept him, because it neither sees him nor knows him. But you know him, for he lives with you and will be in you. I will not leave you as orphans; I will come to you. Before long, the world will not see me anymore, but you will see me. Because I live, you also will live. On that day, you will realize that I am in my Father, and you are in me, and I am in you" (Jn 14:17-20). Notice here that

Jesus makes some startling claims about the relationship between Christians and the Holy Spirit. The world (those who do not follow Christ) does not know this Spirit, but the disciples do. Furthermore, there will come a time when the Holy Spirit will not merely be with the disciples but will live in the disciples. We know that that time came not long after Jesus rose from the dead and ascended into heaven, and the day when the Holy Spirit began to live in Christians is described in Acts 2. From that time on, we who follow Christ have the Spirit of God dwelling within us.

Here we should also notice that Jesus links the Holy Spirit's dwelling within Christians to the fact that the Father and the Son are in each other. Because of the indwelling Holy Spirit, we will recognize that the Son is in the Father and the Son is in us. In other words, the Holy Spirit is the link between the Son's relationship to the Father and the Christian's relationship to the Son. As Jesus continues speaking, he will make this link much clearer. In the meantime, we notice again how interconnected the Father, the Son, the Holy Spirit, Christians, love and obedience are. The very fabric of who we are is an intricate tapestry of relationships and actions. As we try to understand that tapestry more fully, let us look at what Jesus says later in the discourse.

Christian Love: The Same as the Love Between the Father and the Son

One of Jesus' best-known speeches is his vine-and-branches talk in John 15, which is the middle section of the upper room discourse. As beloved as this talk may be, it probably does not have nearly the impact with us that it did with its original audience, since not many of us live in agrarian societies. But for a group of Jews living in ancient Israel, nothing could have been a more appropriate image of the relationship between God, Jesus and Christians than a grape vine. Grapes were one of the primary crops of Israel, since they grew well in the arid climate, especially in the hill country where the contours of the land created natural terraces. They were essential to the lifestyle of the people, since wine was generally safer to drink than the available water was. Grapes were thus closely connected to life, to survival itself, and growing them provided the livelihood for a significant segment of the population.

Let us take a look at part of what Jesus says in this famous speech:

> I am the true vine, and my Father is the gardener. . . . No branch can
> bear fruit by itself; it must remain in the vine. Neither can you bear fruit
> unless you remain in me.
>
> I am the vine; you are the branches. If a man remains in me and I in
> him, he will bear much fruit; apart from me you can do nothing. . . .
> This is to my Father's glory, that you bear much fruit, showing your-
> selves to be my disciples. (Jn 15:1, 4-5, 8)

From these words it becomes clear why Jesus chose this image.
Christians are the branches, the ones who bear the grapes and thus the
most visible producers in the grape-growing operation. But the
branches cannot produce grapes on their own. If they are cut off from
the vine, they become useless. And they must be pruned every spring
and protected from predators. The connection between the branch,
the vine/root and the gardener who tends the vine would have been
clear to the disciples.

Notice also that in this paragraph the fruitfulness of Christians is to
the Father's glory. Remembering that glory is connected to God's presence, we see that one of the ways God shows his presence on earth is
through the actions of Christians, through the love we show for one
another, through the fruit we bear. On our own, we can accomplish
nothing. If we remain (or abide) in Christ, then we can keep God's
commands and bear the sort of fruit that God intends us to. First and
foremost, then, Christian life is a process of abiding in Christ, of rely-
ing on him, of recognizing and maintaining one's connection to him
in all aspects of life. This image helps to explain what Jesus has said
earlier in the discourse. Remember that when he said, "As I have loved
you, so you must love one another" in John 13, I mentioned that there
were various possibilities about how one might understand the connection between Jesus' love and ours. One possibility was that he meant we
should love others because he has loved us. But by this point, it is clear
that this cannot be all Jesus meant there. If we were simply to love because he loved us, then that would mean that we love on our own,

merely by imitating Christ. But we now know that the Holy Spirit lives within us—helping us, enabling us, leading us to love others. And now the image of the vine and the branches removes any possibility that we could or should imitate Christ's love on our own. The connection between his love and ours is closer than this: as we remain in his love, Jesus works through us to make us fruitful, so that the Father's glorious presence may be known.

This brings us to the next part of Jesus' speech, in which he pulls together the various threads of the tapestry he has been weaving so far and articulates most clearly the relation between Christians, himself and God his Father. Jesus says:

> As the Father has loved me, so have I loved you. Now remain in my love. If you obey my commands, you will remain in my love, just as I have obeyed my Father's commands and remain in his love. I have told you this so that my joy may be in you and that your joy may be complete. My command is this: Love each other as I have loved you. Greater love has no one than this, that he lay down his life for his friends. You are my friends if you do what I command. I no longer call you servants, because a servant does not know his master's business. Instead, I have called you friends, for everything that I learned from my Father I have made known to you. (Jn 15:9-15)

Previously Jesus has forged a link between his love for us and our love for one another. Here he extends that link. His love for us is connected to the Father's love for him. Furthermore, he does not say merely that we are to love each other because the Father loved him and he loved us, or even that we are to love each other in the same way as the Father loved him and he loved us. Instead, he says, "Now remain in my love." We are to remain in the very same love with which Christ has loved us, which is in fact the very same love with which the Father has loved Christ. Somehow we are called to do more than simply imitate God's love. We are called to remain in and to carry forward to the world the very love with which the Father has loved his Son from all eternity. The loving relationship between Father and Son, the glorious presence of the Father with the Son, is not simply a model that we are to follow. That relationship is the substance of what Jesus says Christians are to possess. Christ is not simply giving us an example; he is offering himself to us as a person, that we might share in his most deeply personal relationship, the relationship he has with God the Father.

Notice that just as in John 14, so also here, Jesus mentions obedience in connection with love. But here he goes beyond what he has said previously: he links our obeying his commands to his having obeyed the Father's commands. At this point, you may really object to the idea of obedience. Even if you (perhaps grudgingly) accepted what I wrote above—that we are not God's equals and thus that obedience is part of the way we love him—you may balk at what Jesus says here. He is God's equal. He is somehow the same God as the Father. So even if it is appropriate to speak of people's obedience to Christ, how can it be appropriate to speak of God the Son's obedience to God the Father? The answer implied in what Jesus says here is that even among equals, there are relationships which should be characterized as leader-follower or initiator-receptor or even lover-beloved, relationships in which obedience plays a part. God the Son is just as fully God as the Father; he is in every way equal to the Father. But he still obeys the Father and carries out his Father's will on earth. If he is willing to love his Father in this way, then we, who are not God's equals in any way whatsoever, should also be willing to love God and love Christ by obeying.

I will return to this idea in chapter four, but for now we need to recognize again how radically different this is from what we normally think of when we envision human relationships. Jesus is tying our human relationships to his relationship with the Father. God loves him; he loves his Father and obeys him. In obedience to the Father, he comes into the world to love us with the very same love with which he and the Father have loved each other. He calls us to love each other with that very same love, and as we will see later, this will involve a willingness to be both leaders and followers, initiators and receptors of love. But another thing that we need to notice in this passage is that Jesus insists his disciples are not just servants, even though they are to obey him. In fact, "servants" is not his preferred word for describing them, even though many followers of Christ will later use that word to describe themselves. (See Rom 1:1 and Jas 1:1 for examples of this.) Instead Christ calls the disciples "friends." Why? Because someone who is merely a servant is not privy to his master's reasons for doing something; he is simply told what he should do. A servant who is also a friend shares in his master's purposes in a much greater way. He knows the big picture of who his master is and what his master is doing, and thus he sees clearly why he is being called to do his part of the task. God the Father called on his Son to obey, but at the same time, the Son shared fully in both the Father's personal presence with him and in the big picture of the Father's purposes. He knew the Father's love toward him and thus the loving nature of the Father's purposes toward humanity. In a similar way, the Son now calls us to obey, but he also shows us who he is and what he is doing. He gives us a glimpse of the love that lies behind his purposes, and so he calls us his friends rather than just his servants.

This is why typical Christian teaching can be so frustrating if it merely tells us what we are to do without granting us any insight into why the commands are important or how they fit with what God is doing. In the upper room discourse, Jesus shows us that the key to Christianity as it is meant to be is linking our lives to him, and indeed linking our lives directly to his own relationship with God the Father.

CHRISTIAN LOVE AND THE ETERNAL LOVE BETWEEN FATHER AND SON

At some point after Jesus and the disciples leave the upper room, but before Jesus is arrested, he prays a prayer recorded in John 17. In many ways, this high-priestly prayer is an exact complement to the upper room discourse. In the discourse, Jesus has laid out a picture of life as God intends it, and in the prayer, he asks his Father to bring about the kind of life he has just described to the disciples. In this prayer, Jesus prays first for himself (Jn 17:1-5), then for the twelve disciples (Jn 17:6-19) and then for all those who will later become his followers (Jn 17:20-26). Let us look at what Jesus prays for himself:

> Father, the time has come. Glorify your Son, that your Son may glorify you. For you granted him authority over all people that he might give eternal life to all those you have given him. Now this is eternal life: that

they may know you, the only true God, and Jesus Christ, whom you have sent. I have brought you glory on earth by completing the work you gave me to do. And now, Father, glorify me in your presence with the glory I had with you before the world began. (Jn 17:1-5)

In this passage, the phrase that may jump out at you first is "eternal life." We all know that Jesus gives eternal life to those who believe in him. But what is eternal life? Most of us think of it either as a synonym for "heaven" or as meaning "living forever." But neither of these gets to the heart of what eternal life, in the biblical sense, means. "Heaven," the way many people use the word, means little more than the actualization of whatever a particular person happens to like. Heaven is the place where you never have to work or where you can play baseball all day long or where you can eat whatever you want and not have to worry about your cholesterol level. The word *heaven* has been trivialized so much that it is almost meaningless today. And "living forever" can be misleading as well. According to Scripture, all people are going to live forever, in one way or another. One of the marks of the significance God has given to every human being is that all will live forever, either with God or apart from God.[4] But that is not what Jesus means by "eternal life" here. Rather, the phrase translated "eternal life" means "life of the age." It is referring to a future age, to the new kind of life that God will establish at the end of history, a life that will be shared by all those who believe in Christ and follow him. Eternal life is not just living forever; it is living in a certain way, having a certain quality of life that is available only to those who have faith in Christ.

So what is this kind of life like? Jesus says here that eternal life consists of knowing God and knowing Jesus Christ, whom God has sent. Notice right away how personal this description is. Jesus is not just saying eternal life is something that he will give us. He is not saying that because of what he has done, or what he will do or what we do, then we will get *x*, *y* or *z* while living forever in heaven. Eternal life is knowing Christ and his Father, God. At the heart of the central idea of Christianity lies the reality that Christians will know the Father and the Son. This concurs

---

[4]See, e.g., Dan 12:1-3; Mt 13:36-43, 47-50; 2 Thess 1:5-10; Rev 20:11-15; 21:1-8.

very closely with what he has said in the upper room discourse about our sharing in the love between the Father and the Son.

What makes this description of eternal life even more striking is that it comes not as Jesus is praying for us but as he is praying for himself. His giving us eternal life is intimately connected to God's glory, so much so that Jesus speaks of our eternal life in the same breath as he speaks about his glorifying the Father and the Father's glorifying him. God does not just bask in his own greatness and magnificence, he shares it. He shares that greatness within himself among the persons of the Trinity, and he shares that glorious presence with his people as well. So part of the way God shows forth his magnificence is by leading human beings to know him. And knowing him implies knowing both the Father and the Son whom the Father has sent.

In light of this idea, let us look at several other aspects of this passage from Jesus' prayer. We see that the Son's completion of the work God has given him to do (living and dying for our salvation—a work that Jesus has almost finished as he speaks these words) ascribes glory to the Father. That work shows the world just how magnificent God is. But notice verses 1 and 5. Jesus is praying that the Father may now glorify him, just as he has glorified the Father. And he describes that glory with the word "presence" and as something that he has had with the Father before the world began. The glory of God is the majestic presence of God. From all eternity, from before the moment he created the world, God has shared his magnificent presence. How? By sharing that presence between the Father and the Son. Christianity is unique among world religions in claiming both that there is only one God and that this one God exists as three persons, as the Trinity. Here Jesus indicates that the majesty of God shines forth as he shares his presence. Before there was a world or any people to sense that presence, God's glory shone forth in the relationship between the Father and the Son (and the Holy Spirit as well, although Jesus does not mention him here). As we come to know the Son, we too see God's glorious presence, and this is eternal life. The presence that God has shared within himself, between the Father, Son and Spirit, is the heart of that knowledge of God which he gives to us and which constitutes eternal life. Through this part of the prayer, we see that eternal life is much more than just something Christians get because of what Christ has done. Eternal life is a deeply personal knowledge of the one who has shared from all eternity in the glory of the Father. Somehow, the eternally glorious relationship between the Father and Son is shared with us as we follow Christ. The end, the future that awaits Christians, involves sharing in the relationship that has characterized God from the beginning, indeed from before the beginning, before there was human history or even earthly history. And again, this is similar to what we have seen in the upper room discourse.

Even more striking than what Jesus prays at the beginning of this prayer is what he says at the end, as he prays for all who will follow him. He continues to speak of glory and of the "time" before the creation of the world, but now he introduces another key idea, that of oneness or unity. Jesus prays that all believers may be "one" (Jn 17:21). Before I even quote the passage, we need to recognize that *one* is a pretty vague word; there are many different kinds of unity that could lead us to speak of people as "one." People who have a common purpose or who come together to do a common task can speak of themselves as "one." Americans used to pride themselves on being one people, with a common identity and culture, derived from many different ethnic groups. This is what our national motto, *e pluribus unum* ("from many, one") implies. People who consider themselves to be soul mates or kindred spirits or even lovers often speak of themselves as "one." This is what the lighting of the unity candle at many wedding ceremonies is designed to signify. In Eastern religions and philosophies, perhaps the central idea is that a person's soul can become "one" with the universe. In fact, this Eastern idea is increasingly common in the West today, as people speak of realizing their oneness with the universe or actualizing the divinity within themselves. There are many kinds of oneness, and if this passage is really as central to the Christian message as I claim it is, then we need to grasp what kind of unity Jesus is praying for here.

Let us look carefully at the passage itself. Jesus says:

> My prayer is not for them [the twelve disciples] alone. I pray also for those who will believe in me through their message, that all of them may be one, Father, just as you are in me and I am in you. May they

also be in us so that the world may believe that you have sent me. I have given them the glory that you gave me, that they may be one as we are one: I in them and you in me. May they be brought to complete unity to let the world know that you sent me and have loved them even as you have loved me.

Father, I want those you have given me to be with me where I am, and to see my glory, the glory you have given me because you loved me before the creation of the world. (Jn 17:20-24)

There are a number of things in this passage that we need to consider. First, notice that when Jesus prays that Christians may be "one," he explains this idea by saying that he is in the Father, the Father is in him, and Christians are to be in the Father and the Son. For followers of Jesus to be one with each other is somehow tied to the relationship between the Father and the Son, and Jesus uses the word *in* to describe that relationship. Second, notice that the unity between Christians is to be a major sign to the non-Christian world that God has sent Jesus. In other words, part of the way the world is to believe that Jesus is really God's Son is because of the unity or oneness between Christians. Third, and perhaps most important, notice that Jesus ties oneness to love. In fact, he has talked a great deal about love in the upper room discourse, and now as he prays for Christians, he speaks not only of love but also of oneness. Saying that Christians should be one in the same way the Father and Son are one means the same thing as saying that Christians should love one another with the same love the Father has shown the Son. Fourth, notice that Jesus again speaks of eternal glory—of the presence of the Father with him before the world was created—and this time he ties that presence to the Father's love for him.

So what kind of unity is Jesus talking about? He clearly has in mind something much greater than just a unity of purpose, like that which binds people together when they have a common task. He is not talking about a physical or emotional unity, like what binds wife and husband together. And he is not talking about a unity of substance, in which the distinction between God and people is lost, as is often the case in Eastern philosophical concepts of unity. In contrast to all of these, he is talking about a unity of love, and "unity" in this prayer is a synonym for "love" as Jesus has used that word throughout the upper room discourse. To say that the Father and Son are "one" and are "in" each other is to speak of the love they have for each other, and Jesus says they have shared this love from all eternity, from before the time when they made the world. The glory of God has shone forth from all eter-

---

Irenaeus of Lyons on Christians' Participation in God (ca. 180):

Being ignorant of him who from the Virgin is Emmanuel, they are deprived of his gift, which is eternal life; and not receiving the incorruptible Word, they remain in mortal flesh. . . . He undoubtedly speaks these words to those who have not received the gift of adoption but who despise the incarnation of the pure generation of the Word of God. . . . The Word of God was made man, and he who was the Son of God became the Son of Man, that man, having been taken into the Word, and receiving the adoption, might become the son of God. For by no other means could we have attained to incorruptibility and immortality, unless we had been united to incorruptibility and immortality.

Ag. Her., bk. 3, chap. 19, par. 1 (ANF, vol. 1, 448, translation slightly modified)

---

nity past, through the loving presence of the Father with the Son (and the Holy Spirit, but again, Jesus does not mention him here). After God made the world and placed human beings in it, his desire for us was that we share that same glorious love with him and with each other. Jesus prays that those who follow him may be one with each other in the same way that he is one with the Father.

The relationship between the Father and the Son that Jesus describes here provides the basis for some of the early church's best reflection on the concept of *theōsis,* or participation in God. The four church fathers on whom I am concentrating the most—Irenaeus in the second century, Athanasius in the fourth century, and Augustine and Cyril of Alexandria in the fifth century—all recognize that participation in God, or "becoming divine," involves a variety of aspects, such as becoming incorruptible as God is incorruptible. But all four of them recognize that the central aspect of *theōsis*—and thus the heart of the bond between God's life and human life—lies in our adoption into Christ's sonship with the Father. In the sidebar (previous page) from Irenaeus, in which he claims that those who deny the reality of the incarnation have no salvation, notice that in salvation we receive the Logos (God the Son) himself. We do not simply receive something that he gives us, because the Son gives us his very self. And the essence of this gift of himself is that we become sons and daughters of God. We are adopted

---

Athanasius on Adopted Sonship (ca. 358):

God, being first Creator, next, as has been said, becomes Father of men, because of his Word dwelling in them. But in the case of the Word the reverse; for God, being his Father by nature, becomes afterward both his Creator and Maker, when the Word puts on that flesh which was created and made, and becomes man. For, as men, receiving the Spirit of the Son, become children through him, so the Word of God, when he himself puts on the flesh of man, then is said both to be created and to have been made. If then we are by nature sons [of God], then is he by nature creature and work; but if we become sons [of God] by adoption and grace, then has the Word also, when in grace toward us he became man, said "The Lord created me."

Ag. Arian., bk. 2, par. 61 (NPNF[2], vol. 4, 381)

---

into the same relationship he has with God the Father—into his own sonship with the Father. Incorruption and immortality (as well as other benefits of salvation) flow from the gift of God the Son himself; they are not the primary aspects of *theōsis*.

Similarly, Athanasius links participation in God to the gift of divine sonship or adoption, and in doing so, he carefully distinguishes God the Son from believers. In the sidebar just above, notice that the Logos, who was always the natural Son of God, became human, in order that we, who were not sons and daughters of God, might become

---

Augustine on Jesus' Prayer That Believers All Be One (ca. 410):

He [Jesus] is declaring his divinity, consubstantial with the Father
. . . in his own proper way, that is, in the consubstantial equality
of the same substance, and he wants his disciples to be one in
him, because they cannot be one in themselves, split as they are
from each other by clashing wills and desires, and the unclean-
ness of their sins. . . . Just as Father and Son are one not only by
equality of substance but also by identity of will, so these men, for
whom the Son is mediator with God, might be one not only by
being of the same nature, but also by being bound in the fellowship of the same love.

On Trin., bk. 4, chap. 12 (Hill, 161)

---

such. We were created as human beings and have become divine by
sharing in the Son's relationship to the Father. The means to this end
was the Son's action of becoming one of us through the incarnation.
Furthermore, the sidebar just above from Augustine shows that he interprets Jesus' prayer in John 17 in a closely analogous way.

Perhaps the most insightful reflection on this idea during the early
church comes from the fifth-century father Cyril of Alexandria, who
follows Irenaeus and Athanasius in making adoption into the Son's relationship to the Father the key aspect of *theōsis*. Like Athanasius, but with
much more precision, Cyril distinguishes two kinds of unity between

---

Cyril of Alexandria on the Difference Between Christ and Christians (ca. 425):

Shall we then abandon what we are by nature and mount up to
the divine and unutterable essence, and shall we depose the Word
of God from his very sonship and sit in place of him with the Father and make the grace of him who honors us a pretext for impi-
ety? May it never be! Rather, the Son will remain unchangeably in
that condition in which he is, but we, adopted into sonship and
gods by grace, shall not be ignorant of what we are.

Com. Jn., bk. 1, chap. 9 (Pusey, 86, translation modified)

---

the Father and the Son. The first is a unity of substance, and the Father and the Son do not share this kind of unity with us in any way whatsoever. The second, though, is a unity of love or fellowship that the Father and the Son have enjoyed from all eternity precisely because of their

---

Cyril of Alexandria on the Similarity Between Christ and Christians (ca. 425):

> When he had said that authority was given to them from him who is by nature Son to become sons of God, and had hereby first introduced that which is of adoption and grace, he can afterward add without danger [of misunderstanding] that they were begotten of God, in order that he might show the greatness of the grace which was conferred on them, gathering as it were into natural fellowship *[oikeiotēs physikē]* those who were alien from God the Father, and raising up the slaves to the nobility of their Lord, on account of his warm love toward them.

Com. Jn., bk. 1, chap. 9 (Pusey, 106, translation modified)

---

unity of substance. Cyril argues that God does share this kind of unity with us. In the sidebar (previous page) on the difference between Christ and Christians, notice that Cyril insists that we in no way mount up to the level of God. Instead we are adopted as daughters and sons of God by grace, not by nature and in essence, as Christ is. In the sidebar just above, on the similarity between Christ and Christians, notice that Cyril again clearly maintains the distinction between Christians and God, but at the same time he insists that we share in the natural fellowship between the Son and the Father. According to Cyril, we share by grace in the same fellowship or love that the persons of the Trinity share by nature. This is why Jesus can pray that believers may be one in the same way the Father and the Son are one. The Father and the Son are one in two ways, and we can be one with the Trinity and with each other in one of those two ways, by sharing in their fellowship of love.[5]

---

[5]In fact, Cyril develops his own technical terms to distinguish these two kinds of unity. He uses the Greek word *idiotēs* to refer to the identity of substance or nature between the persons of

CONCLUSIONS

In this chapter we have looked in some detail at Jesus' poignant final words to his disciples before his death, and I have argued that what Jesus says here is a key to understanding how Christian doctrine and Christian practice relate to each other. The heart of Christian faith is the eternal relationship that has characterized the persons of the Trinity, and Jesus explicitly describes the relationship between God the Father and himself, God the Son. This relationship links God's life to our lives, precisely because our lives are meant to be a sharing in that relationship. And in what I consider to be the best strand of patristic thought, our sharing in the Father-Son relationship is at the center of what it means for us to participate in God. However, what Jesus says here—as well as what church fathers such as Irenaeus, Athanasius and Cyril write about Christ—requires a great deal more explanation than I have given so far. What he says raises questions about God (How can he be one God if the Father and Son are treated so distinctly?), about the difference between Christianity and other religions (Is Christianity really monotheistic, given this sharp distinction between the Father and the Son?), and about what it means to be a Christian (Are we really supposed to be in God, and what does that even mean?). In the next chapter, I will attempt to address these questions and to explain more fully the link between the life of the Trinity and Christian life.

---

the Trinity. Father, Son and Spirit share *idiotēs* (identity of nature) with one another because they are the same God, the same being. Furthermore, Cyril uses the word *oikeiotēs* to refer to the unity of love and fellowship that binds the persons of the Trinity together. Even more strikingly, Cyril uses the phrase *oikeiotēs physikē* or "natural fellowship" to refer to the unity of love that the persons of the Trinity share precisely because they are of the same substance. They share *oikeiotēs physikē* (natural fellowship) because they share *idiotēs* (identity of nature). Armed with this distinction, Cyril insists that Christians do not in any way whatsoever share the *idiotēs* (identity of nature) of the Trinity (that would be pantheism), but in spite of this, we do share in God's *oikeiotēs* (fellowship). For a comprehensive explanation of Cyril's use of *idiotēs* and *oikeiotēs* to lay out his understanding of our participation in God's fellowship, see Donald Fairbairn, *Grace and Christology in the Early Church,* Oxford Early Christian Studies (Oxford: Oxford University Press, 2003), chap. 3.

Chapter 3

From the Father-Son Relationship to the Trinity, and Back

Among all of the world's religions there are only three great faiths that insist there is one and only one God. These, of course, are Judaism, Christianity and Islam. But from what I have written in the previous chapter, it may not seem like Christianity is very monotheistic. Over and over again in the upper room discourse, Jesus speaks of his relationship to the Father in a way that gives the impression that the two are more like separate gods than like one God. How can there really be only one God, if in fact the Son sees himself as being so distinct from the Father, and from the Holy Spirit as well? This is a good question, and this is the point at which Christianity departs most fundamentally from its monotheistic cousins. In fact, this is perhaps the biggest sticking point about Christianity in the minds of Jews and Muslims. They say that Christians cannot be monotheistic, or the Christians would not affirm the Trinity. In fact, Jesus' claim to be God infuriated the Jewish religious leaders of his day more than anything else he said,[1] and the Qur'an as well rails unrelentingly against the Christian doctrine of the Trinity.[2] Christians owe the religious world some kind of explanation

---

[1]See especially Mt 26:63-67; Jn 8:58; 10:30-33.
[2]See especially the Qur'an 17:111; 19:88-92.

for how we can speak of God as Father, Son and Spirit while still claiming to be monotheistic. And if what I have written so far is correct, then such an explanation is all the more needed. If we are to understand in what sense Christians can be one with God, then we must first grasp the way or ways in which the Father, Son and Spirit are one.

STARTING POINTS FOR DISCUSSING THE TRINITY

Typically, the first question one asks when one grapples with the concept of God as a Trinity is whether to start with the oneness of God or with his threeness. In fact, these different starting points are reputedly the sources of distinct Eastern and Western models of the Trinity. It is often said that from early in Christian history, the Western church has emphasized the oneness of God and the Eastern church has stressed God's threeness. Furthermore, it is usually argued that Augustine solidified this Western understanding in the early fifth century, whereas the fourth-century Cappadocians—Basil the Great, Gregory of Nazianzus and Gregory of Nyssa—crystallized the Eastern understanding.[3] We should recognize that whether one starts with the one or the three depends on how one interprets the flow of biblical revelation about the Trinity, and it is appropriate at this point for me to give a brief summary of that revelation.

There is no question that the overwhelming emphasis in the Old Testament is on the uniqueness of God (the fact that although there are many spiritual beings, there is no other being in or above the universe who deserves the title "God") and the unity of God (the fact that God is not divided within himself—he is not composed of parts that could be separated one from another, nor does he have competing tendencies). The most extended treatment of God's uniqueness in the entire Bible comes in Isaiah 43–45. In these three chapters, the prophet mentions and explains God's uniqueness eleven times (43:10-11; 44:6, 8, 24; 45:5, 6, 14, 18, 21, 22, 24). Other noteworthy Old Testament passages stressing God's uniqueness are Exodus 15:11 (in which Moses and Miriam sing, "Who among the gods is like you, O LORD?"), Deuter-

---

[3]For a good concise summary of this view, see Alister McGrath, *Historical Theology: An Introduction to the History of Christian Thought* (Oxford: Blackwell, 1998), pp. 61-72.

onomy 4:32-40 (in which Moses affirms in Deut 4:39: "The LORD is God in heaven above and on earth below. There is no other"), 2 Samuel 7:22 (in which David declares to God, "There is no one like you, and there is no God but you") and 1 Kings 8:60 (in which Solomon dedicates the temple by praying that "all the peoples of the earth may know that the LORD is God and that there is no other"). The clearest Old Testament statement of God's unity comes in Deuteronomy 6:4-9, the famous Shema, in which Moses says to the people in Deut 6:4, "Hear, O Israel: The LORD our God, the LORD is one." This passage was so central to the faith of ancient Israel that it was repeated constantly throughout the people's life and worship. The truth of God's unity is scarcely mentioned elsewhere in the Bible, because it did not need to be so mentioned. This passage on its own was the heart of the Old Testament understanding of God.

In contrast to this clear evidence about the oneness of God, the evidence for the Trinity in the Old Testament is rather slight, and there is a great deal of dispute about whether the passages in question refer to the Trinity. For example, there are potential indications of plurality within God in Genesis 1:26 ("Let us make man in our image"), Genesis 3:22 ("The man has now become like one of us") and Genesis 11:7 ("Come, let us go down and confuse their language"), as well as Isaiah 6:8 (God asks, "Whom shall I send? And who will go for us?"). But all of these passages could be interpreted another way—as God's talking to angels or as plurals of majesty (that is, God's referring to himself in the plural just as a king might speak of himself in the plural even though he is only one person). Other Old Testament evidence that may point to the Trinity is the use of the words "Son," "Lord" or "Word," in such a way that it might imply the Son/Word/Lord is a distinct person from God (Ps 2:7; 110:1; Dan 7:9-14). Furthermore, there are references to "spirit" in the Old Testament that may imply the Spirit is a person (Gen 1:2; 6:3; Neh 9:20-30; Is 63:10). I generally refer to passages like these as potential hints of the Trinity rather than actual statements that God is a Trinity.

It is not until the New Testament that we find clear indications that the Son and the Spirit are God, just as the Father is. Some of the most direct New Testament statements indicating that the Son (or Christ) is God are John 1:1-5 ("the Word was God"), Philippians 2:5-7 (Christ was equal to God but emptied himself at the incarnation), Col 1:15-20 (Christ is the image of the invisible God) and Hebrews 1:1-3 (the Son is the exact representation of the Father's being). We should also notice Jesus' indications that he understood himself to be God. He exercised prerogatives that only God possessed, such as the ability to forgive sins (Mt 9:1-7 and parallels Mk 2:1-12; Lk 5:17-26), greater power than Beelzebul (Mt 12:22-30 and parallels Mk 3:2-27; Lk 11:14-23), the right to judge the world at the end of the age (Mt 24:31-46) and the right to be worshiped (Jn 9:35-41). He also used the divine name, "I am" (from Ex 3:14-15), in reference to himself (Mt 14:27; Mk 14:62; Jn 4:26; 8:24, 28, 58; 13:12; 18:5). He claimed to be one with the Father (Jn 10:30) and stated that anyone who had seen him had seen the Father (Jn 14:9). Some of the evidence related to the Holy Spirit as God comes in Matthew 12:32 and the parallel, Mark 3:29 (blaspheming the Holy Spirit is unforgivable), Acts 5:3-4 (lying to the Holy Spirit constitutes lying to God) and 1 Corinthians 3:16-17; 6:19-20 (Paul calls believers "temples of the Holy Spirit" and "temples of God"). One should also compare Isaiah 6:9 and Acts 28:25, Psalm 95:7-11 and Hebrews 3:7, and Jeremiah 31:31-34 and Hebrews 10:15. In all three of these cases, the Old Testament passage is introduced with a statement such as "the Lord says," but when it is quoted in the New Testament, it is introduced with something like "the Spirit says."

Does the fact that God revealed his oneness first and only later his threeness mean that our articulation of the doctrine of the Trinity should begin with God's oneness rather than with threeness? One could make a case for doing so, and this is what much of Western trinitarian theology does. We take the Old Testament's statements about God as referring to God in general, and then within this God we distinguish the persons of Father, Son and Spirit. The problem with this is that it tends to turn God into an idea, and the concrete relationship between real persons—Father, Son and Spirit—tends to get lost in the discussion of the idea of God's "essence" or "substance." Another

aspect of modern Western trinitarian thought that tends to de-empha-
size the personal dimension of God's being is the use of analogies to
describe the Trinity. For example, we say that God is one and three in
the same way that water is one and three. (At the right temperature and
pressure, water can exist in gas, liquid and solid phases.) Or we say that
God can be one and three in the same way that a man can be a son, a
husband and a father. But there are significant problems with these
analogies and most others like them. It is true that water can exist in
solid, liquid and gaseous phases at very low atmospheric pressure and
temperature, but no single water molecule can be in more than one
phase at once. The water analogy, if pushed to its logical conclusion,
would imply that God changes from one phase to another, from one
person of the Trinity to another, at different times. Conversely, the
analogy of the father, son and husband points to three different relationships that the same person has with others, not to three distinct
persons in relationship one to another.[4]

In light of these problems, perhaps there is another way of account-
ing for the fact that biblical revelation begins with God's oneness. Re
member that the ancient Near Eastern society that surrounded ancient
Isreal was almost universally polytheistic. Against this polytheistic
background, if God had clearly revealed himself as Father, Son and
Holy Spirit in the Old Testament, the Jews would almost certainly have
understood this to mean that these three were separate gods. Father,
Son and Spirit would then have taken their places alongside Baal,
Molech, Asherah, and the many other gods and goddesses of the
ancient Near East. In other words, the people almost certainly could
not have understood that the three persons of the Trinity were a single
God if God had begun his revelation of himself with these three per-

---

[4]The use of analogies to explain the Trinity in Western theology had its origin in Augustine's
On Trin. However, Augustine's analogies, most notably Lover-Beloved-Love (in bk. 8, par.
10-12) and Memory-Understanding-Will (in bk. 14, par. 5-11), are much more personal than
the ones we often use. Furthermore, they are not meant as descriptions of God; they are attempts to understand something of the way in which we are called to reflect God. He is an
indescribable Trinity, but we see something of who he is by studying his image in ourselves.
Augustine's use of these analogies is so different from ours that perhaps "analogies" is not even
the right word for them in Augustine's thought. They are more like "resemblances" to the
uncreated God in created humanity.

sons. Instead, it was important for God to emphasize strongly and re-peatedly that the "gods" of the nations around Israel were not truly God at all; they were spiritual beings of a lesser status (demons, we would say). Only once the people clearly understood that there was but one true God could they begin to grasp the fact that this one God was somehow also three persons.

If I am right about this, then rather than starting with oneness in general and then using analogies to describe oneness and threeness in the abstract, we should understand the Old Testament's depictions of God as referring concretely to a person, God the Father. Then when we come to the New Testament, we recognize that this Father has a Son and a Spirit, and that these two are persons (thus they can have relationship with the Father and each other), and also that they are not separate gods but are united to the Father and each other so as to be a single God.

A careful reading of the New Testament seems to confirm this. The New Testament writers do not use the word *God* to refer in the abstract to God's essence or substance, nor do they treat the Father, Son and Spirit as some kind of subdivisions within God. Instead, the New Testament uses the word *God* primarily to refer to the Father, and on the basis of this usage, it affirms that the Son and Spirit are God as well, and indeed are the same God as the Father. For example, in 1 Corinthians 8:5-6, Paul writes, "For even if there are so-called gods, whether in heaven or on earth (as indeed there are many 'gods' and many 'lords'), yet for us there is but one God, the Father, from whom all things came and for whom we live; and there is but one Lord, Jesus Christ through whom all things came and through whom we live." Likewise, in the famous benedic-tion that closes 2 Corinthians, Paul writes in 13:14: "May the grace of the Lord Jesus Christ, and the love of God, and the fellowship of the Holy Spirit be with you all." Similarly, in Galatians 4:4-6, Paul writes that "God sent his Son" and "God sent the Spirit of his Son into our hearts." In Ephesians 4:4-6, Paul affirms, "There is one body and one Spirit—just as you were called to one hope when you were called—one Lord, one faith, one baptism; one God and Father of all, who is over all and through all and in all." In these four Pauline passages, the link between the persons of the Trinity is very strong, but the word "God," when used by itself, refers to the Father. The biblical idea is not so much that there is one divine essence in which Father, Son and Spirit participate. Rather, it is that there is one God, the Father, but there are also two other persons who are equal to him and united to him and each other in such a way that they are one being, one God.

THE TRINITY IN THE CHURCH FATHERS

This is precisely the way the early church understood God. In fact, I suggest that the distinction scholars often draw between the Cappadocians (representing the so-called Eastern view of the Trinity) and Augustine (who allegedly forged the so-called Western view of the Trinity) is exaggerated. As I read Augustine's *On the Trinity*, it seems to me that his basic framework is more like that of the Cappadocians than like that of the later Western church.[5] So I suggest that the early church as a whole began with God's threeness, and the shift to a focus on God's oneness as the starting point was primarily a later Western

---

Tertullian of Carthage on the Distinctions of the Three Persons (ca. 215):

> I testify that Father and Son and Spirit are unseparated from one other. . . . Understand then, I say that the Father is one, the Son another, and the Spirit another—every untrained or perverse person takes this saying wrongly, as if it expressed difference, and as the result of difference meant a separation of Father, Son, and Holy Spirit.

Ag. Prax., chap. 9 (Souter, 46)

---

[5]It is true that Augustine sometimes starts with the oneness of God (see *On Trin.*, bk. 8, par. 1 [Hill, 241], 3.21 [140], 5.3 [190] and 5.8 [194]). But at other times, he seems to start with the threeness of God (especially in bks. 2–7, and most notably in 7.3 [221] and 7.8-9 [226-27]). See also 15.42-43 (428). I suggest that in some respects Augustine paves the way for the Western understanding of the Trinity, but his actual understanding is closer to the early Eastern church than to the medieval Western church after him.

development. But whether or not I am right about Augustine, it is clear that this is the way most of the early church understood the Trinity. As the Fathers sought to articulate the doctrine of the Trinity in the second through fourth centuries, their starting point was the identification of the word *God* with the Father. For example, in the sidebar (previous page) from Tertullian of Carthage (who lived in the late second and early third centuries in Latin North Africa), notice that Tertullian assumes the distinctions between the persons of the Trinity. He insists that they are not separate (that is, that they are not three different gods), but he insists nonetheless that they are distinct as persons.

The burning question, then, was not whether the one God included three persons within himself but whether the Son and the Spirit were equal to God the Father (and thus somehow the same God as the Father) or whether they were lower than the Father in their being (and thus merely semi-divine beings, angels or the like). This question emerged openly in the middle of the third century, when the thought of Origen of Alexandria began to raise controversy within the church. There were a number of problematic aspects of Origen's thought, but for our purposes, the major problem was that he subordinated the Son and Spirit to the Father.[6] Origen's teaching was eventually condemned, but not until 553, and in the late third and early fourth centuries, Origen's followers pushed his thought further than their master had intended. One of these followers, Arius, a presbyter in Alexandria in the early fourth century, insisted so strongly on the Son as lower than the Father that he called him a creature, and this sparked the Arian controversy that bears his name. This controversy led initially to the meeting of a general council at Nicaea in 325, later called the First Ecumenical Council. This council condemned Arius and used the word *homoousios* ("of the same substance") to describe the Son's relationship to the Father. The intent of this word was to emphasize the full equality and identity between the Son and the Father, but the word turned out to be problematic because some feared that it might imply that Father and

---

[6]See, e.g., Origen's statement of the Son's inferiority to the Father in *On Princ.*, bk. 1, chap. 3, par. 5 (Butterworth, 33-34).

Athanasius on the Equality of the Son to the Father (ca. 358):

We take divine Scripture, and thence discourse with freedom of the religious faith, and set it up as a light upon its candlestick, saying: Very Son of the Father, natural and genuine, proper to his essence *(homoousios)*, Wisdom only-begotten, and very and only Word of God is he; not a creature or work but an offspring proper to the Father's essence *(homoousios)*. . . . A work is external to the nature, but a son is the proper offspring of the essence; it follows that a work need not have been always, for the workman frames it when he will. . . . A man may be and may be called maker, though the works are not as yet; but father he cannot be called, nor can he be, unless a son exist. . . . The Son, not being a work, but proper to the Father's essence, always is; for, whereas the Father always is, so what is proper to his essence must always be; and this is his Word and his Wisdom. . . . For the offspring not to be ever with the Father is a disparagement of the perfection of his essence.

Ag. Arian., bk. 1, chaps. 9, 29 (NPNF[2], vol. 4, 311, 323-24, translation slightly modified)

Son were a single person. In the complicated aftermath of Nicaea, Athanasius was the leader of a group of bishops who stood firmly for the truth that the Son had to be, and was, just as fully God as the Father in order to be able to save us. In the sidebar just above, notice Athanasius's use of the word *homoousios* ("proper to the essence" in this translation) and his insistence on the difference between a work and a Son. If Christ were a mere work, a creation of the Father, then Christ would not have always existed. But since Christ was and is the Son, then he must have always existed, or God could not have always been a Father. In the midst of this reasoning, notice again the assumption that the word *God* refers to the Father, and the issue is whether the Son is equal to God or less than God, eternal or created.

By the year 362, the church was in general agreement that the Son was and is equal to the Father, and from this time on the question turned to the status of the Holy Spirit. After Athanasius's death in 373, the mantle of leadership fell primarily to the great Cappadocians, Basil the Great, Gregory of Nazianzus and Gregory of Nyssa. Basil took up the question of the Holy Spirit and emphasized that he too was and is equal to the Father. In his treatise *On the Holy Spirit*, Basil assumes the distinction between the Father, Son and Holy Spirit as persons. His argument centers around the fact that the Holy Spirit possesses the

---

Basil the Great on the Holy Spirit (ca. 375):

> If we ponder the meaning of His name, and the greatness of His deeds, and the multitude of blessings He has showered on us and on all creation, it is possible for us to understand at least partially the greatness of His nature and unapproachable power. He is named Spirit: "God is Spirit," and "the Spirit of our nostrils, the Lord's Anointed," He is called holy, as the Father is holy and the Son is holy. For creatures, holiness comes from without; for the Spirit, holiness fills His very nature. He is not sanctified, but sanctifies. He is called good, as the Father is good; the essence of the Spirit embraces the goodness of the Father. He is called upright— the Lord my God is upright—because he is truth and righteousness personified. . . . The Spirit shares titles held in common by the Father and the Son; He receives these titles due to his natural and intimate relationship with them.

On HS, par. 48 (Anderson, 76)

---

same qualities and receives the same titles as the Father and Son, so the three must be equal. As such, they are a single God even though they are distinct as persons. In the sidebar just above, notice that Basil sees the Holy Spirit as the source of our sanctification, and he could not be such a source if he were not God himself. Notice also that he clearly sees the Holy Spirit as a person, not just a force or power of God, and that he speaks of the intimate relationship between the Spirit and the Father and the Son.

Led by the Cappadocians and others, the early church enshrined this understanding of God by ratifying its greatest creedal statement. A first version of this creed (the Creed of Nicaea) had been established at the

---

Nicene-Constantinopolitan Creed (381):

We believe in one God, Father, all-sovereign, maker of heaven and earth, of all things seen and unseen.

And in one Lord Jesus Christ, the only-begotten Son of God, who was begotten from the Father before all the ages, light from light, true God from true God, begotten, not made, of the same substance *(homoousios)* with the Father, through whom all things came into existence, who because of us men and our salvation came down from heaven, and was incarnated by the Holy Spirit and the virgin Mary and was made man, was crucified on our behalf by Pontius Pilate, and suffered, and was buried and arose on the third day according to the Scriptures, and ascended into heaven, and is seated at the right of the Father and is coming again with glory to judge the living and the dead, of whose kingdom there will be no end.

And in the Holy Spirit, the Lord, who makes us alive, who proceeds from the Father, who is worshiped and glorified together with the Father and the Son, who has spoken through the prophets. In one holy, catholic and apostolic church. We confess one baptism for the forgiveness of sins. We await the resurrection of the dead and the life of the coming age. Amen.

(Fairbairn's translation)

First Ecumenical Council in Nicaea in 325, and the expanded version (technically called the Nicene-Constantinopolitan Creed but more commonly known simply as the Nicene Creed) was approved at the Second Ecumenical Council in Constantinople in 381. The sidebar just above contains the text of this creed. Notice that the starting point is the identification of the one God as the Father and that the bulk of the creed concentrates on the equality of the Son and the Spirit to the Father. The working understanding of the Trinity in this creed is that there are three persons who are equal and eternal and who therefore are a single God. The Son and Spirit are identified with the Father even as they are acknowledged to be distinct persons. This, I suggest, is the way the early church, in the West as well as the East,[7] understood God the Trinity.

Let us think about this more carefully. Remember that in the upper room discourse, Jesus not only speaks of himself, the Father and the Spirit as distinct persons, but he also speaks of that distinction as being an eternal one. From before the time when the world was created, the Father has loved the Son and has been "in" the Son. One could not say this if the "persons" were merely different roles that the one God played with respect to humanity, different relationships the one God had with other personal beings or different appearances that the one God assumed at different times. One cannot speak of love and relationship unless one is speaking of distinct persons, so the distinctions between the persons are indicative of who God has always been, from all eternity. So instead of thinking in terms of One, who is somehow also three, we need to think in terms of Three, who have always been in relationship one to another and who are united in such a way that they are a single God rather than three separate gods. I have argued that this is the way the New Testament itself describes God, and it was one of the most fundamental things the church fathers recognized about the biblical witness.

Furthermore, we should notice that this way of understanding the Trinity is foundational to the reading of Jesus' words in John 13–17. If the link between theology and Christian life is really *theōsis*, and if *theōsis* is best understood as our sharing in the Son's relationship to the Father, then there must truly be an eternal relationship between Father and Son as distinct persons in order for God to share this relationship with us when he saves us. This doctrine of the Trinity is not an abstraction whose connection with Christian life is tenuous or even nonexis-

---

[7]It is worth pointing out that creeds of Western origin, such as the Apostles' Creed and the so-called Athanasian Creed, also identify the one God as the Father and then assert that the Son and the Spirit are the same God.

tent. Rather, the doctrine of the Trinity is the gateway to understanding Christian life. A God who was completely alone would have had nothing relational to offer us in salvation; he could have offered only a right status before him or something of that sort. But because God has eternally existed as a fellowship of three persons, there is fellowship within God in which we can also share.

However, even if this concept of the Trinity is foundational to the early church's understanding of Christian life, it may seem to you that such an understanding is utterly impossible. How can three distinct persons who have eternally been in a loving relationship with one another possibly be the same God? This is admittedly a difficult question, but let us now try to address it.

Grappling with the Doctrine of the Trinity

In order to get our minds around this seeming impossibility, let us briefly consider two human beings who have a great deal in common—say, identical twins. If one were to list all the characteristics the twins shared, it would be a long list. They have a very similar appearance and probably similar habits and mannerisms. Most strikingly, they have exactly the same DNA. But in spite of all those similarities, the twins do not have every characteristic in common. To state the obvious, they do not have the same body. In most cases, people who know them well can tell that they do not look exactly alike. Almost never do they have identical or even very similar personalities. They are not the same being even though they have the same DNA, because in spite of that shared genetic blueprint, they do not possess every characteristic in common.

But what if it is possible to have two (or more to the point, three) persons who do possess every characteristic in common? Of course this would not be possible if we were talking about human persons, because three human persons could not inhabit the same body. But let us turn from the analogy of identical twins or triplets to divine persons, who are not in bodily form. What if there are three divine persons who are infinite, bodiless, all-powerful, all-wise and so on? If one could list absolutely every characteristic these persons possess, and if every characteristic is common to all three of them, then in what sense can one say that they are separate beings? Of course, it is hard for us to imagine how they can really be distinct persons if they have every characteristic in common, so one might be tempted at this point to say that they only appear to be distinct persons. I will return momentarily to that issue, but for now the point is that if it is possible for persons to possess every characteristic in common while still being distinct persons, we cannot say that they are separate beings.

This is what the Bible affirms about the Father, Son and Holy Spirit. To speak of God, according to the Bible, is to speak of an infinite spiritual being who possesses certain characteristics that are described throughout Scripture. These characteristics that the Bible describes— perfect love, perfect holiness, all knowledge, all power—are by no means an exhaustive list of all the qualities God possesses, but they give a sufficient picture of his character to separate him clearly from all other spiritual beings.[8] The Old Testament makes quite clear that there is only one being who possesses all of these characteristics (often called "attributes" in Western theological language)—God the Father. But then, the New Testament affirms explicitly what the Old Testament merely hints at—that in addition to the Father who possesses these characteristics, there are two other persons, the Son and the Spirit, who also possess the same characteristics and who therefore are somehow the same God as the Father. So the Bible depicts three divine persons who are identical in terms of characteristics or attributes, although, as we will see shortly, there are other ways to distinguish them in spite of their having the same set of divine attributes. Theologians describe this by saying that they possess a single "substance," "nature" or "essence" or simply that they are a single God.

In fact, at the end of the patristic period, the eighth-century Syrian father John of Damascus makes this point clearly in a passage I quote in the

---

[8]Virtually any Western theology textbook will have an extensive discussion of God's attributes. The ones I mention in this sentence are simply the attributes most crucial for purposes of the argument I am developing here. Among the many biblical passages dealing with these, see the following: All power—Gen 17:1; 18:1-14; 28:3; 35:11; 43:14; 48:3; Ex 6:3; Jer 32:17-27; Ezek 10:5; Dan 3:17; Lk 1:37. All knowledge—Job 28:23-24; Ps 147:4-5; Acts 1:24; Heb 4:13. Perfect love—Ps 103:17; 136; Is 43:4; Jer 31:3; 1 Jn 4:8, 16. Perfect holiness—Is 5:16; 6:3; 45:21; Rev 4:8.

sidebar just below. Notice here that the "nature" of God is not an entity in itself; it is the set of characteristics (attributes, in Western terminology) that define what it means to be God. A person who possesses all of these biblical

---

John of Damascus on the Trinity (ca. 750):

The Word of God, in so far as He subsists in Himself, is distinct from Him from whom He has His subsistence. But, since He exhibits in Himself those same things which are discerned in God, then in His nature He is identical with God. . . . By the three Persons we understand that God is uncompounded and without confusion; by the consubstantiality of the Persons and their existence in one another and by the indivisibility of the identity of will, operation, virtue, power and, so to speak, motion we understand that God is one. For God and His Word and His Spirit are really one God.

Orth. Faith, bk. 1, chaps. 6, 8 (FC, vol. 37, 174, 185)

---

characteristics is God. But three persons who possess all the same divine attributes are not three separate beings; they are a single God.

If this is true then we must return to the question I asked just above: how can persons who are really identical be considered distinct persons? Here there are two things that are worth pointing out. First, the fact that love is a characteristic of God (see especially 1 Jn 4:8) implies that God does something—he loves. But whom does he love? Well, of course, he loves us. But we have not always been here. In fact, no being in the universe has always been here, since the universe itself has not always been here. But the Bible indicates that God has been a loving being from all eternity. The very fact that this is true implies that even though God is a single being, there is still some kind of distinction of persons, so that one person can love another. The Bible also shows us that this distinction is threefold. There are three persons who have loved one another from all eternity: the Father, the Son and the Spirit.

The second thing that is worth pointing out is that even though the persons are identical in terms of characteristics, they are not identical in the way they are related one to another. The Son is begotten by the Father, and the Spirit proceeds from the Father (and perhaps also from the Son as well).[9] That is to say, the relation between the Son and the Father is not identical to the relation between the Spirit and the Father, even though all three persons possess identical characteristics and even though they share in the same relationship of love and fellowship. The distinction I am making here between "relationship" and "relation" is a fine one, but nevertheless an important one. I use the word *relationship* here in the same way I use it throughout this book, in the sense of personal fellowship and communion. I use the word *relation* to refer to the manner in which each person of the Trinity is associated with the others. Thus, one can say that the relationship all three persons share is the same—a personal communion of love exemplified by the fellowship between Father and Son described in the upper room discourse but common to the Spirit as well. Nevertheless, the Father's relation to the Son is not exactly the same as his relation to the Spirit, and these different relations are the key to distinguishing the persons of the Trinity.

Theologically, the relations that distinguish the persons are called properties, and the characteristics that show them to be identical (or, in theological language, "of the same nature") are called attributes.[10] All three persons possess the same attributes, so they have a single nature (since the nature is the complete set of attributes defining what it means to be God), and thus they are a single God rather than three different gods. But the Father and the Spirit are not the begotten persons of the Trinity; only the Son is begotten. In other words, he has eternally been in a relation as Son to Father, not brother to brother or something else. In an analogous way, the Father and the Son are not the proceeding

---

[9]One of the major historical disputes between the Eastern and Western churches has centered around the question of whether the Holy Spirit proceeds from the Father alone or from the Father and from the Son. The original version of the Nicene Creed stated simply that the Holy Spirit proceeds from the Father. (See the sidebar quoting this creed above.) In the sixth century in Spain, the phrase "and from the Son" (one word in Latin—*filioque*) was added to the creed. This altered version of the creed was common in the West by the ninth century, although it was not approved by the pope until the eleventh century. The controversy over this question was at its height in the middle of the ninth century.

[10]For an excellent late patristic discussion of the properties that distinguish the divine persons, see John of Damascus, *Orth. Faith,* bk. 1, chap. 8 (FC, vol. 37, 176-88).

persons; only the Spirit proceeds. In other words, he is not in a filial relation to the Father, the way the Son is, but rather he is in a processional relation; he goes out ("proceeds") from the Father to accomplish his will.[11] If one looks at these relations from the other side, one may say that the Father is begetter of the Son and spirator of the Holy Spirit (that is, the one who breathes out or sends forth the Spirit).

LOVE, UNITY AND THE UNIQUENESS OF CHRISTIANITY

Obviously, the Trinity is the deepest mystery of the Christian faith, and a few pages—or even a few books or a few libraries—do not begin to do justice to such a mystery. Nevertheless, I hope it is clear at this point that Christianity is monotheistic, but the monotheism of Christianity is very different from that of Judaism or Islam. Christian monotheism affirms the presence of three eternal, divine persons who are united in such a way as to be a single God and whose love for one another is the basis for all of human life. These persons are not separate—that would imply that they were different gods—but they are distinct as persons, and this distinction is what makes it possible for God to share love within himself from all eternity. In addition, this way of understanding God has important implications for the way one describes the unity between God and Christians, the unity that Jesus prays for in John 17. Let us now return to that unity and look at it in more detail.

Of the different kinds of unity that I mentioned in the previous chapter, there are two that are highly significant for religious purposes. The first is what we sometimes call a unity of substance, and the second could be called a unity of communion or fellowship. A unity of substance im-

---

[11]On the basis of the ideas of begetting and procession, some of the church fathers argued that the way to distinguish the persons was through the concept of source or cause. The Father is the sole source or principle of the godhead, and the Son and Spirit are God because they are caused by the Father (see, e.g., Gregory of Nyssa's *Not Three Gods* [Rusch, 159-60]). In contrast, others argued that the idea of causation made it hard to maintain the eternality and full equality of the Son and the Spirit (see, e.g., Gregory of Nazianzus's *Or.* 29, par. 2 [Wickham, 70]). It is best, I think, to speak of the persons as being equal and to distinguish them simply by the Son's and Spirit's different relations to the Father—begetting versus procession. For an excellent discussion of the complexities of this issue, see chapter 8 of Thomas F. Torrance, *The Trinitarian Faith: The Evangelical Theology of the Ancient Catholic Church* (Edinburgh: T & T Clark, 1988).

plies that there is fundamentally no substantial difference between the two entities that are united. Ultimately, the two are one thing. When Eastern mysticism (which is increasingly popular in the West today as well) speaks of oneness or unity, this is what it has in mind. People's problem is not that they are disunited from the universe or from what can be called "god." (I place the word *god* in quotation marks because Eastern mystical thought does not generally think of God in anything like the monotheistic sense. "God" is not a being distinct from the universe but an all-pervading, impersonal spirit within the universe.) Rather, the problem is that people simply do not realize their fundamental oneness with the universe. So the religious task is to recognize that we are one with the cosmos, to get in touch with the living divinity within ourselves, to actualize the "self" which is "god." This kind of unity tends to blur the distinction between people and "god," and it turns the spiritual quest into an attempt to get in touch with ourselves, rather than an attempt to know a God who is different from us. Thus there is a kind of self-focus in Eastern mysticism that makes it especially attractive to contemporary Westerners. This kind of spirituality appeals to our belief that we are the most important beings in the universe by affirming that we are, in fact, at one with the very spirit of the universe.

In sharp contrast to that sort of oneness, a unity of fellowship maintains the distinctions between the persons who are united and sees the bond between them in personal, relational terms. This kind of unity is one of love, and it is clear that in his prayer in John 17, Jesus is talking about this second kind of unity. But in order to understand this prayer more fully—and thus in order to understand Christianity itself more fully—one needs to recognize that between the trinitarian persons both kinds of unity are present, but God shares only one of these with Christian believers. God possesses both a unity of substance and a unity of fellowship. The persons of the Trinity are a single God precisely because they share a common nature or substance, or to say it the way I did above, they have every attribute or characteristic in common. But this is not the only kind of unity the persons of the Trinity share; they also share in a unity of love, of fellowship, and that kind of unity is possible precisely because they are distinct as persons. Identical in substance and attributes (characteristics), they nevertheless relate to one another as distinct persons. Therefore, they can be and are united to one another in giving and receiving love.[12]

When Jesus prays that Christians may be one in the way the Father and Son are one, he is talking about this second kind of unity. We are not only distinct as persons, but we are different beings from God as well. We are not fundamentally the same thing as God, and what we are really looking for cannot be found by simply getting in touch with an alleged divinity within ourselves. Christianity therefore asserts that we cannot and do not ever become one with God in substance. To say that would be blasphemy, because it would deny the utter uniqueness of God, his utter superiority to all things he has made, including human beings. (Thus the patristic idea of *theōsis* emphatically does not mean that we become united with God in substance.) But at the same time, Father, Son and Holy Spirit also possess a unity of fellowship. This is what God shares with us. This is what Jesus prays all believers may have. This is what ties our lives to the very life of God, and this is what I think the best strand of patristic thought means by *theōsis*. This, according to Christianity, is what we were created to share.

On this point, Eastern mystical religions effectively bring God down to the level of the universe. The attraction of this kind of spirituality lies in the fact that it puts human beings on a par with the highest spirit in existence. But this is a misleading attraction, because lowering "god" to our level does not elevate us; it just gives us a false sense of our own importance. In contrast, Judaism and Islam properly maintain the distinction between God and all that he has created, but they offer human beings little more than servant status in God's purposes. Or if they do speak of "fellowship with God," they do not mean this in the same way Christianity does. Only Christianity affirms that within God there is love and fellowship. Only the Christian God has such fellowship to share with humanity. Thus only Christianity is willing to say that people are and always will be lower than God, but at the same time, we are not meant to be merely servants. We are meant to be

---

[12]This is the point that Cyril of Alexandria makes by using the words *idiotēs* (unity of nature) and *oikeiotēs* (fellowship).

Christ's "friends," as he says in John 15. We are meant to remain creatures and thus remain lower than God but at the same time to share in the fellowship and love that have existed from all eternity between the persons of the Trinity. This is a deeper, more personal and more profound spirituality than either Eastern mysticism or the world's other great monotheisms offer. This is what Jesus, the Bible and the Christian faith claim people are meant for, even though most Christians do not fully recognize it. Or better, this is whom we are meant for. This God who shares such fellowship within himself offers his very self to us in this way, and he is the center of life as it is meant to be.

CONCLUSIONS

In this chapter, I have tried briefly to set what Jesus says in the upper room discourse into the larger context of Christian doctrine as a whole. The understanding of God as a Trinity is intimately tied to the Christian understanding of what God intends for humanity, and I believe that the writers of the early church have articulated this connection truly and powerfully. As a result of this discussion, I hope it is clear that Christianity is not merely one religion among many equivalent faiths. The vision of life, the vision of humanity's place within the universe and the vision of what (or better, whom) the spiritual person receives are all quite different in Christianity than they are in other religions. Christ refuses to stand in a line-up of interchangeable religious options. What he claims to give people—a share in the fellowship he and the Spirit have enjoyed with the Father from all eternity—is not even on offer in other religions. To say this a different way, the kind of salvation Christ gives us is not offered—or even conceivable—in other religions, and if the Bible is true, this kind of salvation is the only kind there really is. Salvation or heaven apart from Christ is inconceivable, precisely because salvation is Christ; salvation is our sharing in Christ's relationship to his eternal Father.

One could argue that in chapters two and three of this book, I have focused so much on the Father's relationship to the Son that I have neglected the third person of the Trinity, the Holy Spirit. Part of the reason for this is that in general the Bible does not say very much about him. The

Spirit is the inspirer of Scripture, and as he inspired the biblical writers to record God's Word, he did not generally call attention to himself. Instead, he directed our attention to the other two persons of the Trinity, the Father and the Son. Because of the Bible's relative scarcity of references to the Holy Spirit, it is not surprising that Scripture also does not say very much about the Holy Spirit's relationship to the Father and the Son. We may assume that what Jesus specifically says about his own relationship to the Father is also true in an analogous way of his relationship to the Holy Spirit and of the Spirit's relationship to the Father, but Scripture does not spell that out directly.

In addition, we need to recognize that the Spirit's task with respect to us is not so much to exemplify the relationship between the persons of the Trinity as it is to bring us into that relationship. Even though he surely shares the same eternal loving relationship with the Father as the Son does, he is not the person to whom we look in order to describe the trinitarian relationship. Rather, he is the one who unites us to that relationship. So as this book continues, I will have the opportunity at several points to return to the way the Holy Spirit unites us to the relationship that is shared among all three trinitarian persons but that the Bible describes mainly as the Father-Son relationship. These forthcoming discussions of the Holy Spirit in various places will, I hope, fill the gap left by my relative lack of attention to him so far.

At this point, one could easily raise the question: "What does it mean for us to share in the fellowship between the persons of the Trinity?" What does it mean for us to be in Christ in the way the Father and the Son are in each other? Here we move even deeper into the fundamental mystery of the Christian faith, and I suggest that it might be better to ask not what it means but rather what it looks like for us to share in this relationship. What does it look like in everyday life for human beings to reflect and share in the love between the persons of the Trinity? If Christ's fellowship with his Father is indeed the scarlet thread of the Christian faith, then when we have a share in that relationship, what do we look like on the ground? These are the questions we will consider in chapter 4 of this book.

Life as It Was Meant to Be

A REFLECTION OF THE
FATHER-SON RELATIONSHIP

In this chapter, as we look at the way human life was meant to reflect the relationship between the Father and the Son, it is appropriate to start by examining the beginning of human history, before sin disrupted God's intention. Once we have looked at humanity as originally created, I would like to turn our attention to contemporary society today in order to describe some of the major differences between life as God meant it to be and life as it is now. In this way, I hope to flesh out my discussion of what it looks like for us to share in the fellowship that has eternally existed between the Father, Son and Spirit.

THE SPIRIT, THE IMAGE OF GOD AND HUMANITY IN THE BEGINNING

The book of Genesis deals with the beginning of the universe and human life. Genesis 1 contains a day-by-day account of God's creation of all things, culminating with the creation of human beings on the sixth day. We read: "Then God said, 'Let us make man in our image, in our likeness, and let them rule over the fish of the sea and the birds of the air, over the livestock, over all the earth, and over all the creatures that move along the ground.' So God created man in his own image, in the image of God he created him; male and female he created them" (Gen 1:26-27). There are several things about this passage that are controversial, but I will try to draw some conclusions without spending undue space on the controversies. First, it is fairly certain that "image" and "likeness" are synonyms. Some patristic writers and a few modern scholars have tried to see them as distinct, but the probability is that they are used more or less interchangeably.[1] Second, it is not clear exactly what characteristic of human beings constitutes the image of God within us. Some have suggested that it is our reasoning capacity, others have said it is our free will, others have pointed to our spiritual nature, and still others have even speculated that it is our threeness (body, soul and spirit) as an image of the Trinity. But nowhere does the Bible spell out specifically what the image of God entails.

Third, whatever the image of God consists of, it is clear that this image sets human beings apart from the rest of creation. We are somehow distinct from all other creatures God made, and that distinctness qualifies us to govern the rest of creation. In fact, the image of God (whatever it is, exactly) does not merely distinguish us from animals and plants (which are fairly obviously lower than us on the created scale); it also distinguishes human beings from angels. Even though angels are spiritual beings and are "closer" to God than people are (their main task is to surround God and worship him[2]), Scripture never says that they are created in the image of God. (As one of my students helpfully put it, angels are greater than people in "altitude," but this does not mean they are more like God than we are.) Human beings alone bear this distinction, and all human beings bear the image of God. The passage makes an explicit point of stating that all mankind, male and female, is created in the image of God.

---

[1]Among patristic writers who distinguished "image" and "likeness," Origen is the most famous. Commenting on Gen 1:26-27, he writes that human beings were created in the image of God but called to aspire to the divine likeness through our own effort. See *On Princ.*, bk. 3, chap. 6, par. 1 (Butterworth, 245). In sharp contrast, Athanasius and Cyril of Alexandria (among others) insist that "image" and "likeness" are synonyms, describing characteristics which God gave humanity at creation. See Athanasius, *On Incar.*, chap. 13 (Thomson, 165-67), and Cyril, *On Sol.,* par. 3 (Wickham, 195).
[2]See, e.g., Ps 103:20; 148:2; Is 6:1-4; Rev 5:11-12.

Moreover, the fact that human beings bear the image of God does not merely distinguish us from the rest of creation, it also distinguishes us from God and at the same time explicitly links us to the God who created us in his image. Three times in the New Testament, the biblical writers refer to the Son (or Christ) using image language. In 2 Corinthians 4:4, Paul calls Christ "the image of God," and in Colossians 1:15, he refers to Christ as "the image of the invisible God." Similarly Hebrews 1:3 declares, "The Son is the radiance of God's glory and the exact representation of his being." These three passages remind us that although we are created in the image of God, we are not the very image of God itself. This exact image is Christ, the Son.[3] But even so, we more than all other creatures are meant to reflect the Son, to be the created images that bear witness by our lives to the one true image of God. This means that there is a direct link between human beings and God the Son.

The Son is the eternal, uncreated image of God, and he has eternally shared in fellowship with his Father (and the Spirit). Furthermore, one of the ways he has shared that fellowship with the Father was by carrying out the Father's will through the creation and sustaining of the universe (see Jn 1:1-5; Col 1:15-20; Heb 1:1-3). Humanity is the created image of God, and humanity was initially called to exercise dominion over the universe (Gen 1:28). If the function of humanity was originally to exercise a role within creation similar to that which the Son has exercised over creation, and if humanity and the Son were linked by the possession of the image of God, then one may reasonably infer that human beings were originally meant to share in the Son's fellowship with his Father as well. The passage does not state this directly, but the close analogy between the roles of the uncreated Son and created human beings, coupled with the link Jesus later draws between his own relationship with the Father and believers, strongly suggests that the created image bearers were meant to share in the fellowship that the uncreated image has enjoyed with his Father. If this is correct, then we may understand the fellowship with God that Adam and Eve

---

[3]Athanasius reflects on the distinction between the Son as the very image of God and human beings as the created images in *On Incar.*, par. 13 (Thomson, 165-67).

enjoyed prior to the Fall as specifically their participation in the Son's own fellowship with God.

In addition to this direct link between human beings and Christ, there also seems to be a link between humanity and the Holy Spirit in the descriptions of creation. We have seen that Genesis 1 gives a bird's-eye view of creation as a whole, culminating with the creation of humanity at the end of the chapter. Genesis 2 is a more detailed look at the creation of human beings, and as part of that in-depth treatment, verse 7 reads, "The LORD formed the man from the dust of the ground and breathed into his nostrils the breath of life, and the man became a living being." Most of the church fathers, as well as most modern scholars, see Genesis 2:7 as God's giving Adam a soul.[4] However, this passage is tantalizingly similar to Jesus' later words after his resurrection. John 20:21-22 tells us, "Again Jesus said, 'Peace be with you! As the Father has sent me, I am sending you.' And with that, he breathed on them and said, 'Receive the Holy Spirit.'" Notice that in both of these passages, God/Jesus breathes on Adam/the disciples. In light of these similarities, Genesis 2:7 may mean that God breathed not the breath of life but the Spirit of life (that is, the Holy Spirit) into Adam, just as Jesus later breathes on the disciples as a way of communicating the Holy Spirit to them. The parallels between the passages in Genesis and John are striking, and the strand of thought in the early church which I believe is most fruitful for us today does see these two passages as parallel. This strand of thought argues that in Genesis 2:7 God gave Adam the Holy Spirit himself, thus linking him to the Son in whose image he was created and causing him to share in the fellowship of the Trinity. Likewise, when God gives the Spirit anew through redemption, he is restoring people to a state akin to the original sharing in the life of the Trinity that humankind lost through the Fall. In the sidebar on the next page, Cyril of Alexandria envisions the closest possible link between Genesis 2:7 and John 20:22, as he argues that the holiness the

---

[4]For an extended ancient defense of the idea that the verse refers to God's giving Adam a soul, rather than giving him the Holy Spirit, see Augustine, *City of God,* bk. 13, chap. 24 (Bettenson, 540-46). Modern commentators typically assume that the passage refers to the giving of a soul and do not consider the possibility that it might refer to God's giving the Holy Spirit.

Cyril of Alexandria on Genesis 2:7 and John 20:22 (ca. 435):

> Seeing that he [Adam] ought to be not merely rational with an
> aptitude for doing good and right but also a participator in the
> Holy Spirit, he [God] breathed into him, so that he might have
> brighter marks of the divine nature within him, the breath of life.
> This is the Spirit furnished through the Son to rational creation and
> shaping it into the sublimest, that is, the divine, form. . . . Christ's
> act was a renewal of that primal gift and of the inbreathing be-
> stowed on us, bringing us back to the form of the initial holiness
> and carrying man's nature up, as a kind of firstfruits among the
> holy apostles, into the holiness bestowed on us initially at the first
> creation.

On Sol., par. 2 (Wickham, 189-91, translation slightly modified)

disciples receive after the resurrection is a participation in the Holy
Spirit and that this is the same holiness that God initially bestowed on
Adam, also through participation in the Holy Spirit.

If this strand of patristic thought is correct, then Adam and Eve as
originally created shared directly in the person of the Holy Spirit and
mirrored in a created way the uncreated Son, the exact and perfect image of God. Thus humanity as originally created was linked directly
and personally to the Trinity. In fact, even if Genesis 2:7 is not referring to the inbreathing of the Spirit into humanity, other details of the
creation account provide links to the Trinity. In Genesis 2:15-17, God
gives Adam a command not to eat of the fruit of a certain tree. As we
have seen, commands are opportunities for us to love God. Just as the
Son obeys God the Father in John 15:10, so too human beings were
called to love God by obeying him. In doing so, people were to share
in the Son's relationship to his Father. Moreover, such participation in
the Father-Son relationship was not meant to be purely vertical. Rather,
people were meant to share that same fellowship among themselves as
well. Genesis 2:18 indicates that even when Adam was surrounded by
God's presence and by all the wonders that God had made, he was still

"alone" in a sense that was somehow "not good" (a startling phrase in the midst of a creation account replete with the statements "it was good" and "it was very good"). So God created Eve from Adam's rib, gave her to Adam as his wife (Gen 2:21-22), and commanded the two of them to be fruitful and multiply (Gen 1:28). These passages hint that God intended human beings to share his presence both with God and with each other. He even wanted to ensure that there would be more people around who could share this presence with each other. To state this in the terms I have been developing in this book, the relationship between the persons of the Trinity was so valuable that God created people in his image to share in that relationship. This sharing was meant to take place not merely through people's relationship to God, but also through human relationships with one another. Humanity was initially linked to God and called to image forth the Son's relationship to God. Human life as God meant it to be, as God created it initially, was life in the Trinity.

LIFE IN THE TRINITY: THEN AND NOW

What I have written above has two potential problems. First, it is still too abstract and in need of concrete details. As we have asked before, what does it mean or look like to share in the fellowship of the Trinity? Second, it surely sounds too idyllic to square very well with what we know of life today. Accordingly, at this time I would like to turn our attention from the Bible's (and the early church's) depiction of life before the Fall to life in contemporary Western society today. I believe the contrast between life as we know it and life as God meant it to be will help us to grasp more fully what life in the Trinity was (and still is!) meant to look like.

Face it—ordinary life involves a lot of chaos. Dealing with parents, children, siblings, friends, relatives, teachers, students, spouses, co-workers and so on can be a challenge at best and can lead to all-out verbal war at worst. Dealing with deadlines, financial worries, and the perpetual conflict between what we need and what we want can be draining at best and debilitating at worst. For the vast majority of us, no matter what our age or station in life, living involves some turbulent waters. And I suspect that when we look at the chaos that so often dominates our everyday lives, we tend to think the only way to deal with it is either to eliminate it or to tolerate it in silence. As many of us know, neither of these works particularly well, since chaos does not normally stay eliminated, and we are not normally able to stay quiet about it forever. In the remainder of this chapter, I would like to suggest that these two choices are neither the only options nor the best options. Chaos does not need to be either eliminated or tolerated; it can be redeemed. And redeeming the chaos of normal life requires the recognition that this life, especially this life, is meant to be a reflection of the love between the Father and the Son.

The word *redeem* means "to buy back," and the idea is that something which has been taken is restored to its rightful owner. When I assert that the chaos of everyday life can be redeemed, what I mean is that there is something that chaos has taken from us, and it is possible for people to see it restored, to see life return to the way God originally meant it to be. What is that something? In short, it is perspective. The chaos we face on a daily basis seems to be unending and meaningless, because we have lost the perspective which alone can give it meaning. As we think about perspective together, I would like to break my discussion of it into four parts. These are significance, peace, the value of work and the conduct of human relationships.

Significance in a different guise. It is often said that one of the most basic human needs is for a sense of significance. All of us need to believe that what we do matters, that our lives are important. This is part of the reason we often speak of our need "to be a part of something bigger than ourselves." But one of the ways modern Western society has sapped people's sense of significance is that it tied that significance to things that are generally out of reach. Look through the pages of *People* magazine, the *Parade* section of the Sunday newspaper or the endless webpages devoted to famous people, and you will quickly conclude that what we think makes a person significant is celebrity. We fawn over movie stars, athletes and self-made women and men who have pulled themselves up by their bootstraps, gained fame and fortune. and are now determined to show the rest of us that they are every bit as important as we seem to think they are. For that matter, we also fawn over people who have not pulled themselves up by their bootstraps but who were born with celebrity status.

What does this cult of celebrity do to us? For starters, it completely distorts our sense of proportion. A famous actress's break-up with her current guy is no more a tragedy than your own or your roommate's or your neighbor's. We quickly lose sight of how important certain things really are, or are not, when we dive headlong into the worship of our favorite celebrities. But our cult of celebrity has a more insidious effect on us than this. It sends us a constant, subliminal message that we are not really important. The vast majority of us will never be featured in *People* magazine, nor is anyone outside our circle of friends going to care whether we win the cheerleading competition, where we go to college, whom we marry or how our children like their new school. Most of us will not get our names in the paper more than a small handful of times in our lives, and even then, it will not be in *Parade*. Most of us are not going to see a million dollars at one time, get a tickertape parade, bask away our lives on the shore of a tropical island or even stay in a nice hotel room on the beach over spring break or in the best suite on a cruise ship when we take that once-in-a-lifetime vacation. And our society sends us a regular text message that says, "You're not as significant as the people who get to do those things."

So what do we do? Since we cannot do what it would take to become celebrities, we try to attach ourselves to the celebrities. The teenage boy waits outside the gym for the basketball player to autograph his T-shirt, the smitten young woman follows her favorite actor so devotedly that he has to get a restraining order against her, and people stand around the coffeemaker at work and talk about the latest plot twist of their favorite drama without even stopping to realize that the characters involved in that plot twist are not even real people, just characters in a television show. If our society is going to tell us that we are not significant and cannot do what it would take to become important, then we are determined to become virtually important, to pretend that we somehow have a connection with the people our society says are really significant. The connections are, of course, imaginary. But for that matter, the reasons for declaring that the actresses and athletes are important are also fairly trivial in the broad scheme of things. And in the society that invented virtual reality and seems to regard it as being more important than real reality, there is something sadly fitting about the fact that we find our sense of significance through an imagined connection to an imaginary character in a world that exists only on a Hollywood movie set.

Now, you may want to say that the last couple of paragraphs are unfair to the artistic side of movies, television shows and even athletics. Point taken. You may think they constitute an overly harsh criticism of our culture. Point also taken. But my point in writing those paragraphs has not been simply to criticize. Instead, my main point here is to show that beneath the superficiality of virtual celebrity lies something that really is important, namely, the idea buried within each of us that to be significant, we need to be attached to someone who is significant. Note carefully the progression of the last few paragraphs: What makes people significant in their own right is something that is out of reach to most of us. So for most of us, the only way to be significant is to be connected to someone else who is significant. And even though the way we express this idea is thoroughly skewed, the fundamental intuition lying beneath it is exactly right. Christianity teaches us that our significance does not ultimately lie in what we accomplish or what we do; it lies in the one to whom we belong.

This is precisely where the discussion of Genesis 1–2 becomes so crucial. The implication of the creation account is that we do not need to do anything to acquire significance. Instead, we already possess a significance greater than that of any other created beings, simply by virtue of being made in the image of God. We belong to him. We are created resemblances of his uncreated Son. We share (or at least Adam and Eve used to share) in the fellowship that has characterized the persons of the Trinity from all eternity. There is nothing we need to do—indeed, nothing we could possibly do—that would make us any more significant than we already are.

Significance does not lie in what one can accomplish on one's own. It does depend on the one to whom one is connected. But everyone possesses true significance, because all are created in the image of God. There is no one else one could attach oneself to who could give a person greater significance than that person already possesses, by virtue of this connection to God. Furthermore, this significance is linked to creation, not to whether a person follows Christ. It is not just Christians who are inherently significant in God's eyes. All people bear the image of God in a way that unites them to one another and distinguishes them from the rest of the beings in the universe.[5] We do not have to be on the celebrity-chasing carousel. We do not need fame or even a connection to the famous ones. We already have something more, a direct connection to God, and this connection is the source of real significance. As we grasp the fact that this connection brings with it the opportunity to share in and reflect God's intratrinitarian relationship, then all of life begins to appear in a new light. The work we do, the human relationships we try to develop, the success we try to attain—these things need not be attempts to gain significance for ourselves. Rather, we can see them for what they are—opportunities to work out the implications of the significance we already have as people created in the image of God, people meant to share in his glorious presence.

Peace of a different kind. During the upper room discourse, Jesus talks about peace on two different occasions. The first comes in John 14, just after the passage on obedient love that we have already considered. Jesus says to the disciples: "All this I have spoken while still with you. But the Counselor, the Holy Spirit, whom the Father will send in my name, will teach you all things and will remind you of everything I have said to you. Peace I leave with you; my peace I give you. I do not give to you as the world gives. Do not let your hearts be troubled

---

[5]The Bible affirms that although the image of God in humanity was distorted with the Fall, it was not obliterated. Human beings all possess the image of God, no matter how sinful or distant from God they are. See Gen 9:6, which explains that the reason murder is wrong is that God made humanity in his image. See also Jas 3:9, which states: "With the tongue we praise our Lord and Father, and with it we curse men, who have been made in God's likeness." The seriousness of these offenses against other people is tied to the fact that all people still bear the image/likeness of God.

and do not be afraid" (Jn 14:25-27). There are three things about this passage that call for some explanation. In the last sentence, the verbs for "be troubled" and "be afraid" are more specific in Greek than they are in English. The idea is that the disciples already are afraid; their hearts already are troubled. Jesus is not telling them to avoid becoming afraid; he is telling them to stop being troubled and afraid.[6] So the peace that he offers to the disciples (and to us) here is the antidote to the fear and anxiety that the disciples already feel. Of course, for us as well as for the disciples, ordinary life is full of anxiety-producing moments. Concerns like whether you will make it through high school or college with your sanity intact, whether you will be able to pay the bills, whether your family will make it through one day without flared tempers or whether the children will turn out okay are all around us. Mixed in among them are bigger concerns like whether the world our grandchildren live in will be as safe as the one we grew up in and whether the ideals we consider important (whatever those may be) will survive another generation as the world seems bent on destroying them. We are fearful and anxious a lot of the time. And most of us wish that the concerns would simply go away. But they do not go away, and Jesus does not seem to want them to, which brings us to the second noteworthy thing about this passage.

Jesus does not simply say he will give us peace. He says, "*My* peace I give you." And he explicitly says that this peace, his peace, is not like the kind of peace the world has to offer. When the world is able to serve up peace at all (which, we have to admit, is not very often), the peace it gives us is merely negative—the absence of open hostility and conflict. All the world can hope for is a truce, and this is part of the reason most of us are conditioned to think that the best thing for us would be to eliminate the conflicts, concerns and stressors of life. But Jesus is offering us something different here—not the elimination of the storm but the promise that one can find calmness in the midst of that storm. And this kind of peace is far more valuable than a mere ceasefire. Where there is merely a ceasefire, the hostilities will certainly come back, so

---

[6]This is the force of the present negative imperatives *mē tarassesthō* and *mēde deiliatō*.

the world's kind of peace can only be temporary at best. But calmness in the midst of the storm can be deeper and more permanent, since it does not depend on external factors. This is the sort of peace Jesus promises to those who follow him.

The third noteworthy thing about this passage is that the peace Jesus offers is connected directly to the Holy Spirit's ministry within a person. Jesus draws a subtle distinction between the way he has been teaching the disciples and the way the Holy Spirit will teach them once he begins to live within each of them. Jesus teaches through words, externally. This teaching is priceless, but what makes it even more valuable is that the Holy Spirit works internally, to remind people of precisely those parts of Jesus' teaching that they most need to remember at any given point in their lives. And as they face all the nonpeaceful aspects of life from this point on, the Holy Spirit will remind them of what they have learned so that even as the storm rages about them, they can be people at peace with God and with themselves. In the same way, Christians today learn Jesus' teaching through the Bible, and the Holy Spirit reminds us of precisely what we need to remember to be women and men of peace. The gist of this passage, then, is that God offers a peace far more personal and more significant than what most of us even wish for—an internal peace that does not depend on eliminating the sources of stress and hostility.

But what is the nature of this peace? What exactly do we need to remember in order to be calm in the midst of storms? Jesus takes up this question in the second passage dealing with peace, which comes at the end of the upper room discourse, just before his high-priestly prayer. At the end of John 16, the disciples finally begin to understand what Jesus is saying, and they affirm that they believe he has come from God. Jesus rejoices, but at the same time, he is somber in a strange way. He says, "But a time is coming, and has come, when you will be scattered, each to his own home. You will leave me all alone. Yet I am not alone, for my Father is with me. I have told you these things, so that in me you may have peace. In this world you will have trouble. But take heart! I have overcome the world" (Jn 16:32-33).

Remember that Jesus is soon to be arrested, tried and crucified. Yet here his mind is not on those impending events, but rather he is thinking about the fact that his own disciples will leave him all alone as he goes to his death. The men in whom he has invested three years or so of his life, the men who have just now proclaimed that they know he came from God, are about to abandon him. Jesus' words "You will leave me all alone" are haunting in their poignancy, because perhaps what most of us fear even more than chaos and conflict is isolation. The people who surround us may be sources of stress, frustration and hostility, but most of us fear their absence a great deal more than we get annoyed by their presence. And Jesus too, evidently, rues the solitude, the abandonment he is about to walk into. Yet Jesus' great consolation as he faces that abandonment is that he will not be alone, because God the Father will still be with him. Notice how utterly personal his words are here: he does not say "the Father" or "our Father"; he says, "*my* Father." For him, the ultimate source of peace—and indeed in his moment of greatest anguish, the only source of peace—is his relationship with his Father.

Immediately after this heart-wrenchingly personal confession, Jesus turns his attention back to the disciples. He has told them these things about himself so that in him the disciples may have peace. Notice that this goes beyond what he has said about peace earlier in the discourse. Here, Jesus specifically indicates that peace is to be found in him, and he is about to use similar language when he prays for the disciples in John 17. For Christ, peace in the midst of abandonment comes from being in God the Father. For people, peace in the midst of isolation or chaos or trouble comes from being in Christ. To tie this to what we have seen previously from the upper room discourse, the peace that Christ offers to Christians is a peace that flows from people's participation in Christ's relationship with God the Father.

Jesus closes the upper room discourse by reminding the disciples that they will have trouble in this world, and he says, "But take heart! I have overcome the world." The triumphal note he sounds here is quite a contrast to the piquant sadness of a few sentences earlier. But Jesus is not talking about some sort of military victory over all those opposed to him. (The Bible indicates that such a victory will come, but not until the end of history.[7]) Instead, here he indicates that he has provided a way to transcend the chaos and conflict that characterize life in this world. Victory and peace do not involve eliminating the world or its conflicts, nor do they involve Christians' stepping out of the world altogether. Instead, the victory is one of perspective, of attitude. We can live above the chaos because we are in Christ, just as he can face his closest friends' abandonment of him because he is in his Father.

From these two passages in the upper room discourse, we can see that being in Christ, sharing in the Son's fellowship with the Father, gives us a radically new perspective toward the stresses of life. Our tendency is to wish that those stresses could be removed, eliminated. But the chaos of life cannot be removed, and even if it could, we would not want it removed. As long as we surround ourselves with other people, there are going to be sources of conflict, concern and stress. Eliminating those sources would involve removing ourselves from other people, and that, we can be assured, would be worse than the difficulties of human interaction. Instead, the chaos needs to be redeemed. And part of that redemption comes as we recognize that the imperfect, stressful, conflict-ridden relationships that make up our lives are grounded in a perfect, harmonious, loving relationship—the relationship between the Father and the Son. The relationships we have with other people are, of course, very imperfect reflections of that relationship—after all, muddy water does not yield clear images. But those relationships are meant to be reflections nonetheless, and recognizing this fact may help us to see through the mud with a little more clarity, to pay attention to the perfect relationship that our imperfect ones reflect. And as we glimpse that relationship, we find the peace that we need in order to pursue these relationships with a renewed sense of hope. "In *me*," Jesus says, "you will have peace."

Work toward a different end. Why do people work? When I ask that question, I mean by the word *work* not merely employment for which one is paid but also doing schoolwork, raising children, taking care of

---

[7]See, e.g., Dan 2:44-45; 7:19-27; Zech 14; Rev 19–20.

one's room or one's apartment or one's house and yard, keeping up with one's correspondence and other affairs, and so forth. I mean attending to all the duties that accompany life. Why do we do it all? Many people would answer that we work because we need money to pay the bills and we do all the rest because we cannot afford to pay someone else to do them. But is that really the only reason? If any given couple were instantly to become independently wealthy, would they really quit their job or jobs, pay someone to take care of their children, house and yard, and move to an uninhabited island for the rest of their lives? I doubt it. In fact, I suspect that none of us would give up all of our responsibilities merely because money was no longer a problem. Why not? Because to some degree the reason we work is that the things we are working on are important to us. Even if money is not an issue, how we do in school or college or grad school is still important to us, or at least, we consider the diploma that comes at the end to be important enough to pour several years of our lives into getting that piece of paper. How our children turn out is important enough that virtually none of us would hand the responsibility for their care completely over to someone else, no matter how rich we were. And if money were suddenly not an issue, many of us would not even quit our jobs, or if we did quit them, we would look for some other job that we found more fulfilling. We work, we attend to everyday tasks, in part because we sense the importance of what we are doing.

I alluded above to some of the reasons why we consider those tasks and activities to be important. We are trying to show that we are significant or we have a need to feel needed or we want to convince others (or ourselves) that what we do matters. But if you accept what I wrote above about significance, then you will recognize that the whole question of work needs to be revisited in light of the fact that we are created in the image of God. We do not have to work ourselves to death in order to be significant; we already are significant. We do not have to be the basketball star or the valedictorian or climb the corporate ladder to become rich and famous so that once we get to the top, we will be important. We already are important. We do not have to be tight with the boss so that a connection to the one in power will give us significance. So how should we view our work, both paid employment and all the other tasks that life hands us? It would be tempting to say that since our significance is a given, and thus since our sense of self-worth or identity is not tied to what we do or how hard we work at it, then we need not try very hard. If our importance is not tied to our work, then our work is not important, so why bother? Throughout Christian history, critics both inside and outside the church have leveled this accusation against the Christian faith: If salvation or fulfillment is really a gift, if we are significant just because God has given us such significance, and thus if one does not have to work, then what incentive is there for one to live faithfully and do rightly? It is often claimed that people will not be as devout as they would be if they believed such devotion was necessary for their spiritual well-being.

In fact, a superficial reading of the Bible seems to encourage this sort of indifferent attitude toward work. In John 6, just after Jesus' famous feeding of the five thousand, people go looking for him. After they find him, Jesus points out that their motivation for seeking him was simply that they wanted another free lunch, and he says, "Do not work for food that spoils, but for food that endures to eternal life, which the Son of Man will give you" (Jn 6:27). The people are apparently a little sheepish that he has seen through them so easily, and they start paying attention. They ask what they need to do in order to do the works of God. Jesus answers, "The work of God is this: to believe in the one he has sent" (Jn 6:29). This answer appears to imply that people should not do anything; they should just believe in Christ. And admittedly, there are many Christians who are convinced that they do not have to do anything and even should not do anything. They think they do not need to be righteous, because salvation is purely a gift. But people who understand Christianity this way are missing two important points. First, they are missing the subtlety of what Jesus is saying here. He is using the phrase "work for" in the sense of "seek." His criticism of them is that they are seeking merely physical food, when they could be seeking spiritual, eternal food. The one thing that is truly worth longing for, striving for, is something that God gives us, spiritual food that comes from a relationship with Christ. That food comes to us as we believe in Christ. So the "work of God"—the sort of longing or striving that is pleasing to God—is longing for Jesus and trusting him for one's life.

The second thing that people often miss is that when the truth of Jesus' words (here and elsewhere) takes hold of a person, that person becomes anything but passive and apathetic. In fact, just the opposite occurs. A relationship with Christ is so liberating that it inspires a person to work harder, and for different things, rather than giving the person an excuse to do nothing. One of the best examples of this sort of transformation is the apostle Paul, who was an enthusiastic persecutor of Christians until Christ knocked him down (literally) in Acts 9 and reconfigured his entire identity with the stunning truth that this Jesus, whom Paul was persecuting, was in fact God. Nearly twenty years after this event, Paul looks back on it in connection with a discussion of Christ's resurrection. He writes that after Jesus was raised from the dead, he appeared to many people, and then last of all, he appeared to Paul. He continues: "For I am the least of the apostles and do not even deserve to be called an apostle, because I persecuted the church of God. But by the grace of God I am what I am, and his grace to me was not without effect. No, I worked harder than all of them—yet not I, but the grace of God that was with me" (1 Cor 15:9-10). In this passage, we should recognize two things. First, Paul is not taking any of the credit for what he has become since his conversion to Christianity. He says that God's grace transformed him, turning a persecutor of the church into one of Christianity's greatest preachers. Second, the result of this transformation has been that Paul has worked harder than any of the other apostles, all the while recognizing that it was God's grace working with and through him. This is what happens when a person becomes a true follower of Christ. That person does not become complacent or apathetic, but rather he is spurred on to work even harder by the realization that God is at work in and through him. Becoming a Christian enables one to see one's work (whatever kind of work that is) in a new way, as the opportunity for God to work through the person.

Paul makes this point clear at the end of the same chapter. After a lengthy and stirring description of the resurrection, he concludes that when we have been raised, death will have finally been "swallowed up in victory" (1 Cor 15:54). Then Paul writes: "Therefore, my dear brothers, stand firm. Let nothing move you. Always give yourselves fully to the work of the Lord, because you know that your labor in the Lord is not in vain" (1 Cor 15:58). The first part of this verse encourages Christians to remain steadfast in affirming and living by the resurrection. Nothing is to move us from the truth that Christ has been raised, and so we too will be raised from the dead. Confidence about the future (about our resurrection) is rooted in the past (the accomplished fact of Christ's resurrection). By looking both to the past and to the future, Christians can find the motivation they need to work hard in the tasks God has given them to do. Then as a final bit of motivation, Paul reminds us that our labor in the Lord is not in vain, and this reminder needs a bit of explanation. Why is the labor of Christians not in vain? The context of this chapter shows that it is not in vain because it is an outgrowth of God's work in bringing those people to himself so that they might believe and follow him, because it is tied to God's own work of leading other people to himself, and because it is working toward God's ultimate purpose of bringing about the final resurrection of Christians, so that they will be with him forever.

But in addition to these points, there is another reason why the Christian's labor is not in vain—because it is labor "in the Lord." Here again we see the phrase that we have encountered in the upper room discourse. Jesus has said that he is in the Father and the Father is in him. Jesus has also said that believers are in him in the same way he is in the Father. Here Paul writes that believers labor "in the Lord," and clearly he is referring to the same idea that Jesus has talked about earlier. When we share in the fellowship that characterizes the persons of the Trinity, we also have the privilege of sharing in the work that those persons carry out. We are in the Lord, and so we labor in the Lord. And this means that our work—far from becoming insignificant—takes on a surpassing importance. We are the ones through whom the love between the Father and the Son is expressed on earth today, and we are also the ones through whom the purposes of God are carried out today. Just as Jesus loved his Father by doing his

Father's work, so we love the Father, Son and Spirit by carrying out God's work in the world.

Once again, we should remember the question I posed earlier: What does it look like for people to share in the relationship within the Trinity? So far in this chapter, we have seen that sharing in this relationship leads to a transformed perspective in three major areas—a new sense of significance based not on what we do but on our connection to God, a new kind of peace that is more than just the absence of conflict and a new appreciation of work as the means by which we act out the love between the persons of the Trinity. Now we need to look more specifically at the way these changed perspectives manifest themselves in our friendships, our families, our workplaces and our churches. It seems to me that a changed perspective will not simply lead us to work harder and more cheerfully; it will also lead us to work differently.

Human relationships on a different plane. If I had to choose a single word to describe the way people typically interact with one another, unfortunately I would have to choose the word *manipulation*. People seem to be remarkably bent on using the system—and each other—for their own benefit. This is so common and so accepted that the phrase "looking out for number one" is almost a badge of honor today. In large corporations, the competition for promotions is often so intense that it would hardly be feasible for a person to act charitably toward the woman in the next cubicle. Any kindness shown to her, any attempt to help her in her work, could cost you your chance to climb the corporate ladder, and it could even cost you your job. The quest for personal power dictates the way one acts toward one's coworkers, and once one gets far enough up the ladder to obtain real power over others, one is almost expected to use it in order to preserve one's position by keeping potential usurpers farther down the ladder. This is not the way it works in all companies, but it is far more common than we might like to admit. And in academia the pressure is just as intense. From nervous parents asking their daughter's second-grade teacher whether she is being prepared well enough for the SAT, to the relentless race for college scholarships, to the sense that one B on your college transcript might spell the end of your potential medical career, to the "publish or perish" reality that haunts you once you become a professor, the ladder is laden with pressure from the bottom to the top. What is more disheartening, however, is that this sort of mentality does not get left at the academy or the office. It pervades family relationships and friendships as well. Wives and husbands are sometimes remarkably adept at manipulating their spouses. Even young children become masters at the art of throwing a well-timed, public tantrum in the knowledge that their parents will then promise them virtually anything just to get them to be quiet.

Here, as elsewhere, one could argue that I am being overly harsh, and I will plead guilty to that charge. There are employers who try to foster cooperative relationships among their employees and employees who work together kindly. There are many people who want to play by the rules, not just manipulate them. There are students who see their relationships with their teachers and other students as cooperative rather than unduly competitive. There are children who respect and obey their parents. But are they the majority? My guess is that they are not, that most of the time the system works through the kind of manipulation I have described in the previous paragraphs.

At this point, you may be ready to point the finger at me and say, "Christians think they are better, but they are not." Here as well, I freely plead guilty. In the churches, the situation ought to be quite different, but it usually is not. Many churches are torn apart by factions vying for power with a viciousness that could rival anything you would ever see in the corporate world or the academy. In many churches, people are more concerned that the music always follow the style they are most familiar with than they are that music be directed toward the worship of God. Worship services sometimes turn into performances for the edification or entertainment of the people, rather than opportunities for the people to unite in praising God. Denominational hierarchies can be just as political as anything that goes on inside the Washington Beltway. Of course, there are many churches in which things are not this way. But far too often, in the church as well as in the broader society, things operate this way.

In one of his most scathing criticisms, the apostle James writes,

"With the tongue we praise our Lord and Father, and with it we curse men, who have been made in God's likeness. Out of the same mouth come praise and cursing" (Jas 3:9-10). Sadly, this criticism sums up the way people so often act, both inside and outside the church. However pious we may be, however much we praise God, we sometimes (or often, or even habitually) act deceitfully and manipulatively toward people. Whether or not we curse them outright, the way we often treat them amounts to cursing them. James reminds us that those people are created in the likeness of God, which means that there is an intrinsic connection between the way we speak of God and the way we speak of them, the way we treat God and the way we should treat them. Our actions toward each other should grow out of our reverence for God, but so often they do not. In one of the simplest and most haunting statements in the Bible, James immediately goes on to write, "My brothers, this should not be" (Jas 3:10). Indeed, it should not be. But if things should not be this way, what should they be like? What should appropriate relationships in the home, the church, the academy and the workplace look like?

To answer this question well would take many books. But I would like to try to outline briefly a direction in which an answer might lie. Earlier we saw that our society's notion of significance ties people's importance to their ability either to climb the ladder themselves or to attach themselves to important people. In contrast to this, we saw that the Bible insists all people are significant by virtue of being created in God's image. A corollary of this idea is that all functions that people have, at least all legitimate functions, are also significant. If it is not true that the man or woman at the top of the totem pole is the only significant one, then it also is not true that the job at the top of the ladder is the only significant one. In fact, the job at the bottom of the ladder is equally significant, equally important. A famous baseball player once gently reminded his adoring fans that the job a garbage collector performed was more necessary to the welfare of society than his job was. Jobs or roles need not be ranked according to greater or lesser importance, since all of them are important. That we have different roles does not mean that some of us are important and others are unimportant.

The apostle Paul makes this point clear in two passages (Rom 12:3-8; 1 Cor 12:12-26) in which he calls the church "the body of Christ" and compares the roles of different people within the church to the functions of different parts of the human body. In both of these passages, Paul subtly rebukes the attitude that says, "I do not need the other parts of the body," or "I am more important than the other parts of the body," and in both passages he reminds Christians that all parts of the body are important, all need one another. He urges people to exercise the function for which they have been gifted rather than boasting that their function is better than someone else's or trying to acquire a supposedly better function than they have. So the first thing we need to recognize is that in order for home, school, church and work relationships to look more like God wants them to, they must grow out of a shared recognition that all of us, and all of the different functions we exercise, are important.

This point leads directly to something else we have already dealt with, the fact that the Son submits to the Father—he obeys him and carries out his will. In our way of thinking, this would mean that the Son is inferior to the Father. But our way of thinking is wrong on this point. The Son is not only equal to the Father, he is identical in terms of characteristics or attributes. But even so, he submits to the Father. Doing so does not diminish him one bit—after all, he is still God. From this we can recognize not only that submitting or obeying or following is important, but that following is just as important as leading. God the Father who initiates and gives the love within the Trinity is not more important or more significant than God the Son who receives that love and responds through obedience to his Father. In the sidebar on the next page Augustine indicates that even though the Father and Son are absolutely equal, there is still a sense in which one may speak of a priority of the Father. In their being, the two are equal (as is the Holy Spirit). But in each one's relation to the other, the Father holds a certain priority— he sends, and the Son is sent. He directs, and the Son obeys.

We should recognize that the analogy between the Father/Son relation and our interaction with other people is not a complete one. We are separate beings from one another as well as distinct persons. We do

---

Augustine on the Son's Obedience to the Father (ca. 410):

> If . . . the reason why the Son is said to have been sent by the Father is simply that the one is the Father and the other the Son, then there is nothing at all to stop us believing that the Son is equal to the Father and consubstantial and co-eternal, and yet that the Son is sent by the Father. Not because one is greater and the other less, but because one is the Father and the other the Son; one is the begetter, the other begotten; the first is the one from whom the sent one is; the other is the one who is from the sender. . . . For he was not sent in virtue of some disparity of power or substance or anything in him that was not equal to the Father, but in virtue of the Son being from the Father, not the Father being from the Son.

On Trin., bk. 4, par. 27 (Hill, 172)

---

not have a complete unity of will, a complete absence of competition, as is the case among the trinitarian persons. Initiating and receiving, leading and following are not nearly as smooth among us as they are among the Father, Son and Spirit. Nevertheless, our human relationships are meant to mirror the relationship between the persons of the Trinity. As a result, we can and must recognize that among us, receiving, following and obeying are just as important as initiating, leading and loving. (Jesus' washing of the disciples' feet drives this point home as well.) The family, the church and the world need leaders, but they need followers just as much.

When we recognize that all legitimate functions are important and that God the Son was and is willing to submit to his Father in obedient love, this understanding should dramatically change our attitudes toward relationships in the home, school, church and world. Following or obeying is a calling, a gift, an important function that God has given us the privilege of carrying out. Leading by initiating love is similarly a privilege, but no more important. To follow is to walk in the footsteps of God the Son, to live out his relationship to the Father. To lead is to walk in the footsteps of God the Father, to live out his relationship to the Son (and the Spirit). Thus it is not surprising that the New Testament letters have extensive discussions of the kinds of leader-follower relationships that should characterize husbands and wives, parents and children, masters and servants (somewhat analogous to employers and employees today), and church elders/shepherds and their flocks/congregations (see Eph 5:21–6:9; Col 3:18–4:1; 1 Pet 2:13–3:7; 5:1-7 for some of these discussions). This does not condone oppression of the followers by the leaders, and in fact these passages have some harsh words toward leaders who misuse their leadership roles to put others down. For both leaders and followers, love is the guiding motivation.

With all of this in mind, we should recognize that following is not something we do grudgingly and temporarily as we await our opportunity to move up the ladder—remember that the Son always willingly submits to his Father; he is not simply biding time until he no longer has to obey. Nor is leading something we do spitefully or for our own benefit—remember that the Father's initiative is one of loving the Son and the Spirit, sharing his purposes fully with them, giving them complete partnership in his actions. Rather, leading and following are appropriate, equal tasks, both of which are necessary to the health of the family, the church, the school, the corporation, the society, the world. These functions are a matter of calling; they are a privilege, a way of reflecting something of God's own intratrinitarian interaction in our everyday lives. When people realize this, then the way they go about their everyday tasks should be significantly transformed. This is the way it should be. This is what life in the Trinity should look like.

CONCLUSIONS

In this chapter, I have tried to draw a brief sketch of what life was meant to look like at the beginning of human history and then to flesh that sketch out a bit by contrasting what life too often looks like today and what it would look like as Christianity affirms it should be. Even though this sketch has been short, I hope there has been enough here for you to glimpse something of the way the love between the persons of the Trinity should play itself out in transformed attitudes and relationships among human beings.

At this point, one might well ask two questions. First, how can anyone live like this? The answer to this question pertains directly to the Holy Spirit, whom I have had occasion to discuss several times in this chapter. The key to life as God originally meant it to be was the power of the Holy Spirit in Adam and Eve. Human beings were not able, and were not supposed to be able, to reflect the Father-Son relationship on their own. Rather, God gave them the Spirit's power to unite them to the Trinity, to cause them to participate in the Father-Son relationship and to enable them to reflect that relationship in their daily lives. From the beginning, the Spirit was the source of human life, and the Spirit made humanity able to reflect the life of God which people were called to image. If Cyril and others in the early church are right, what made Adam alive was the inbreathing of the Spirit into him, but even if this interpretation is not correct, the Holy Spirit's power was key to humanity's initial life in the Trinity.

The second obvious question is why we do not live like this anymore. Put simply, the reason is that we have lost the power (and maybe also the indwelling) of the Spirit, and thus we have lost our participation in the life of the Trinity. We cannot reflect a relationship if we are not participating in that relationship, and Christian theology affirms that through the Fall, humanity lost the initial blessing God had given to Adam and Eve. As soon as that happened, relationships between people became manipulative rather than cooperative, selfish rather than giving. As a result, most of us do not have the kind of perspective, attitudes or relationships that God intended us to have. Today even those who bear the name of Christ do not live consistently in the way God intended. Christians might hang our heads in shame at that inconsistency, as I often do. Non-Christians often point to the decidedly nontransformed lives so many of us Christians live as evidence that the whole story of Christian theology is not true. But that would be a mistake, because Christianity is not the only religion or philosophy that has to explain why its adherents do not live up to its lofty ideals. Any worldview has to answer that question. And through its understanding of the Fall, Christianity has a compelling answer: humanity turned away from God, left the relationship for which we had been created, rebelled against God. In some ways, the Fall is the most difficult part of the Christian message, not because it is hard to understand but because its implications are hard to accept. In chapter five, we will turn, with the help of the church fathers, to this difficult but crucial subject.

Chapter 5

What Went Wrong?

OUR LOSS OF THE SON'S
RELATIONSHIP TO THE FATHER

I concluded chapter four by asserting that the reason our human relationships and attitudes do not look much like the way Christianity says they should is that humanity has lost its participation in the Son's relationship to the Father. How did this happen? Christianity claims unapologetically that the loss is the result of sin. Of course, one could scarcely imagine a word more out of favor in our society today than *sin*. It conveys in no uncertain terms that some of the things we do are wrong and that we are responsible for the wrong we do. It is our fault, not anyone else's. To speak of sin is to admit that when things go badly for us, we are not always the victims. We have no recourse to finger pointing, looking around for someone to else to blame. It is no wonder that we do not want to admit sin or even talk about it.

SIN: AN UNCOMFORTABLE BUT INESCAPABLE REALITY
However, if we are going to be honest, we have to admit that no other word offers an adequate explanation for what we see around us or

within ourselves. Why do we try to manipulate the system for our own good rather than for the good of all? Why are people often so cruel to one another? Why do people shed blood so readily over ideas or even over long-standing hatreds with no known ideas behind them? Some have tried to argue that the corrupting influence of society lies behind these atrocities, and surely they are partly right. Victor Hugo's epic nineteenth-century novel *Les Misérables* recounts the life of Jean Valjean, a man who steals a loaf of bread to feed his family and spends the rest of his life fleeing from the persistent police inspector Javert, who is determined to punish him. In this story, it is society that comes off looking more sinful than Valjean, who is the victim of a system that drove him to poverty and then to crime. Surely there is much truth in Hugo's portrayal. There is a social, corporate dimension to sin that corrupts people and drives them to do evil. But we have to recognize that this is not the whole story. We do not sin simply because society drives us to do so or even simply because (as in Valjean's case) desperate need drives us to do so. Beyond these influences, we also find sin darkly attractive; there is something about doing wrong that is exciting and intriguing to us. When I was a teenager, one of the biblical passages that convicted me the most about my own sinfulness was Proverbs 9:17-18, which declares, "Stolen water is sweet; food eaten in secret is delicious! But little do they know that the dead are there, that her guests are in the depths of the grave."

In the early church, one of the Fathers who probed the depths of sin most deeply was Augustine, and perhaps his most insightful description of sin comes when he recounts an event from his own life. When he was sixteen, Augustine and a number of other youths stole green pears from his neighbor's tree. As the sidebar on the next page shows, there was no logical reason to steal these pears, no advantage to the boys in doing so. But as he later peers into this event from his own past, Augustine shows us the deep, dark attractiveness of doing evil merely to do evil. Most of us will recognize that we feel the pull of sin for its own sake just as strongly as Augustine did. It is hard to chalk sin up exclusively to the influence of society when one glimpses the negative pull of sin.

Furthermore, to say that people are inherently good until they are corrupted by society does not do justice to the fact that evil manifests itself in people at such a young age. We like to think of young children as being innocent and even angelic, but anyone who thinks children

---

Augustine on the Attractiveness of Sin (ca. 398):

Of what I stole [pears] I already had plenty, and much better at that, and I had no wish to enjoy the things I coveted by stealing, but only to enjoy the theft itself and the sin. There was a pear-tree near our vineyard, loaded with fruit that was attractive neither to look at nor to taste. . . . We took away an enormous quantity of pears, not to eat them ourselves, but simply to throw them to the pigs. Perhaps we ate some of them, but our real pleasure consisted in doing something that was forbidden. . . . And now, O Lord my God, now that I ask what pleasure I had in that theft, I find that it had no beauty to attract me. . . . It brought me no happiness, for *what harvest did I reap from acts which now make me blush,* particularly that act of theft? I loved nothing in it except the thieving, though I cannot truly speak of that as a "thing" that I could love, and I was only the more miserable because of it.

Conf., bk. 2, chaps. 4, 6, 8 (Pine-Coffin, 47, 49, 51)

---

are merely angelic has evidently not spent much time around them. A friend of mine once defined sin as what happens when you have two children in the same room with one toy. My experience has been that it would not matter if there were a hundred toys in the room; as soon as one child picked up one of the toys, the result would be pretty much the same! How do young children learn to be so bad? They do not have to learn; they have an inherent tendency within them that inclines them to be bad, just as we all do. In fact, in the sidebar on the next page, Augustine insists that even newborn infants would sin if they could. The reason they do not seem to be doing things wrong is not that they

---

---

are inherently good but that they are not physically capable of doing much damage yet. This inherent tendency to do wrong is what the Bible calls sin.

Like it or not, sin is all around us, and it begins to manifest itself far too early in each person's life for us to attribute it entirely to the influence of a corrupt society. Instead, something is fundamentally wrong with us, and that something is a large part of the explanation for why we do not act the way God meant us to act. To say it bluntly, as the Bible does, we are all sinners, and we have been that way our entire lives.

THE FALL: AN ACTUAL EVENT

However, even though we have been that way our whole lives, the human race has not always been that way. When God created humanity, people were sharing in the love between the Father and the Son, and were sharing that fellowship with one another. Something went tragically wrong with the human race at some point in its early history, and the effects of that tragedy—the Fall—are felt in the sinfulness of each person who has lived since then. Of course, many scholars believe that the whole story of Adam, Eve and the snake is mythological. They argue that there never was a time when humanity was much different than it is now but rather that the story is a literary way of indicating we are sinners. That explanation might be plausible, except for one thing. If we say that God is good, as the Bible does, and if we say that God meant us to share fellowship with him, then if we also say that humanity has always been sinful and estranged from God, then we are effectively saying that God did not create us the way he meant to. To say this would fly in the face of everything the Bible asserts about God's ability to accomplish the good purposes he wants to accomplish.[1] Furthermore, if humanity had always been sinful, then we would not really be responsible for what we do wrong—God would ultimately be at fault. We would be back to being victims again, in this case, victims of a God who botched the job of creating us the way he meant to. But one thing the Bible makes clear is that we are all responsible for our own sin.[2]

If we are going to say that we are all sinful now (and both the Bible and our experience lead us to say this), and if we are going to say that the situation we find ourselves in is not the way God meant it to be (remember James's haunting statement from 3:10, "My brothers, this should not be"), then we have to recognize that the human race has not always been like this. Prior to the account of the Fall in Genesis 3 comes the account of creation in Genesis 1 and Genesis 2, and that account is replete with God's approving words "It was good." In fact, Genesis 1 ends with the statement, "God saw all that he had made, and it was very good" (Gen 1:31). Even though Genesis 1–3 was written according to historical reporting standards vastly different from ours and thus may contain elements we would call mythical, we do not do justice to these crucial chapters if we claim that they do not describe actual events, and thus if we claim that the situation in which the human race finds itself now is the way things have always been. Instead, God intended to make a good world in which people participated in

---

[1]Among the many passages in Scripture that indicate God's ability to accomplish what he purposes, see especially Job 42:2; Ps 115:3; 135:6; Prov 19:21; Is 14:26-27; 55:10-11; Heb 6:13-20.

[2]The book of Leviticus is especially noteworthy for its enumeration of sins against the Lord and its insistence that people who commit these sins will bear their guilt. For example, see Lev 4–5. See also Ezek 18:19-29; Jas 2:10-11. People are responsible for all sin, whether great or small, whether intentional or unintentional, whether active or passive.

the relationship between the Father and the Son, in which people ruled over creation, in which people shared the Father-Son relationship with one another. And God's evident satisfaction with what he

---

Athanasius on the Pre-Fall Condition of Humanity (ca. 315):

For God did not only create us from nothing, but he also granted us by the grace of the Word to live a divine life. But men, turning away from things eternal and by the counsel of the devil turning towards things corruptible, were themselves the cause of the corruption in death. They are, as I said above, corruptible by nature, but by the grace of the participation of the Word they could have escaped from the consequences of their nature if they had remained virtuous. For on account of the Word who was in them, even natural corruption would not have touched them. . . . Since this [their turning to things corruptible] happened, men died, and corruption thenceforth took a strong hold on them, and was more powerful than the force of nature over the whole race, the more so as it had taken up against them the threat of God concerning the transgression of the law.

On Incar., par. 5 (Thomson, 145)

---

had made at the end of Genesis 1 indicates that he had, in fact, achieved his intention. The sin that we find in and around ourselves today was not always there. Somehow the human race fell into the mess it now finds itself in, and it fell through its own fault, not through God's fault or even God's intention. This is why we say there must have been an event at some point in early human history that tainted the human race so completely that all people since that terrible event have been sinful. There must have been a historical fall into sin. In the sidebar just above, Athanasius makes clear that there was an actual time when humanity was unfallen, that pre-Fall humanity was participating in God (what I call sharing the Father's relationship to the Son) and that humanity of its own accord turned away from this condition through an actual event, a transgression.[3]

You may find this hard to swallow. So do I. But if we accept the fact that we are sinful now, and if we accept Scripture's insistence that God did not want us this way, then we have to say that somewhere along the line, the human race fell. And compelled by this unpleasant but fairly unimpeachable logic, we are forced to take seriously the Bible's depiction of an actual event that transformed people from the way God meant them to be into the sinful, rebellious creatures we have been ever since. So at this point we need to grant the Bible a hearing, however hard it may be to accept what it is saying on this point. Let us look together at Genesis 3, the account of the human race's fall into sin.

SNAKES, SMOKESCREENS AND THE FALL

You know the story. After God creates Adam and Eve and places them in the garden, a snake shows up and tries to talk Eve into eating the fruit of the one tree from which God had told Adam they could not eat. Eve initially puts up some resistance but then gives in, eats the fruit and offers it to Adam, who eats it as well (without putting up any resistance, at least not that the text mentions). The two then try to hide from God, get into arguments with each other, try to blame someone else for their disobedience and wind up being thrown out of the garden. All of this is recounted in Genesis 3. You probably also know that the snake somehow represents Satan, a former angel who rebelled and became the archenemy of God, although you might be surprised to learn that one

---

[3]The early church was virtually unanimous in understanding Gen 1–3 as implying a historical fall from a previous condition of blessedness. There were a few exceptions, most notably Origen in the third century and Theodore in the late fourth and early fifth centuries. Origen held firmly to the idea of a fall from a higher condition but believed that this fall was pretemporal, coming before the creation of the physical universe. Theodore argued that the idea of the Fall was a reflection of the fact that humanity has always been mortal and sinful, and in this way, Theodore was similar to modern interpreters who argue that Gen 3 does not imply a historical fall. Significantly, the church condemned the thought of Origen and Theodore at the Fifth Ecumenical Council in 553. For Origen's cosmology, see *On Princ.*, bk. 1, chap. 8, par. 1, and bk. 3, chap. 1, par. 21 (Butterworth, 66-68, 204). Theodore's work is hard to access in English, but one may find my treatment of his thought useful. See Donald Fairbairn, *Grace and Christology in the Early Church,* Oxford Early Christian Studies (Oxford: Oxford University Press, 2003), pp. 29-34.

has to go all the way to the other end of the Bible before the snake is explicitly identified with Satan (see Rev 12:9). Furthermore, you may have heard that humanity's disobedience was the snake's fault. He tricked Eve, she disobeyed, and then Adam had little choice but to do likewise. But on this last point what you often hear is wrong. Let us look carefully at what happened.

God created Adam and Eve in his own image, which gave them a position of unique privilege in the created world. Human beings were the crowning achievement of God's creation, the beings most like him, the ones he intended to rule over the universe. Adam and Eve were also sharing in the presence of God and sharing God's own fellowship with one another. They had the best position of any created beings, although there was still room for them to foster and grow in their relationships to God and to each other. The only way their lot could have been better would have been if they had been equal to God, which was and is impossible. And their way of retaining all of this grandeur that God had given them was to obey the one commandment God had given them. God is a known entity to them; indeed, they know him as well as they know themselves. They have every possible reason to trust him. He also said in Genesis 2:17 that if Adam ate the fruit of that one tree, he would die. Now Adam may not have known what death was, but he must have realized that it was something bad. And God said that to avoid it, he needed to obey this commandment.

Contrast this history of interaction with God to what Adam and Eve know of the snake. He appears on the scene suddenly, with no explanation of where he came from. And as soon as he shows up, he begins twisting what God has said. He asks Eve in Genesis 3:1 whether God really said not to eat of any tree in the garden. Eve responds in verse 2 that they may eat from all the trees except one, which they are not to eat or touch, lest they die. (Notice that in Genesis 2:17 God did not say they could not touch the tree; Eve has added this.) Then the snake says, "You will not surely die. . . . For God knows that when you eat of it your eyes will be opened, and you will be like God, knowing good and evil" (Gen 3:4-5). Notice three things about this assertion. First, a talking animal whom they have no reason to trust or take seriously is directly contradicting what the God whom they have every reason to trust has told them. God said they would die if they ate that fruit; the snake says they will not. Right here we need to recognize that the blame for the coming disobedience does not lie just with the snake. Certainly he is trying to trick them, but his story has utterly nothing to commend it, whereas God's statement of what will happen has everything to commend it. Adam and Eve can and should know to heed God rather than the snake.

The second noteworthy thing about the snake's words is that he holds out to Eve a nonpossibility as if it were a possibility. It is not possible for a created being to become uncreated. Uncreatedness is not a quality you can acquire; if you have not always had it, you are never going to have it. It never has been possible and never will be possible for a created being to become God. (Remember here that when the church fathers speak of *theōsis* or deification, they do not mean that people can become gods in essence.) God had already given them the best deal of any created beings. There was no upward mobility on offer. But as the snake holds out to Eve this nonpossibility, she is apparently able to imagine it as a possibility. You can almost hear her saying to herself, "Sure, I have a wonderful situation, but could it somehow be better? Well, if I were as great as God, that would be better." Never mind that being as great as God is not a possibility; she can imagine that it is. And as she imagines, she becomes discontented with her current lot, even though it is the best lot a creature can have. The real issue here is not eating an apple or some other kind of fruit. It is rebelling against God because Adam and Eve became envious that God was greater than they were, and with their envy came discontentment with their creaturely status and a latent distrust in what God had said.

The third noteworthy thing about the snake's words is that he says if Adam and Eve eat the forbidden fruit, they will know good and evil as God does. While this passage is debated, one should recognize that in Hebrew, the word "know" *(yāda')* is much stronger than it is in English. The snake seems here to mean "know" in the sense of "decide." He is not talking simply about knowing that this is right and that is wrong; he is talking about having the authority to determine what is right and what is wrong. This is the specific way in which he claims they will be like God—they will get to call the shots on what you can and cannot do in their little kingdom. But this is not a prerogative that human beings have. God is the one who determines what is right and wrong; people's task is to live by the determination God has made. Again, the snake is offering a nonpossibility.

Augustine on the Fall (ca. 420):

We can see then that the Devil would not have entrapped man by the obvious and open sin of doing what God had forbidden, had not man already started to please himself. That is why he was delighted also with the statement, "You will be like gods." In fact, they would have been better able to be like gods if they had in obedience adhered to the supreme and real ground of their being, if they had not in pride made themselves their own ground. For created gods are gods not in their own true nature but by participation in the true God. By aiming at more, a man is diminished, when he elects to be self-sufficient and defects from the one who is really sufficient for him. This then is the original evil: man regards himself as his own light, and turns away from that light which would make man himself a light if he would set his heart on it. This evil came first, in secret, and the result was the other evil, which was committed in the open.

City of God, bk. 14, chap. 13 (Bettenson, 573)

He is lying, and as I have emphasized, there is no good reason why Adam and Eve should believe him.

Reflecting on this passage later, Augustine recognized that at its source, humanity's disobedience stemmed not merely from the temptation the snake offered them but from a pride that made them discontented with the created condition they had and therefore distrustful of God. In the sidebar just above, notice that Augustine sees Adam and Eve's original blessedness as a participation in God. They already were deified—they already were "gods"—in the sense that they shared in the relationship between Father, Son and Spirit. To try to be like God on their own, in some other way than by participation, was and is impossible. When Adam and Eve did try to be gods on their own, they were diminished, not improved. And at the heart of this fall lay pride leading to distrust.

Apart from such pride and a lack of confidence in God that flowed from it, there would have been no reason to take the snake's lies seriously. Apart from this pride there would have been no reason to long for anything they did not already have. They did not have to be gods, since they were already sharing in the Son's relationship to the Father. What more could they possibly have wanted? Nothing. But pride and the discontent/distrust that flowed from it led them to listen to the snake and to disobey the only commandment God had given them. Augustine and other church fathers recognized something we often fail to grasp: that blaming the snake for human disobedience is a smokescreen, a way of deflecting attention away from the real problem, the real source of guilt. It was not the snake's fault that Adam and Eve sinned; it was theirs. And it is not the devil's fault when we sin either; it is ours. To point fingers elsewhere is a smokescreen, and the Bible will not let us hide behind such a smokescreen.

What happened when Adam and Eve sinned? To state the obvious, they did not become gods. Instead, every aspect of their lives and their character was warped, twisted, distorted from the way God had created it. Previously they had freely shared everything with God and with each other (Gen 2:25 affirms that they "were both naked, and they felt no shame"), but now they try to hide from each other by making garments for themselves, and they try to hide from God by taking refuge under some trees in the garden (Gen 3:7-8). Previously they were in complete harmony with God and each other (remember that after each day of creation in Gen 1, God saw that "it was good," but after the creation of humanity, he saw that "it was very good" [Gen 1:31]), but now they make excuses before God and try to blame someone else for their sin (Gen 3:11-13). God pronounces curses upon them, taking two of the most central aspects of their lives (working the garden and bearing chil-

dren) and making those things painful rather than joyous. He says to the
woman, "I will greatly increase your pains in childbearing; with pain
you will give birth to children" (Gen 3:16). And to the man he says,
"Cursed is the ground because of you; through painful toil you will eat
of it all the days of your life" (Gen 3:17). In Hebrew, the word for "pain"
in verse 16 and the word for "painful toil" in verse 17 are the same word
(iṣṣābôn). As a consequence of human sin, God alters the natural processes of life and even somehow alters the earth itself, so that what was
meant to be joyful labor is now toil tinged with pain and difficulty.

Most tragically, God alienates them from himself, a fact that is fit-
tingly demonstrated by his casting them out of the garden he had previously made for them and placing angelic guards in front of the entrance
to ensure that they cannot return (Gen 3:23-24). God had said that if
they disobeyed, they would die, and die they did. The Bible speaks of
death in two ways. First is physical death, the separation of the soul
from the body and the consequent decay of the body. Second is spiritual death, alienation from God. As long as Adam and Eve obeyed, as
long as they retained their participation in the Son's relationship to his
Father, they would not have died either physically or spiritually. God
would have preserved their bodies and their souls intact. But at the moment of their disobedience, they died spiritually, they became estranged
from God.[4] The instantaneous and obvious change in their character
between Genesis 2:25 and Genesis 3:7 makes this clear, as does God's
casting them out of the garden at the end of the chapter. And just as
surely, Adam and Eve died physically. God evidently slowed down his
sustaining work by which he would have preserved their bodies intact,
and he allowed them to begin the slow march toward old age, death
and decay. Adam's death itself is noted in Genesis 5:5.

Once again, as mythical as this account may sound, treating it as a
literary way of describing humanity's perennial condition rather than as

---

[4]This alienation is not a complete separation from God, because if God were to withdraw his
presence entirely, this would involve withdrawing his sustaining work as well, and people
would cease to exist. Throughout this book, I will use the words *alienation* and *estrangement*
to refer to people's state after the Fall because these words convey the personal dimension of
the fallen human plight. We who were meant to share in the relationship of the Trinity have
become, through our sinfulness, personally and relationally distant from God.

a historical account of a change in humanity's condition creates more problems than it solves. It is crucial to affirm that humanity is sinful and estranged from God and that this sin/alienation is not God's fault. Affirming both parts of that statement requires one to recognize that the condition the human race is in now is a radical departure from the way God created it and intended it to be. The Bible affirms that the departure came near the beginning of human history through the disobedience of our first parents. It was humanity's fault, not God's or even primarily the snake's. To place the blame elsewhere is nothing but a smokescreen, and not until one allows the smoke to clear can one begin to think truly about the condition of human beings in our world today.

POST-FALL HUMANITY: BORN DEAD

Later in the book of Genesis, it becomes clear that the twisting of Adam and Eve's character that accompanied this first disobedience corrupted their descendants as well. In the next generation, Cain kills his brother Abel (Gen 4:8), and within a few generations God laments that "every inclination of the thoughts of his [humankind's] heart was only evil all the time" (Gen 6:5). Surveying these chapters and the related passage

---

Athanasius on the Worsening of Human Sin After the Fall (ca. 315):

In the beginning they [human beings] had been inventors of evil and had called upon themselves death and corruption; and in the end they turned to vice and exceeded all iniquity, and not stopping at one wickedness but inventing ever more new things, they became insatiable in sinning. For adulteries and thefts were committed everywhere; the whole earth was filled with murders and violence; there was no care for the law but for corruption and vice; and every wickedness, singly and in concert, was committed by all. Cities warred with cities, and peoples rose up against peoples; the whole world was torn apart by seditions and battles; and everyone competed in lawlessness. Not even acts against nature were alien to them.

On Incar., chap. 5 (Thomson, 147)

Romans 1:21-32, Athanasius comments in the sidebar on the previous page that humanity went downhill so rapidly that generation by generation, people were getting worse. The human race went from being everything God intended to being a pale reflection of its former self. We do not know how sin passes from one generation to the next, and there were various views about this issue in the early church (see the sidebar just below for an excellent statement by Augustine of one such view), but everyone who has children knows all too well that it does so pass. Once our first parents forfeited the perfect life given to them, all of their offspring—all of us—have been born in the state they found themselves in after their fall.

When most of us think of sin, we probably have in mind a few specific actions that are particularly horrific. But the Bible's depiction of sin is quite a bit more sweeping than our idea. The main concept is conveyed by a Hebrew word *(ḥāṭāʾ)* that is used nearly six hundred times in the Old Testament and a Greek word *(hamartanō)* used nearly

---

Augustine on the Transmission of Sin (ca. 420):

> Because of the magnitude of that offence [the Fall], the condemnation changed human nature for the worse; so that what first happened as a matter of punishment in the case of the first human beings, continued in their posterity as something natural and congenital. This is because the descent of man from man is not like the derivation of man from the dust. Dust was the raw material for the making of man; but in the begetting of a human being man is a parent. Hence, although flesh was made out of earth, flesh is not the same as earth, whereas the human parent is the same kind of thing as the human offspring. Therefore the whole human race was in the first man, and it was to pass from him through the woman into his progeny, when the married pair had received the divine sentence of condemnation. And it was not man as first made, but what man became after his sin and punishment, that was begotten, as far as concerns the origin of sin and death.

City of God, bk. 13, chap. 3 (Bettenson, 512)

---

three hundred times in the New Testament. Both of these words originally came from the sphere of archery and meant the same thing: "to miss a mark." The Bible makes clear that one can miss a mark by ignorance of what one is supposed to hit (see Lev 5:15-16), by deliberately aiming at a different target (see Is 1:4) or by aiming at the right standard but falling short of it (see 1 Sam 12:23). Another biblical word for sin (ʿābar in Hebrew or parabainō in Greek) conveys the idea of transgressing, crossing a boundary that God has established and forbidden us to cross. Adam and Eve's eating the forbidden fruit was a transgression, and for other examples, see Jeremiah 34:18 and Daniel 9:11. It is as if God has drawn a line in the sand and said, "Do not cross this," but people do. A third aspect of sin is rebelling against God's authority (pašaʿ in Hebrew or apeitheō in Greek), and thereby breaking off the relationship God desired. Amos 1–4 contains repeated references to the ways Israel has rebelled against God. A fourth aspect of sin in the Bible is translated "iniquity," and the Hebrew word behind this (ʿāwōn) conveys the idea of twisting or distortion. Sin is not just wrong actions; it is a distortion or perversion of one's entire character. See Job 33:9 and Proverbs 12:8 for examples of this.

It should be clear from these passages that in God's eyes, sin involves a person's whole being. The Christian church has long spoken of sin in "thought, word and deed" in order to emphasize that it involves more than just what we do. Furthermore, the church speaks of "sins of omission" as well as "sins of commission," since the Bible makes clear that it is a sin not to do the right thing, just as it is a sin to do the wrong thing (see Jas 4:17). Some people's sin is more blatant and obvious than others', but whether a person obviously rejects God and everything that is good and true, or silently ignores God and the good, or even seeks God and tries to do right but does not succeed, in the eyes of God that person is sinful. The apostle Paul makes this uncomfortable truth especially clear in two passages from his letters. In Romans, he spends about two chapters (1:18–3:20) emphasizing that all people, without exception, are sinful. His conclusion on this issue is, "All have sinned and fall short of the glory of God" (Rom 3:23). This passage makes clear the idea that sin is missing a mark. The target we are to shoot for is the glorious presence of God, and all of us, without exception, fall short of that target in one way or another.

In another important passage, Paul writes to people who are now Christians about their lives before conversion:

> As for you, you were dead in your trangressions and sins, in which you used to live when you followed the ways of this world and the ruler of the kingdom of the air, the spirit who is now at work in those who are disobedient. All of us also lived among them at one time, gratifying the cravings of our sinful nature and following its desires and thoughts. Like the rest, we were by nature objects of wrath. (Eph 2:1-3)

In this passage, the "ruler of the kingdom of the air" is Satan, whom sinful people are said to follow. Notice the different ways sin is described here. Paul writes that we follow the ways of the world, that we are disobedient, that we gratify sinful cravings rather than seeking to overcome them, that we follow sinful desires and thoughts. But the most arresting parts of this somber passage are the beginning and the end. Paul says that we were dead in our transgressions and sins and that by nature we were objects of God's wrath. As much as God loves us, as much as he longed (and longs) for the human race to share in the fellowship he has within himself, our sin has alienated us from him to such a degree that we must be described as spiritually dead even though we are physically and emotionally alive. We are objects of God's wrath because of our sinfulness. We are spiritually born dead. These are strong words, but as hard as they are for us to accept, they do convey accurately how devastating the effects of sin are.

People often object to Paul's scathing descriptions of sinful humanity, and one of the objections is that even if we are all sinners, most of us are not really *that* bad. It is argued that Christians have no right to say all of us are as evil as the Hitlers, Stalins and Husseins of the world. This is true, and Christianity does not claim that everyone is equally sinful. If you are familiar with the theological term "total depravity," you have probably also heard the mistaken idea that it means there is no good whatsoever in any person. But this is not what theologians mean when they use this term, for such an idea would be at odds with the biblical truth that even sinful people still bear the image of God. There is some good left in all people. Instead, the word *total* refers to the fact that sin affects every aspect of a person's being, to a greater or lesser degree. The point is not that everyone is completely sinful, or even that everyone is equally sinful. The point is that all people are sinful in their actions, their words, their thoughts, their emotions, their wills—in every aspect of their beings. No facet of a human being is left untouched by the devastation wrought by humanity's Fall. But even with that misconception corrected, Paul's words are still hard indeed. Why should we be said to be born dead, even if we are sinful to some degree? Are not we better than the Hitlers and Stalins?

As soon as we ask this question, it should be clear that we are grading on a curve. Our standard for "acceptable" righteousness is somewhere between Hitler and Mother Teresa, and we subconsciously think that as long as we are not the worst of people, we ought to pass the test and be acceptable to God. But remember that the mark, the target God calls us to aim for, is the perfect, glorious presence of God. We were created to reflect and share in the fellowship of the Trinity, to live out perfectly the relationship between the Father and the Son. As sinful people after the Fall, we do not do this anymore. We fall short of the target. Admittedly, some people fall a lot farther short than others, but *all* fall short. At this point one might object that perfectly living up to God's glorious standard is too hard a test. Maybe so. But remember that God did not originally place a test in front of humanity. Rather than giving a test that humanity had to pass to become acceptable to him, he gave Adam and Eve a share in the love that united the Father, Son and Spirit. All they had to do was remain in that love through simple obedience. But once they lost it, for themselves and for the entire human race that would descend from them, then the task of gaining that back is something completely beyond the capacity of sinful human beings. In fact, it is so far beyond our capacity that Paul describes us as "dead in our transgressions and sins." Not weakened, not sick, but dead. Can a dead person gain back a relationship with God that has been lost? Can dead people do anything to better their circumstances? No. When the Bible claims that people are spiritually dead, it implies quite obviously that there is nothing we can successfully do to restore ourselves to the condition in which God first placed the human race. While we were spiritually alive, we could have maintained and developed our fellowship with God through the power of the Holy Spirit. But now that we are born dead, we can no more regain that fellowship than a corpse can breathe life back into its own nostrils.

Again, this does not mean that no good whatsoever remains in people. Nor does it imply that human beings are incapable of anything noble or admirable. But sin has so twisted our character that when it comes to our ability to work our way back into a relationship to God, we can do no more than if we were actually dead. And this leads to the urgent question, What can be done if we are born dead and can do nothing to help ourselves? Let us now turn our attention to that question.

A HUMBLING YET LIBERATING TRUTH:
THERE IS NOTHING *WE* CAN DO

One of the words Christians use the most often is *salvation*. In fact, we use it so often, and speak of our salvation in such glowing terms, that we often forget that the word is a profoundly negative one. It means "deliverance" or "rescue," and it implies that people are in some sort of dire straits from which they cannot extricate themselves. One of my Old Testament professors was fond of reminding his students that the Hebrew word for salvation, *yĕsû ʿâ* (which is also the Hebrew name for the person you and I call Jesus), is the word written on the front of ambulances in Israel today. Just as the ambulance races to the scene of an accident to rescue the dying, so Christianity is fundamentally about rescuing the already dead. The use of the word *salvation* thus implies that the task of restoring us to our share in the Son's relationship to the Father is not something we can accomplish; it is something that must be done for us by another. And this is perfectly consistent with Paul's words in Ephesians 2 that we are dead in our transgressions and sins. The sobering truth is that even though the human race got itself into this mess, human beings can do nothing to get ourselves out of it. The glorious news that accompanies that sobering truth is that we do not have to get ourselves out of the mess, because the same God who created us has entered our world to rescue us. But before we get to that good news, we need to reflect on the implications of saying there is nothing we can do to rescue ourselves.

It is very hard to do nothing. Or rather, it is very hard to admit that there is nothing one can do. In any situation, any emergency that befalls us in ordinary life, we want there to be something we can do to make things better. To be able to do nothing gives us a profound sense of helplessness, and most of us have difficulty coming to grips with such helplessness. Furthermore, when we are talking about something so obviously important as our ability to fulfill the purpose for which we have been created, to say that we can do nothing is an enormous affront to our pride. We insist that there must be something we can do to improve our situation, to make things right, to get back to the way everything is supposed to be. Our sense of self-importance rebels against Christianity's characterization of us as born dead. Right?

But notice the phrase "our sense of self-importance" in the last sentence. Remember that we tend to tie our sense of significance to what we do, but Christianity does not allow us to do this. By tying our significance to the fact that each of us is created in the image of God, the Christian faith implies that significance is not something that can be earned; it is something that is given to us by God. This fact is comforting, because it means that no one can take away our significance, nor do we have to climb the ladder or befriend the right people to keep it. But at the same time, this fact is also humbling. We did not earn that significance; God gave it to us pure and simple. He did not declare us to be significant only after watching us do something significant. He did not recognize that we were important in our own right. Instead, he granted us importance and significance. In the same way, after the Fall, God does not wait for humanity in general, or individual people in particular, to do something so grand that we earn back the significance he gave us previously. Rather, even though we have made a mess of ourselves, he has still chosen to consider us so significant that he would do what was necessary to restore us to the fellowship he gave us at creation. Both when we are speaking of our original creation and when we are speaking of our need for salvation, Christianity insists that significance is something God has conferred on us. And thus our sense of self-importance should not be tied to whether we can do anything to save ourselves from the effects of the Fall.

In this way, Christianity compels us to adopt a perspective on our own sinfulness that is both humbling and liberating. It is humbling because we have gotten ourselves into a predicament from which we, as people born dead, cannot extricate ourselves. And many people are never able to get around this humbling point. It goes against our nature to accept such a humbling truth, so we do not accept it. We may unconsciously turn Christianity into a creed that is primarily about what we are supposed to do, a set of rules that we can follow. Christianity does involve many moral and ethical principles, but these lie toward the edges of the faith, not at the center. Part of the reason so many Christians manage to bring these to the center is that we desperately want to think that Christianity is about what we do, that we can accomplish what God requires. Or when we are unwilling to accept that there is nothing we can do to improve our situation, we may turn elsewhere besides Christianity. Other religions are much more willing to tell us that we can, should and must do this or that to achieve our purpose. In fact, Islam considers the Christian doctrine of sin to be a cop-out and prides itself on saying that Allah makes no unreasonable demands— you can do what he wants you to.[5] Admitting that we can do nothing is perhaps the hardest thing for prideful human beings to do.

But if this admission is hard for us, it is also the essential starting point for Christian faith, and once we are able to make this admission, it is the most liberating thing one could imagine. Because as much as our pride wants to tell us that there must be something we can do, our honesty also tells us that whatever it is we are supposed to do, we do not do it very successfully. Any creed or philosophy that caters to human pride by assigning tasks by which we may earn our salvation is also setting people up for an overwhelming sense of failure when they do not successfully do what they are called to do. And generally speaking, the people who are most honest and have the

---

[5]See, e.g., the Qur'an 6:153.

most spiritual sensitivity are the ones who are crushed by that sense of failure. Many people are able to live with the delusion that they are doing well enough, but those who really take the commandments seriously are the ones who are racked with guilt, frustration and despair over their inability to work their way back to God. And they are the ones who see the lay of the land accurately. Then, when such people finally grasp the truth that yes, they cannot get it done themselves, but no, that is not a cause for despair, then they begin to breathe the liberating air that comes from allowing God to do everything because we can do nothing. Only when we truly despair of ourselves and our own ability are we ready to see how staggering is Christianity's claim that God has done for us what we could not and cannot and will not do for ourselves. To admit we can do nothing is hard, but it is necessary, and most of all, it is liberating.

At this point, I need to address an important objection to Christianity that is often raised in connection with the ideas I have been discussing in this book. People throughout Christian history and all over the world have objected to Christianity's exclusivity, its claim that only followers of Christ can be saved. This claim has been an embarrassment to many Christians, and many have avoided it or even denied it. Put simply, why does God not allow those who faithfully follow other religions or other philosophies into heaven along with Christians?

This question has a great deal of emotional import. Our sensitivity, our sense of kindness and even our sense of decency make us want to answer it by saying, "he would, and he does." And in addition to its emotional clout, the question would have a lot of intellectual traction if heaven were a generic sort of place where everyone who is above the curve of average goodness would be welcome. But heaven is not such a generic place. We have seen from John 17 that heaven, eternal life, is knowing the one true God and Jesus Christ whom he has sent. Salvation is a person's sharing in the fellowship that unites the Father, Son and Spirit. To say that one could receive this fellowship by following some other religion or merely by being moral on one's own is to say that one could be united to Christ while having no discernible connection to Christ. If salvation is Christ, then to say one could be saved apart from Christ would be to say that one could have Christ without having Christ! If we understand biblically what salvation is, then it becomes painfully obvious that one cannot possibly have this kind of salvation without being joined to Christ. And Christianity asserts that this kind of salvation is the only kind there is.

Furthermore, to ask why people cannot be saved by faithfully following some other religion is to forget that people cannot be saved by their own efforts to follow Christianity either. We are born dead, helpless to save ourselves by anything we do. Our efforts to follow the principles of the Christian faith cannot and do not save us. To say that the human race is in a predicament from which it cannot extricate itself is to say that no human solution, no set of human rules or principles, is going to save us, no matter how good those principles are or how well we follow them. So no matter what the ethical code is—that of Islam or Confucianism or Hinduism or even Christianity—our efforts to follow it will not get us there.

To combine these points, there are two reasons why following another religion will not bring us salvation. First, no matter how good a religion's moral code is, we will not succeed in following it perfectly. Second, other religions do not even aim at what the Bible says is the correct target—sharing in the glorious fellowship between the Father and the Son. They aim at some other target, some different kind of salvation. For both of these reasons, all people, even religious people, miss the target of God's glorious presence whenever they try to hit that target themselves. Paul's words that we considered earlier in this chapter come back to haunt us now: "All have sinned, and fall short of the glory of God."

CONCLUSIONS

In this chapter, we have looked at the Fall as an actual historical event that fundamentally altered the condition and the inclination of humanity. Before the Fall, Adam and Eve shared in the Father-Son relationship, ruled over creation and shared love with one another. Through their pride, they became discontented with their condition as creatures and sought not merely to participate in God through the Spirit but to become like God on their own apart from God's work. This pride led to distrust of God and open disobedience, and humanity's sin twisted and marred the human character. All of Adam and Eve's descendants have been born spiritually dead, estranged from the Father-Son relationship and related to one another in an adversarial way. Furthermore, there is nothing we can do that would bring us back into fellowship with God.

Admittedly, this is strong medicine, and it is very hard to take. But the despair that this chapter might seem to produce is not the end of the story. In the same book in which Paul writes the bitter words, "All have sinned, and fall short of the glory of God," he also writes: "Therefore, there is now no condemnation for those who are in Christ Jesus, because through Christ Jesus the law of the Spirit of life set me free from the law of sin and death. For what the law was powerless to do in that it was weakened by the sinful nature, God did by sending his own Son in the likeness of sinful man to be a sin offering" (Rom 8:1-3). This is the rest of the story, the hope that emerges only when we have the honesty to admit that on our own we are helpless and even dead. This is the story to which I will turn in earnest in chapter seven. In the meantime, though, it is appropriate to examine the way God worked with humanity between the Fall and the sending of his Son into the world. The books of the Old Testament describe God's preparation of the people of Israel and the world for Christ's coming. This will be the subject of chapter six.

Chapter 6

The Promise

GOD'S PREPARATION
OF THE WORLD FOR HIS SON

Among the ironies of Christian theology is the fact that one of the most crucial theological questions—how one should view the Old Testament writings in light of Christ—gets little attention in many systematic theology textbooks. It is not uncommon for such texts to move directly from the Fall to the incarnation, leaving thousands of years of God's interaction with his people virtually untouched. The reason for this surprising gap is that the question of how to relate the Old and New Testaments is usually regarded as an issue for biblical theology rather than for systematic theology per se. But the distinction between these two disciplines is somewhat arbitrary, and given the integrative nature of this book, it is appropriate to deal with Old Testament history as God's way of preparing the world for the coming of his Son.

Furthermore, there is another reason for treating the Old Testament period in a book such as this. The theologians of the early church were vitally concerned with the Old Testament and sought to read its books as Christian documents. The way they went about doing this is often criticized today, but I believe some of that criticism is unwarranted. I think the church fathers understood something important about the way the Old and New Testaments related to each other, and thus we today have something to learn from the way they handled the Hebrew Scriptures. At the same time, I think the Fathers made some mistakes in the way they linked the Old and New Testaments, so my exposition in this chapter will by no means follow them exactly. In order for us to delve into the world of Old Testament/New Testament connections, I need to begin with a discussion about the differences between the way modern interpreters and the Fathers have handled the Bible as a whole.

BIBLICAL INTERPRETATION: THEN AND NOW

Among scholars and students today, the field of biblical interpretation is divided into two distinct yet overlapping categories: exegesis and hermeneutics. Exegesis is the microlevel task of understanding a particular passage of Scripture accurately in its original context. Put simply, the question exegesis tries to answer is, What did this passage mean to its original audience? Hermeneutics is the macrolevel task of placing a given passage in the context of the book in which it falls, the group of writings (Gospels, letters, historical narrative, poetry, prophecy, law) of which it is a part, the Bible as a whole and the various traditions for interpreting the Bible.

For our purposes at this point, the most important thing is that in our contemporary way of interpreting the Bible, we begin with exegesis and only then turn to hermeneutics. To expand on this idea, we believe that the starting point for understanding any Bible passage correctly is the direct context of the passage. We look at the historical background to the passage, its literary context, its syntactical structure in the language in which it was written and the precise usages of the important words in the passage. We study the immediate context of the passage as carefully and exhaustively as we can before we move out from that passage to take other relevant passages or relevant theological ideas into consideration. We move from the narrow to the broad. And our reason for this is that we believe starting with the broad would lead us to read our own theological ideas into the passage rather than reading the passage's own meaning out of its context. In fact, the word *exegesis* means "reading out," in contrast to *eisegesis,* which would be reading our own ideas into the passage. In our minds, to impose our own ideas onto the passage would be subjective and unfair to the passage or to the truth it seeks to communicate. Only by starting with the passage in and of itself, we think, can we be objective and truly grasp what the passage really means. The fact that we speak of exegesis (in contrast to eisegesis) and then hermeneutics reinforces this idea that to be objective, we must start with the text and then read out its theological implications rather than imposing our preconceived notions on the text.

At this point, we have to recognize that the way we are trying to ensure accuracy in biblical interpretation is fundamentally different from the way the early church went about the same task. The Fathers had no qualms whatsoever about reading preconceived theological ideas into a given passage, as long as they got those ideas from elsewhere in the Bible. In fact, they regarded any attempt to avoid such a reading to be un-Christian. The Fathers believed that the entire Bible was a book about Christ, and therefore they were determined to read every passage of Scripture as being directly or indirectly about Christ, the Christian's relationship to Christ or the church's relationship to Christ. When modern people examine the Fathers' biblical interpretation, we are quick to accuse them of allegorizing, of reading into certain texts ideas that are not there. For example, we often insist that the Song of Songs is a book about human love, not about the love between Christ and the church. When the Fathers read it as a book about Christ's relationship to his church, some of us are scandalized, and we point to this kind of interpretation as a reason not to take patristic exegesis seriously. But we evidently forget that in Ephesians 5, Paul explicitly links the husband-wife relationship to Christ's relationship with his church. If those two relationships are in fact analogous, why can we not say that a book of the Bible that is obviously about the first one is also about the second one? Similarly, why can we not accept that Hagar and Sarah, in addition to being historical women, were also types that foreshadowed something God was going to do in the future, when Paul specifically says this is the case in Galatians 4:21-31? For that matter, why can we not accept that God's love for Israel in the book of Hosea somehow mirrored God's love for his own Son, when Matthew 2:15 links the two by quoting Hosea

11:1: "Out of Egypt I called my son"? From these examples we see that the New Testament indicates that certain events, people and relationships in the Old Testament did prefigure greater realities. Whether the original human author of the passage in question knew it or not, whether the original human audience of the passage could have recognized it or not, the Holy Spirit evidently intended a connection between those people and events in the Old Testament and the greater realities of the New Testament. The New Testament passages dealing with these events disturb us because they smack of allegory. But these New Testament passages did not remotely bother the early church. Rather, the Fathers saw these as the key to unlocking the riches of the Old Testament, and they scoured the Hebrew Scriptures for hints, prefigurings and foreshadowings of Christ and the church.

Note carefully what is happening here. In interpreting the Bible, we start with the immediate context of the passage in question, and we generally refuse to allow any interpretation of that passage that cannot be drawn from the passage itself. In sharp contrast, the church fathers started with the whole Bible, with its entire message, and they read each passage in light of that entire message. We start from the narrow and work to the broad. They started from the broad and read each narrow passage in light of their understanding of the Bible's broad, overall message. We and the Fathers start the process of interpretation from opposite ends of the contextual spectrum, and this is part of the reason we are so quick to write them off as allegorizers. They see connections between biblical passages that we do not think are there. This fact shows up clearly in the passage from Irenaeus that appears in the sidebar at the top of the next page. His purpose here is to refute the biblical interpretation of the Gnostics, second-century heretics who believed that there were two distinct gods, one of the Old Testament and the other of the New Testament. Notice that Irenaeus's criticism of their style of biblical interpretation is not focused on details; it concentrates on the big picture. The Gnostics get the overall message of the Bible wrong, and so they are wrong on the individual passages as well.

In fact, the Fathers worked from the broad to the narrow consciously and deliberately. They coined the phrase "rule of faith," by

---

Irenaeus on False Biblical Interpretation (ca. 180):

> Their manner of acting is just as if one, when a beautiful image of
> a king has been constructed by some skillful artist out of precious
> jewels, should then take this likeness of the man all to pieces,
> should rearrange the gems and so fit them together as to make
> them into the form of a dog or a fox, and even that but poorly
> executed; and should then maintain and declare that *this* was the
> beautiful image of the king which the skilled artist constructed. . . .
> In like manner do these persons patch together old wives' fables
> and then endeavor, by violently drawing away from their proper
> connection, words, expressions and parables whenever found, to
> adapt the oracles of God to their baseless fictions.

Ag. Her., bk. 1, chap. 8, par. 1 (ANF, vol. 1, 326)

---

which they meant the totality of what the Bible teaches and what the
church has said about the Bible. Then they read all passages of Scripture in light of this rule of faith. In the sidebar just below by Irenaeus,
notice that the key to interpreting the parables (which he finds to be
obscure and therefore difficult) is clearer statements elsewhere in
Scripture, not the context of the parables themselves. And, in the
sidebar (next page) by Augustine, notice that when there is ambiguity about a certain passage, one should first consult the rule of
faith (which he describes as both the clearer passages of Scripture

---

Irenaeus on the Interpretation of Scripture (ca. 180):

> All Scripture, which has been given to us by God, shall be found
> by us perfectly consistent; and the parables shall harmonize with
> those passages which are perfectly plain; and those statements
> the meaning of which is clear shall serve to explain the parables;
> and through the many diversified utterances [of Scripture] there
> shall be heard one harmonious melody in us, praising in hymns
> that God who created all things.

Ag. Her., bk. 2, chap. 28, par. 3 (ANF, vol. 1, 400)

---

and the church's authoritative statements about it), and only if that fails should one consult the context of the passage. Here Irenaeus and Augustine are putting into concrete expression what the entire early church did in practice: using the whole Bible and the church's teach-

---

Augustine on the Interpretation of Scripture (ca. 398):

When words used literally cause ambiguity in Scripture, we must first determine whether we have mispunctuated or misconstrued them. When investigation reveals an uncertainty as to how a locution should be pointed or construed, the rule of faith should be consulted as it is found in the more open places of the Scriptures and in the authority of the Church. . . . But if both meanings, or all of them, in the event that there are several, remain ambiguous after the faith has been consulted, then it is necessary to examine the context of the preceding and following parts surrounding the ambiguous place.

On Doc., bk. 3, chap. 2 (Robertson, 79)

---

ing based on the Bible to interpret each individual biblical passage. This does not mean simply that one should consult clearer passages on the same subject as the ambiguous passage. In addition, it means that one must clearly see the whole of Scripture—the whole picture of the king, in Irenaeus's illustration above—before one can correctly interpret any of the individual passages.[1]

However, there is another difference between our biblical interpretation and that of the church fathers than simply working from narrow to broad or from broad to narrow. As I have mentioned above, we tend to stick to interpretations for a given text that the human author of the passage could have meant and the human audience could have understood at the time. But as the church fathers drew numerous connections between the Testaments, they relied on their perception of what the

---

[1]For a more detailed treatment of the early church's biblical interpretation, see Donald Fairbairn, "Patristic Exegesis and Theology: The Cart and the Horse," *Westminster Theological Journal* 69 (2007): 1-19.

Holy Spirit meant, not what the human author could have known or intended. Whether we admit it or not, we are influenced by the idea that the Bible is primarily a human book, and our preoccupation with the human author's intent at the time leads us to the kind of interpretation we adopt. Moreover, we are also influenced by the modern idea that the Bible is not so much a single book as it is a collection of unrelated or scarcely related human accounts of the human experience of God. The reason we must look only at this passage of Scripture in interpreting this passage is that we think other parts of Scripture are not really relevant for interpreting this passage. As evangelicals, we reject the ideas that the Bible is primarily a human book, that it is a collection of disparate accounts and that other passages of Scripture are not relevant to the interpretation of the one we are dealing with at any given time. But even though we reject these premises, they were the premises of the biblical scholars who forged the dominant method of biblical interpretation that we use today. Whether we like it or not, whether we admit it or not, we are influenced by a method of biblical interpretation that treats the Bible as a set of unrelated human testimonies to the divine-human encounter.

ROOTS OF PATRISTIC AND MODERN
OLD TESTAMENT INTERPRETATION

At this point, we as evangelicals should notice a significant incongruity latent in our situation. We accept (albeit with reservations) a method of biblical interpretation that historically arose among scholars who rejected most of our core convictions about the Bible—that it is from God, that it is a book telling a single story, that its various writings are fundamentally unified, that its central subject is Christ. Furthermore, without giving the matter a lot of thought, we reject allegory as a way of interpreting the Hebrew Bible, a way that is found in the New Testament and that was widely used in the early church, even though that kind of interpretation grows out of the same convictions that we share. It is indeed ironic that when a church father who shares all of our basic convictions argues for a connection between this Old Testament passage and that New Testament reality, we reject his argument out of hand because our masters in the school of modern interpretation (masters who do not share our convictions) have branded such exegesis as allegory. And it is even more ironic that our adherence to a plain-sense, nonallegorical method is so intense that the New Testament itself disturbs us when it connects the Testaments in a way that sounds like allegory to us. We wind up thinking that Paul and Matthew were allowed to handle the Old Testament this way because they were divinely inspired, but surely we must not handle the Old Testament this way.

If we recognize the incongruity I have been discussing, then we should also see that there is more than "mere allegory" going on when the church fathers interpret the Old Testament. In contrast to modern liberals (who might see no unifying theme in Scripture) and in partial contrast to modern conservatives (who tend to organize Scripture around concepts such as the covenant or the dispensations which have governed God's dealings with humanity), the church fathers tended to see the scarlet thread, the unifying theme of Scripture, as Christ. Again, this unifying theme places the emphasis in a rather different place than we do. We today start with ourselves and ask how God relates to us. The church fathers started with God, and especially with Christ, and asked how we participate in Christ. This is why virtually all of patristic thought saw *theōsis*—humanity's becoming somehow a participant in the divine life—as the link between God and humanity. Furthermore, this is why one strand of patristic thought, the one I think is most fruitful for us today, understood *theōsis* in terms of the Father's relationship to the Son and saw our participation in this relationship as the scarlet thread of the Christian faith. If one does theology in the way the church fathers did, with the life of the three trinitarian persons at the heart, then one will seek to find those trinitarian persons—especially the preincarnate Son—throughout the Old Testament.

When we recognize that we evangelicals and the church fathers both believe there is a unifying theme or scarlet thread uniting all of Scripture, and when we acknowledge that the early church understood this thread in a more God-focused way than we do, we may be willing to admit that we potentially have a lot to learn from patristic biblical interpretation. If this is the case, then it is appropriate now to consider an extended illustration of the patristic way to link the Old and New Testaments. An excellent example comes in Irenaeus's *Demonstration of the Apostolic Preaching* (written ca. 190), which is noteworthy for two major reasons. First, Irenaeus is the earliest church father to present an extended, positive statement of Christian belief in a nonpolemical context. Second, he is one of the best early representatives of the strand of thought that focuses on the personal, relational dimensions of salvation.

IRENAEUS AS AN EXAMPLE OF PATRISTIC
OLD TESTAMENT INTERPRETATION

Irenaeus's *Demonstration of the Apostolic Preaching* has no stated divisions, but its content lends itself to a fairly clear division into two parts. The first is Irenaeus's exposition of the apostolic preaching, and the second is his demonstration that this preaching is truly biblical because the message the apostles preached was foretold by the Hebrew prophets. The first part may be further divided into three subsections, describing (1) the central truths of who God is and who human beings are before God, (2) the history by which God prepared humanity for redemption, and (3) the redemption accomplished through Christ. The second part may be divided into four subsections, demonstrating that the Old Testament prophets foresaw (1) the eternal existence of the Son, (2) the human birth of the Son, (3) the human life, death and resurrection of the Son, and (4) the calling of the Gentiles.[2] From this structure, one can see that Irenaeus treats the Old Testament twice, once in terms of its historical preparation of the world for the incarnation and then again for its specific prophecies of Christ. Clearly, the organizing principle for handling the Old Testament is its foreshadowing of Christ.

More specifically the first part of the work begins with the Trinity and then describes human life in terms of communion with God or sharing in the life of the Trinity. Within this trinitarian framework, the central idea (based on Paul's comparisons between Adam and Christ in Rom 5:12-21 and 1 Cor 15:21-22) is that the Son will recapitulate humanity, undoing Adam's disobedience and restoring people to com-

---

[2]See Behr, 18-23, for this structure.

munion with God.[3] This idea in turn controls Irenaeus's interpretation of key Old Testament texts. For example, after the flood when God makes a covenant with Noah and requires death as the penalty for murder, Irenaeus elaborates on the reason the biblical text gives for this. The text of Genesis 9:6 says simply, "for in the image of God has God made man," but Irenaeus expands this by writing, "and the image of

---

Irenaeus on Christ as the Recapitulation of Adam (ca. 190):

Whence, then, was the substance of the first-formed? From the will and wisdom of God and from virgin earth—"For God had not caused it to rain," says Scripture, before man was made, "and there was no man to till the ground." So, from this [earth] while it was still virgin, God "took mud from the earth and fashioned man," the beginning of mankind. Thus, the Lord, recapitulating this man, received the same arrangement of embodiment as this one [Adam], being born from the Virgin by the will and wisdom of God, that He might also demonstrate the likeness of embodiment to Adam, and might become the man, written in the beginning, "according to the image and likeness of God."

Preach., par. 32 (Behr, 61)

God is the Son, according to whose image was man made; and for this reason, He appeared in the last times, to render the image like himself."[4] In Irenaeus's hands, the connection between the Son as the true image of God and each human being as a created image of God means not only that human beings are valuable and should not be killed but also that we will one day be made like Christ as he recapitulates humanity. Similarly, Irenaeus finds a striking parallel between the original creation of Adam and the virgin birth of Christ. In the sidebar just above, notice that Irenaeus directly connects God's creation of Adam from virgin soil to the human birth of God's Son from the virgin Mary.

---

[3]*Preach.*, par. 6 (Behr, 43-44).
[4]*Preach.*, par. 22 (Behr, 53-54).

This sort of interpretation is usually troubling to us—we brand it as allegorizing—but we should notice two things about it. First, Irenaeus does not in any way denigrate the historical accuracy of the Genesis account, and in fact, most of the church fathers affirm the historicity of the narratives they are describing, even when they see additional significance in those narratives beyond the historical sphere. And second, notice that what governs this interpretation—what keeps Irenaeus from reading anything he pleases into the Genesis account—is the biblical concept of Christ as the second Adam.

This sort of interpretation becomes even more common in the second part of *Demonstration of the Apostolic Preaching*, because here Irenaeus is combing the Old Testament to find as many references to Christ as he can. In this part, Irenaeus makes some connections between the Testaments that we also make, such as affirming that Isaiah 7:14 and Isaiah 9:6

Irenaeus on Psalm 24 (ca. 190):

> David again says the same thing, "Lift up your gates, O princes, and be lifted up, you everlasting gates; and the King of glory shall enter in," for the "everlasting gates" are the heavens. But, because the Word descended invisible to creatures, He was not known to them in His descent; [yet] because the Word was incarnate He also ascended, visible, on high. And having seen Him, the principalities, the lower angels, cried to those in the firmament, "Lift up your gates, O princes, and be lifted up, you everlasting gates; that King of glory shall enter in." And when they were astonished and said, "Who is He?" those who already saw Him testify a second time, "The Lord strong and mighty, He is the King of glory."

Preach., par. 84 (Behr, 91)

---

predict the incarnation of the Son.[5] He makes certain connections that some of us would accept but others would reject, such as seeing two of the three visitors to Abraham in Genesis 17 as angels but the third as the preincarnate Son of God.[6] Irenaeus also makes connections between the

---

[5]*Preach.*, par. 53-55 (Behr, 74-76).
[6]*Preach.*, par. 44 (Behr, 68).

Testaments that we may refuse to recognize, such as finding in Psalm 110 the truths that the Son has existed before all, that he judges all people and specifically opposes those who hate him, and that this Son is immortal by virtue of being an eternal priest.[7] He interprets the famous passage about the lion lying down with the lamb (Is 11:1-11) as meaning that those who have believed in Christ have been transformed and have abandoned their earlier animosity toward one another.[8] He interprets Isaiah 65:2 ("All day long I have held out my hands to an obstinate people") as a sign of the cross, rather than as an illustration of God's love for Judah.[9] And in an interpretation virtually all of us today would reject, he insists in the sidebar on the previous page that Psalm 24:9-10 is a conversation between the lower and upper angels on the occasion of Christ's ascension.

ASSESSING THE EARLY CHURCH'S
OLD TESTAMENT INTERPRETATION

The way Irenaeus handles the Old Testament in *Demonstration of the Apostolic Preaching* is typical of the early church as a whole. The Fathers take Christ as the controlling theme by which to link the Old and the New, and they are exuberant in finding references to Christ in the Old Testament. We today are prone to write off this kind of interpretation as allegorizing, largely because of our fear that it will lose its grounding in the texts and will lead to false readings. But it should be clear that neither Irenaeus's interpretation nor that of most other church fathers is ungrounded. Their interpretation is grounded in and controlled by their conviction that the whole Bible is a book about Christ. So we are back to the central difference with which we began this chapter: we ground (or at least claim to ground) our interpretation in the details of each passage and its background; the church fathers grounded their interpretation in the overall message of the Bible. Let us think about the implications of this apparent impasse a little bit further.

One way of looking at interpretive styles is to ask whether they might lead to mistakes, to false interpretations. Clearly, the church fa-

---

[7]*Preach.*, par. 48 (Behr, 72).
[8]*Preach.*, par. 61 (Behr, 80).
[9]*Preach.*, par. 79 (Behr, 89).

thers' way of handling the Old Testament is prone to mistakes. But
another way of looking at the issue is to recognize that all interpretive
styles could lead to mistakes and to ask what kinds of mistakes a given
style is prone to. What kinds of mistakes does one tend to commit if
one sees the entire Bible as pointing to Christ? And what kinds of mistakes does one commit if one sees no connection between the books of
the Bible or if one sees the connection in terms of something more
peripheral to the Christian faith than Christ? When I ask the questions
this way, it should be clear that the sorts of mistakes to which the early
church was prone are not as dangerous as the ones to which we are
prone. However overexuberant they may have been, they did not go
wrong on the fundamental idea of Scripture, because they were looking for that fundamental idea everywhere. Today, in contrast, some
interpreters insist that the Bible is about different people's experience of
God, which can lead either to saying that any kind of experience of any
sort of God is equally valid or to saying that my own experience of God
must be normative for everyone else. Other interpreters insist that the
Bible is about how we are supposed to live once we are redeemed,
which leads us to place too much emphasis on ourselves and to pay
little attention to the relation between God's action and ours. Still
others say that the Bible is about humanity's legal standing before God,
which means that we underemphasize or ignore the personal aspects of
salvation. These different misconceptions about the central subject of
Scripture are not equally severe, and so the problems to which they lead
are not equally dangerous. But all of them result in our focusing our
attention too much on areas that are not at the center of the faith. And
no grounding in the tools of exegesis can prevent us from making the
mistakes to which these misconceptions lead, because the mistakes do
not grow out of tools or methods; they grow out of the assumptions
with which people use the tools.

With this in mind, we can recognize that it is less dangerous to dis-
cern the Bible's central message clearly but read that message too en-
thusiastically into all passages than it is to read each passage individually
without an adequate grasp of the central message. This is the lesson we
can and should learn from the early church. I freely admit that the

church fathers were overly exuberant, and thus they read too much into certain Old Testament passages. But at the same time, I think they had the most important thing right. They correctly understood that the key to good interpretation is discerning the whole message of Scripture well, and they correctly saw that the Bible as a whole is fundamentally about Christ. In light of this fundamental lesson, I would like to spend the rest of this chapter sketching out a way of looking at the Old Testament that focuses on Christ, that bridges the gap between the Fall and the incarnation, and that remains true to the church fathers' fundamental insights while trying to avoid some of the pitfalls into which they fell through their overexuberance.

THE LINK BETWEEN THE TESTAMENTS: THE PROMISE OF THE SON

How then can we relate the Old and New Testaments using the early church's fundamental conviction that the Old Testament is about Christ? I believe we need to pay careful attention to two things: the fact that Christ is the fulfillment of the entire Old Testament hope and the fact that during the history of Israel, people's understanding of Christ became increasingly specific as time and revelation progressed. It seems to me that if we think in terms of both the end fulfillment—Christ—and the progressive unfolding of who that Christ was to be, we will be able to relate the Testaments in a way that is faithful to the message of the whole Bible while being less prone to read too much into a given Old Testament passage. I suggest further that a helpful motif to use in dong this is the idea of promise. Shortly after the Fall, God gave humanity a promise that a single person would come to undo the effects of that Fall and bring humankind back into the fellowship of the Trinity. Then throughout the Old Testament period, God revealed with increasing specificity where this promised person would come from, why people would need him, what he would do, and most important, that he would be not merely a human person but a divine person, the Son of God.

I believe that this idea of promise is fundamental to the Old Testament and that it is even more foundational than the concept of covenant or the question of how God relates to humanity at different periods in redemptive history. The concept of promise places the focus on God, because God has made the promise, and the content of the promise is that God will send his own Son to us. Thus the idea of promise provides the context in which the question of God's relationship to humanity is addressed. Or, to say it differently, the promise underlies and provides the groundwork for God's covenant (or covenants) with human beings. In keeping with the purpose of this book to integrate Christian theology around the Father-Son relationship, I would like to concentrate only on those elements of the unfolding promise that directly pertain to the identity of the promised person, the Son of God.

The promise: a single person. God initially gives his promise almost immediately after the Fall, as he pronounces his curses upon the serpent, Eve and Adam. God speaks to the serpent first, saying, "Cursed are you above all the livestock and all the wild animals! You will crawl on your belly and you will eat dust all the days of your life. And I will put enmity between you and the woman, and between your offspring and hers; he will crush your head, and you will strike his heel" (Gen 3:14-15). The word translated "offspring" here *(zera')* literally means "seed," and it can refer to a single descendant or to all of the descendants considered collectively. The crucial interpretive question in this verse has to do with whether God is speaking of one descendant or of the descendants of Eve in general. While modern commentators typically assume the word is referring to the descendants collectively, there is also evidence that the pre-Christian Jewish translators of the Septuagint (the Greek translation of the Hebrew Scriptures, begun about 250 B.C.) understood the word *seed* in this passage as a reference to a single person.[10] Furthermore, in Galatians 3:16, during a discussion of the "seed" (albeit not a discussion of this passage but of passages later

---

[10]This evidence has to do with the pronoun one uses with the word *seed*. In Hebrew, *zera'* is masculine, so one would use the masculine pronoun "he" *(hû')* whether one wanted to speak of one descendant or all of them. But in Greek the word for "seed" *(sperma)* is neuter, so if one wants to use the word to refer to all the descendants, one follows it with the neuter personal pronoun "it" *(auto)*. In contrast, if one wants to use the word "seed" to refer to a single descendant, one uses a masculine or feminine pronoun: "he" *(autos)* or "she" *(autē)*. In this passage, the Septuagint uses the masculine pronoun *autos,* indicating that "seed" refers to a single male descendant of Eve.

Irenaeus on Christ as the Fulfillment of Genesis 3:15 (ca. 180):

He has therefore, in his work of recapitulation, summed up all things, both waging war against our enemy and crushing him who had at the beginning led us away captives in Adam. . . . For from that time, he who should be born of a woman, [namely] from the Virgin, after the likeness of Adam, was preached as keeping watch for the head of the serpent. This is the seed of which the apostle says in the epistle to the Galatians, "that the law of works was established until the seed should come to whom the promise was made." This fact is exhibited in a still clearer light in the same epistle, where he thus speaks: "But when the fullness of time was come, God sent forth his Son, made of a woman."

Ag. Her., bk. 5, chap. 21, par. 1 (ANF, vol. 1, 548-49)

---

in Genesis where the word is also used), Paul insists that the singular word implies a single person, Christ. And not surprisingly, this is the way the early church understood the passage as well. In the sidebar just above, Irenaeus not only interprets the word *seed* to refer to a single person, Christ, but also sees a reference to the virgin birth in the fact that the promised person is called the seed of the woman rather than the seed of Adam. At the beginning of human history, just after the Fall, God gave a promise that a single person would come from among Eve's descendants and that *this* man, this person, would crush the head of Satan. From the beginning, people were to recognize that we were not able to restore ourselves to the fellowship of the Trinity. Instead, we were to await the promised seed, the man whom God would send.

The promised person: a blessing for the world. In the progressive unfolding of the promise, the next major step comes in Genesis 12. God appears to Abram while he is living in Haran (in what is today northern Iraq) and tells him to leave his people and country for another land (Canaan, which will later be called Israel). At the same time God makes the following promise to Abram: "I will make you into a great nation and I will bless you; I will make your name great, and you will be a blessing. I will bless those who bless you, and whoever curses you I will curse; and all peoples on earth will be blessed through you" (Gen 12:2-3). Several aspects of this promise are noteworthy, but for our purposes, the most significant is that Abram's descendants will constitute a nation which God blesses in order that through that nation he may bless all peoples (equivalent to what we would call "people groups" or "ethnic groups" today) of the world. Abram and his descendants will not be the only ones who will be blessed. Instead, that nation will be the channel through which God will bless all the families of the earth. Thus the choosing of Abram and his descendants was not a means of excluding the rest of humanity; it was for the purpose of blessing the whole world through Abraham.

Notice that in this passage, the word *seed* does not occur, and so there is no explicit link between the promise of Genesis 3:15 and the promise God makes to Abram here. However, later in the book of Genesis, God repeats this promise in one form or another four times: to Abram (whose name has subsequently been changed to Abraham— see Gen 17:5) in Genesis 18:18 and Genesis 22:18, to his son Isaac in Genesis 26:4, and to Isaac's son Jacob in Genesis 28:14. Significantly, in the last three of these four passages, the repetition of the promise includes the word *seed*. After God prevents Abraham from sacrificing Isaac, he says to Abraham, "Because you have done this and have not withheld your son, your only son, I will surely bless you and make your descendants as numerous as the stars in the sky and as the sand on the seashore. Your descendants will take possession of the cities of their enemies, and through your offspring all nations on earth will be blessed, because you have obeyed me" (Gen 22:16-18). Then in the repetition of the promise to Isaac and then Jacob, the language is almost the same: the descendants will be numerous, and through the seed/descendant all nations will be blessed.

If one were to read these passages solely in light of Genesis 12:2-3, then one would naturally understand them as referring to the descendants of Abraham in general. Abraham's seed will be numerous—a great nation will come from him—and through this large nation God will bless all nations of the world. However, the introduction of the word *seed* in these passages when it was not present in Genesis 12 serves to tie this promise directly to the prior promise of Genesis 3:15, and *that* promise was that a single person, a single descendant, would come from Eve's descendants to crush the head of the serpent. In light of this explicit connection, we need to understand the promise of a great nation as the means of fulfilling the promise of a single seed. The one person whom the world is to expect will come not just from the descendants of Eve (the whole human race) but specifically from the descendants of Abraham, indeed from Isaac (not his half-brother Ishmael) and from Jacob (not his brother Esau). Jacob, of course, is the father of the nation Israel, but it is not Israel as a whole that will bless the world. Instead, the one promised person who will come from that nation will bless the entire world.

The promised person: a king from the line of David. A great deal of God's revelation of the promise in the Old Testament has to do with the people's need for the forgiveness of sins that person will accomplish, and this is part of the purpose of the Old Testament law given after the exodus from Egypt. However, in the interest of concentrating only on the revelation of the promised person, we should now turn our attention to the period of the early monarchy. After David becomes king of Israel around 1010 B.C. and achieves peace in his realm, he builds his palace and then expresses the wish to build a house for God, a permanent temple to replace the tabernacle. In 2 Samuel 7, God sends the prophet Nathan to commend David for this desire and to let him know that his son Solomon will be the one who builds the temple. Nathan tells David:

> The LORD declares to you that the LORD himself will establish a house for you: When your days are over and you rest with your fathers, I will raise up your offspring to succeed you, who will come from your own body, and I will establish his kingdom. He is the one who will build a house for my Name, and I will establish the throne of his kingdom forever. I will be his father, and he will be my son. When he does wrong, I will punish him with the rod of men, with floggings inflicted by men. But my love will never be taken away from him, as I took it away from Saul, whom I removed from before you. Your house and your kingdom will endure forever before me; your

throne will be established forever. (2 Sam 7:11-16)

Once again, the word *seed* (translated "offspring" here) ties this passage to the previous unveilings of the promise. This passage immediately refers to David's son Solomon, who will build the temple and whom God will discipline when he does wrong. But ultimately this prophecy looks beyond Solomon to the person promised in Genesis 3:15. This person will come from the line of David (not just the nation of Israel as a whole) and will be a king whose kingdom will endure forever. Furthermore, Nathan says that God will be a father to that person, and he will be a son to God. This refers in a general way to David, Solomon and the rest of their descendants, but it refers specifically and preeminently to the promised person. This is perhaps the first hint in the Old Testament that the promised seed will be God the Son. Again, one could not expect David to recognize the significance of calling his descendant a son to God, but from the vantage point of Christ, we may see that the ultimate fulfillment of this prophecy is indeed the second person of the Trinity.

The promised person: God himself. As Israel's history progresses, the people fall deeper into sin, and this sin is punished by the division of the monarchy into two kingdoms in 931, the fall of the northern kingdom to the Assyrians in 722 and finally the destruction of Jerusalem and the fall of the southern kingdom to the Babylonians in 586. Much of the prophetic literature during this time period consists of God's calling attention to the people's disobedience and his warnings that they must turn back to him or suffer punishment. The prophets also give increasing attention to the work that the promised person will accomplish,[11] and most significant for our purposes, they begin to state more clearly that he will be more than just a man. The two most noteworthy examples of this trend come in Isaiah 9 and Micah 5, both written in the eighth century.

---

[11]See especially Is 52:13–53:12; Jer 31:31-34. In the former passage, the servant (the seed of the promise) will take upon himself the infirmities, sorrows, transgressions and iniquities of all people. In the latter passage, the prophecy of the new covenant recalls the previous aspects of the promise: God's people will be holy, he will be their God and they will be his people, all people will know God, and God will forgive the people's sins.

Isaiah 9 is a prophecy that the gloom and darkness into which the people have sunk will ultimately be undone through the birth of a child who will become an everlasting king. Isaiah 9:6-7, among the most famous verses in the Old Testament, reads: "For to us a child is born, to us a son is given, and the government will be on his shoulders. And he will be called Wonderful Counselor, Mighty God, Everlasting Father, Prince of Peace. Of the increase of his government and peace there will be no end. He will reign on David's throne and over his kingdom, establishing and upholding it with justice and righteousness from that time on and forever. The zeal of the LORD Almighty will accomplish this." Here again the connections between this passage and the previous statements of the promise are clear. The promised child who will reign on David's throne and whose kingdom will never end is the person promised in Genesis 3:15, implied in Genesis 12, promised in 2 Samuel 7. But what is especially noteworthy in this passage is that two of the names for this person are to be "Everlasting Father" and "Mighty God." In light of these names, the person who is promised will not simply be a son but will be the Son, the second person of the Trinity. The baby who is to be born will be God himself.

Equally striking is another famous passage, Micah 5:2. During a discussion of a grave threat to Israel, the prophet speaks of a ruler who will come forth to shepherd his people and provide protection for them. Micah 5:2 reads: "But you, Bethlehem Ephrathah, though you are small among the clans of Judah, out of you will come for me one who will be ruler over Israel, whose origins are from of old, from ancient times." The Jews understand this as a prophecy that the promised person (by now called the Messiah, meaning "anointed one") would be born in Bethlehem (see Mt 2:1-8). But even more noteworthy than the first half of this verse is the second part. Micah says that the ruler who will come out of Bethlehem will be one "whose origins are from of old, from ancient times." The phrase translated "from ancient times" here can be rendered more precisely as "from days of eternity."[12] Furthermore, the word for "will come" and "origins" are the same word:

---

[12]The NIV text note makes this point. The word in question, ʿōlām, is the same word that is used twice in Ps 90:2, translated, "from everlasting to everlasting you are God."

Micah's point is that one will go forth who has been going forth from all eternity.[13] His language here is similar to John the Baptist's later statement, "A man who comes after me has surpassed me because he was before me" (Jn 1:30). Both Micah and John speak of one coming later who has existed before; that is, they imply that the person who will be born has eternally existed and is thus God.

CONCLUSIONS

In this chapter, we have seen that in the eyes of the church fathers (in contrast to many modern biblical interpreters), proper interpretation of the Old Testament requires one to have an accurate understanding of the total message of the Bible, so that one may read each individual passage in light of that overall message. Furthermore, we have seen that the early church overwhelmingly saw that central message as Christ. Therefore, Christ is the link between the Old and New Testaments, just as Christ's relationship to his Father is the link between divine life and Christian life, between God's action and human action. I have argued that even though the early church's exuberance in finding Christ in the Old Testament led to mistaken exegesis of certain passages, the Fathers were correct in their overall assumption that the link between the Testaments should be Christ.

Furthermore, in this chapter I have attempted to trace the Old Testament's developing revelation of the promise that is fulfilled in Christ. In doing so I have used passages that the church fathers (and indeed, the vast majority of believers for most of Christian history) have seen as referring directly to Christ. However, I have also tried to show that one need not have known the end of the story to be able to see Christ in the developing Old Testament revelation. Instead, from the beginning people should have been able to recognize that God had promised a single person in whom they should place their hope. As time went on, God made clear that this person would come from Abraham, from Is-

---

[13]Contemporary commentators are much less willing than the early church to interpret these Old Testament passages as pointing to the deity of the Messiah. Here, as elsewhere, modern interpretation asks what the initial readers could have understood, but patristic interpretation brings the later revelation of who Christ was into the picture and insists that these passages prefigured that later revelation.

rael and then from David's line. God made clear that the people needed this person to accomplish forgiveness of sins and usher in an eternal kingdom. And finally, God began more and more to show that this person would be divine, that he would be God. With the fuller revelation of the New Testament behind us as well, we can (and the church fathers did) look back and recognize that the references in the Old Testament to "a son" were references to the Son, to the second person of the Trinity. But while the Jews could not have guessed this at the time, since they had so far been given only hints of the Trinity, they were given enough to recognize that somehow this person whom God would send was himself God.

As a result, we can see that the link between the Old and New Testaments is stronger than modern interpreters often make it out to be. Furthermore, we can recognize that our common criticism of patristic Old Testament interpretation is not always warranted, because if my focus on the idea of a promised person is correct, then the proper way to draw the connection between the Testaments is much closer to the way the church fathers made that connection than we typically allow. From beginning to end the Bible is the story of God's love for his people, a love on the basis of which he promised to send a person through whom all nations of the world might be blessed. This person, we now know, is Christ. The love which prompted God to promise us this Christ, we now know, is the love which the Father and the Son have shared from all eternity. God promised us his Son in order to share with us the love he shares with his Son. The several millennia of Old Testament history served to prepare Israel and the world to recognize and receive this Son when he came into the world. And that entrance of God the Son into the world is the subject to which I will turn in chapter seven.

Chapter 7

The Incarnation

THE ONLY SON BECOMES
THE FIRSTBORN SON

Now that we have considered the relation between the Old and New Testaments, and thus the way God has prepared the world for the coming of his Son, we are ready to turn back to the centerpiece of history, the events that lie at the heart of what Christianity calls *redemption*. This word refers to the fact that because of our sin, we have been enslaved to a foreign master, and we need to be bought back so as to be restored to our rightful owner, God. I will break this treatment of redemption into two chapters, this one focused on the incarnation and the life of Christ, and the following one on the death and resurrection of Christ. Thus it is now time to return to John's Gospel, for John is the one who explains most clearly the incarnation, the act by which God the Son stepped into human life by becoming a real human being without ceasing to be God. As we seek to understand John's teaching with the help of the church fathers, I will rely most heavily on Athanasius and Cyril of Alexandria, the church's greatest teachers on the incarnation and perhaps the best representatives of the strand of patristic thought that I am elaborating in this book.

GOD'S SENDING OF HIS SON

John begins his Gospel with some of the most memorable words in the whole Bible: "In the beginning was the Word, and the Word was with God, and the Word was God. He was with God in the beginning. Through him all things were made; without him nothing was made that has been made. In him was life, and that life was the light of men. The light shines in the darkness, but the darkness has not understood it" (Jn 1:1-5). In this passage, the "Word" is the Son of God, the second person of the Trinity who after the incarnation will be called the Christ or Jesus. To see that the one John calls the "Word" is indeed the Son, one can turn to Hebrews 1:1-2, where the writer claims: "In the past God spoke to our forefathers through the prophets at many times and in various ways, but in these last days he has spoken to us by his Son, whom he appointed heir of all things, and through whom he made the universe." Notice how similar the passage in Hebrews is to this passage in John. Both affirm that this one of whom they are speaking is the one through whom God made the universe. The writer of Hebrews calls him the "Son," and John calls him the "Word." Clearly, the same person is in mind in both cases.

Why does John call him the "Word" here? Of course, the word is the means of communication, the basic unit of speech. It is the way we express the reasoning of our minds. In fact, the word translated "word" here *(logos)* can also be rendered "reasoning," "account," "speech" or even "explanation." By using this word *logos,* John indicates that the second person of the Trinity is the one by whom God communicates to humanity. He is God's communication par excellence, the last and greatest way God has spoken to us. The writer of Hebrews conveys exactly the same idea by saying that God had spoken through the prophets, but now he has spoken through his Son. In addition, John knows that his readers, Greek speakers from various different cultures of the ancient world, will all recognize the word *logos,* since the pagan Greeks used this word to refer to the divine being by whom the supreme God communicated to the world.

Notice what John writes about this Word, this Son of God: he was in the beginning with God. The first verse of the Bible says, "In the beginning God created the heavens and the earth" (Gen 1:1). Here John indicates that at the time God created the heavens and the earth, the Word was already present, already with God. Thus this Word has always been with God, from eternity past. By writing this, John is setting the stage for what Jesus will later say—that we are to share in the glory he had with the Father before the world existed. But notice also that John does not simply assert that the Word was with God; he also writes that the Word was God. Here we have both an identification of the Word with God such that they can be said to be the same God and a distinction between them such that the Word can be said to be with God. Furthermore, John indicates that all things that have been made (that is, all noneternal things, all created things) were made through the Word. Genesis has told us that God made everything. (In Hebrew thought, the expression "the heavens and the earth" was a way of saying "everything.") Here John tells us that the way God made everything was through the Word. Therefore, we see that in a few short phrases, John gives us the fundamental truths of the relationship between the Son and the Father. The two are distinct as persons, and yet they are united so as to be a single God. They are together in love, and the Son/Word is the one through whom the Father/God works. Jesus spells out this relationship in more detail later in the Gospel.

Having sketched this relationship in a concise way, John then turns his attention to the personal entrance of this Word into the world. He briefly describes the role of another John (whom the other Gospel writers call "John the Baptist") in bearing witness to the Word, and then he writes:

> He [the Word] was in the world, and though the world was made through him, the world did not recognize him. He came to that which was his own, but his own did not receive him. Yet to all who received him, to those who believed in his name, he gave the right to become children of God—children born not of natural descent, nor of human decision or a husband's will, but born of God. (Jn 1:10-13)

The beginning of this passage indicates that the Word came first to the Jews, the people to whom he belonged in terms of human descent. Most of them did not receive him, but the crucial point John makes has to do with those who did believe in him, whether Jews or Gentiles. John writes that "he gave them the right to become children of God" and affirms that they were "born of God." Remember that the Word is God the Son, and those who believe in the Son become sons and daughters of God—not natural children, but spiritual sons and daughters, as we are born spiritually from God. How does believing in the Word enable one to become a child of God, even to be born of God? John explains this striking claim in the next verse: "The Word became flesh and made his dwelling among us. We have seen his glory, the glory of the One and Only who came from the Father, full of grace and truth" (Jn 1:14). Let us look carefully at the three main assertions John makes in this spectacular verse.

First, John writes that the "Word became flesh" and lived among us. By "flesh," John does not simply mean that the Word took on a body or a visible form; he means that the Word became human, without ceasing to be God. In the Bible, "flesh" often refers to human beings,[1] and the vividness of the word is designed to show that he was really human, physical as well as spiritual, and not some sort of ghost. In fact, John will later write that we have seen, heard and even touched the Word of life (1 Jn 1:1-2). The Word, the Son, has come down from heaven, somehow become human as we are and lived a human life among us.

The second assertion John makes in this verse is that as we have seen the incarnate Word, we have seen "the glory of the One and Only who came from the Father." The Greek word translated "one and only" *(monogenēs)* is sometimes rendered "only-begotten," and it refers to the fact that the Word is the unique Son of God. God has only one true Son—the Word, the second person of the Trinity. Even when Christians are called children of God (as in the previous verse) or sons of God (see, for example, Rom 8:14-17)—and by implication, also daughters of God—we are not children of God in the same way that the Word is God's Son. He is equal to God, eternal and always the Father's Son. We are created, servants of God, on a lower level, and we are adopted into

---

[1]See Lk 3:6 (where the NIV renders "all flesh" as "all mankind"); Rom 3:20 (where the NIV renders "no flesh" as "no one"); Eph 6:12 ("flesh and blood" as a synonym for "human beings"); 1 Pet 1:24 (where the NIV renders "all flesh" as "all men").

God's family. This is what John means when he writes that we are born
of God, and Paul uses the word *adoption* in Romans 8 and elsewhere. So
as the Word became human, people were able to see the uniqueness of
the One and Only, the true Son of God. Furthermore, notice here that
John uses the word *glory*. We do not just see the Son of God; we see the
glory of the unique Son. Remember again that glory implies presence.
When we see the incarnate Word, we see something of the unique
presence of God with him, something of his unique relationship with
God the Father. Once again, John is introducing in brief form what
Jesus will spell out in more detail later: The loving fellowship between
the Son and the Father becomes clear to us when we see the Word
made flesh, and somehow the true Son's relationship to his Father leads
to our becoming adopted children of God.

The third claim John makes in this verse is that the incarnate Word
is "full of grace and truth." The Greek words John uses here *(charis* and
alētheia) are intended to echo two Hebrew words *(ḥesed* and *ʾĕmet)* that
are extremely common in the Old Testament, especially in the Psalms,
where they often occur together.[2] The first of these *(ḥesed),* rendered
"grace" here, is normally rendered "lovingkindness" or "tender mer-
cies" or "unfailing love" in the Old Testament. It conveys two basic
ideas: the depth of God's love for us and the constancy of that love. The
second word *(ʾĕmet),* rendered "truth" here, is often translated "faith-
fulness" in the Old Testament. These two words sum up the constant,
consistent, faithful and personal love of God toward his people. John
indicates that in the incarnate Word we see the fullest possible display
of God's love. Indeed, we see this love displayed in two directions—
toward his Father and toward us, his people.

THE INCARNATE SON: DISTINCT FROM US AND YET LINKED

As the great thinkers of the early church reflected on these passages
from John's Gospel, they developed a pair of phrases that distinguish
Christ from Christians and yet also link him to us. Those phrases were
"Son by nature" and "sons by grace" (or "sons by adoption"). The

[2]See, for example, Ps 115:1; 117:2.

Word, Jesus Christ, is the one, true, natural Son of God, who is one of the persons of the Trinity, equal to (and in terms of attributes, even identical to) the Father. He is the only one who has eternally been in a filial relationship with God the Father. In contrast, those who believe in Christ are sons and daughters by adoption, by grace. We are brought into the relationship through God's action; it is conferred on us rather

---

Cyril of Alexandria on the Distinction Between the True Son and Sons by Adoption (ca. 423):

> The concept of sonship means this when applied to one who is so naturally [that is, when applied to Christ], but the matter is otherwise with those who are sons by adoption. For since Christ is not a son in this manner [by adoption], he is therefore truly a Son, so that on account of this he may be distinguished from us, who are sons by adoption. For there would be sonship neither by adoption nor by likeness to God if he did not remain the true Son, to whose likeness our sonship is called and formed by a certain skill and grace.

Thes., chap. 32 (Fairbairn's translation)

---

than being our natural birthright. Thus, in the writings of the early church, the phrases "by nature" and "by grace" clearly distinguish Christ/the Word/the Son from those who are born of God by believing in the Son. For an illustration of this distinction, see the sidebar just above from Cyril of Alexandria.

At the same time, however, the phrases "Son by nature" and "sons by grace/adoption" link us to Christ by referring to us both as "sons." By becoming human, the Word has become one of us. In a sense, he has become our brother, and Paul refers to him in Romans 8:29, as the firstborn among many brothers. Notice that the Bible uses both the phrase "one and only" and the word "firstborn" to describe God the Son. How can one be the only Son if one is also the first son among many brothers and sisters? Reflecting on this, the church fathers concluded that the Word, when considered as God, is the only Son. But when the same Word is considered after the incarnation as a human being, he is the first of many brothers and sisters. Athanasius explains this succinctly in the sidebar just below. The Son has become human in order to make himself our adopted brother, so that we, having become his adopted sisters and brothers, could then become the adopted daughters and sons of his natural Father, God. The Son by nature has made us sons and daughters by grace.

Not only do the church fathers emphasize that Christ is Son in a different way from us, they also stress that he had to be so. If Christ were merely a man who was indwelt by God, a man who climbed back up to God, then he could not have given us grace and salvation. One who receives grace from the outside, whether by earning it or by

---

Athanasius on the Son as Only-Begotten and Firstborn (ca. 358):

If then he is Only-begotten, as indeed he is, "Firstborn" needs some explanation; but if he is really Firstborn, then he is not Only-begotten. For the same cannot be both Only-begotten and First-born, except in different relations—that is, Only-begotten, because of his generation from the Father, as has been said; and Firstborn, because of his condescension to the creation and his making the many his brethren.

Ag. Arian., bk. 2, chap. 62 (NPNF[2], vol. 4, 382)

---

receiving it as a gift, cannot pass that grace on to others. If grace or salvation were a thing, then one who had received this could in turn pass it on to others. Christ could have been a man who gained this thing as a reward and then handed it over to us. But as we have seen, salvation is not a thing. Rather, salvation is Christ; grace is Christ. To say this differently, salvation is our sharing by adoption in the Son's own relationship to the Father. Because salvation is Christ, then only Christ can give himself to us. Only the one who is naturally the Father's Son, who has from all eternity shared in loving fellowship with the Father, is able to grant us participation by adoption in his own relationship to the Father. In the sidebar on the next page by Athanasius, notice that the reason salvation cannot be earned is that salvation is adopted sonship. The content of salvation is inseparable from the person of Christ, who is the real and natural Son of God. Athanasius writes that Christ could not have received the prerogatives as a reward for his virtue. Salvation is Christ himself, adoption into his own relationship with the Father. Because of what (or better, who) salva-

---

Athanasius on Christ as the Natural Son of God (ca. 358):
> For how in that case [if Christ were not the natural Son] can any at all know God as their Father? for adoption there could not be apart from the real Son, who says, "No one knoweth the Father, save the Son, and he to whomsoever the Son will reveal him." . . . And if all that are called sons and gods, whether in earth or in heaven, were adopted and deified through the Word, and the Son himself is the Word, it is plain that through him are they all, and he himself before all, or rather he himself only is very Son, and he alone is very God from the very God, not receiving these prerogatives as a reward for his virtue, nor being another beside them, but being all these by nature and according to essence.

Ag. Arian., bk. 1, chap. 39 (NPNF², vol. 4, 329)

---

tion is, this salvation cannot be earned and can be given only by the true and natural Son of God.[3]

As the early church understood John's Gospel, the incarnation was the movement of God that made it possible for human beings who had lost their relationship with God to be restored to that fellowship again. God called us to share in the loving relationship between the Father

---

[3]These are the ideas that lay at the heart of the christological controversy in the fifth century. Theodore and his student Nestorius saw grace as a thing that one who received could then pass on to others. Specifically, they understood grace as God's aid in the human task of aspiring to perfection. Christ the man received this grace, and thus he was "divine" in the sense that God the Son cooperated with him and aided him by indwelling him. As he reached perfection, he was able to pass this grace on to us. In sharp contrast, Cyril (and, I believe, virtually the entire church as well) saw grace as God the Son's giving us himself. Thus, in order for us to receive this grace, Christ had to be God the Son, not merely a graced man, as Theodore and Nestorius argued.

and the Son, to live that relationship out in the world. But because humanity lost that fellowship through the Fall, God the Son personally stepped into human existence in order to make us his adopted brothers and sisters. As we are adopted into God's family, we are once again given the privilege of sharing the fellowship that unites the persons of the Trinity. The Father, Son and Spirit share this by nature, by virtue of the fact that they possess the single divine nature and are the same God. We are not sons and daughters by nature and never will be, but through the grace of the incarnation, we are given anew the fellowship that the natural Son shares with his Father.

John communicates this staggering truth to us in outline form at the beginning of his Gospel, and Jesus, the Son, gives us more of the specifics in the upper room discourse. Cyril of Alexandria offers perhaps the boldest summary of the link between the incarnation and our sharing in divine fellowship when he comments on Jesus' discussion of believers as Christ's own sheep in John 10. In the sidebar just below, notice the distinction between Christ and us (he has an identical nature to God, but we do not) and the link between Christ and us (he has taken our flesh when he was made man, so we are closely related). Above all, notice that the fellowship we have with God is the same as that which the Son has with the Father. They have that fellowship because they share the same nature; we have it because we have been linked to God through the incarnation.

Cyril of Alexandria on Christians as Christ's Sheep (ca. 425):

For the Word of God is a divine nature even when in the flesh, and although he is by nature God, we are his kindred because of his taking the same flesh as ours. Therefore the manner of the fellowship *(oikeiotēs)* is similar. For just as he is closely related to the Father and through their identity of nature the Father is closely related to him, so also are we [closely related] to him and he to us, in so far as he was made man. And through him as through a mediator we are joined to the Father.

Com. Jn., bk. 6, chap. 1 (Randell, 84, translation modified)

At this point, several major questions present themselves. The one that might be foremost is the issue of how the incarnation could be possible. How could God enter the human race and live a really human life? We can imagine God appearing briefly in a human form, taking on some sort of visible guise as he speaks to us. But can we conceive of God, the infinite Creator of the universe and Son of the Father, becoming a helpless baby? And if he were to do this, in what way could he possibly still be God? A second question that emerges is how the life of the incarnate God could have any connection to our sinful human lives. In what way could the Son of God really be our brother, so that we could become adopted children and thus receive a share in his relationship with his Father? And a third potential question is how any of this deals with the problem of sin, the problem that led us to lose our fellowship with God in the first place. These are significant questions, and I will attempt to address them in the remainder of this chapter and the next one.

ARTICULATING THE DOCTRINE OF CHRIST

When one attempts to make sense of the incarnation, one should begin from the foundational insight about the Trinity that we have considered earlier—there are three divine persons who are equal, eternal and even identical with respect to attributes, and therefore these three persons are the same God. If the divine nature is the complete set of characteristics or attributes the Bible ascribes to God, then the Father, the Son and the Holy Spirit possess this identical divine nature. Possessing this divine nature from all eternity, the three persons have thus eternally lived the divine life—a life that involves sharing in fellowship and love. In this way, one may speak of the second person as Son of God by nature. However, Scripture affirms that this same Son has come down to earth and lived among us, that is, he has lived a human life among human beings. In order for this to happen, he has "become flesh"—he has taken upon himself a full set of human characteristics so as to enable himself to live that human life. If the divine nature is the set of divine attributes that makes it possible for the three persons to live the divine life, then in the same way, a human nature is the set of human attributes and components that makes our sort of life possible. To live as a human being, one needs to be both spiritual and physical (to have a soul and a body), one needs a human mind, human emotions and so forth. If one were to list all such characteristics—attributes and component parts that all human beings have in common—then these collectively would constitute a human nature.

Furthermore, it should be clear that a nature does not exist by itself. A nature is a complete set of characteristics, and these characteristics must have a person in whom to reside. (For example, hunger is not something that exists on its own; it is a characteristic that a particular person exhibits at a given time.) In each of us, our human nature resides in the particular human person that each one of us is. However, what the early church recognized about the incarnation was that the human nature of Christ resides not in a merely human person but in the divine person, God the Son. To say this differently, God the Son—one of three and only three persons who possessed the divine nature—added to his own person a complete human nature, a full complement of the characteristics and components that make one human. In this way, the same person—the second person of the Trinity—was both divine and human. He was divine because from all eternity he had possessed the divine nature. After the incarnation he was also human because he took upon himself "flesh," that is, all the characteristics that define one as a human being. Because this same person, whom we now call Jesus Christ, was both divine and human, he was able to live on two levels at the same time. He continued to live on the divine level as he had done from all eternity—sharing fellowship with the Father, maintaining the universe (see Col 1:17) and whatever else God does. But now he began to live on a human level at the same time—being conceived and born as a baby, growing up in Nazareth, learning Scripture as any other Jewish boy would, becoming hungry, thirsty and tired, and even dying.

The fathers of the church expressed this idea beautifully when they spoke of God the Son doing some things as God and doing other things as man. The same person did things that were appropriate for humanity and other things that were appropriate, or even possible, only for God. But the person who did these things was the same, God the Son. He sim-

Augustine on Christ "as God" and "as Man" (ca. 410):
> So it is that the Son of God, who is at once the Word of God and
> the mediator between God and men the Son of man, equal to the
> Father by oneness of divinity and our fellow by taking of human-
> ity, so it is that he intercedes for us insofar as he is man, while not
> concealing the fact that as God he is one with the Father.

On Trin., bk. 4, chap. 12 (Hill, 161)

ply did some things in keeping with his divine nature that he had possessed from all eternity and other things appropriate to his human nature
that he had begun to possess at the incarnation. In the sidebar from Augustine just above, notice that the person of Christ is the Son of God. This
person is one with the Father when one considers him as God, and he is
the one who prays to the Father on our behalf when one considers him as
man. God the Son does what is appropriate to God and what is appropriate to humanity. Similarly, in the sidebar from Athanasius on the next
page, notice that Christ both gives and receives grace. As the Word (that
is, as God), he gives grace from the Father. But he gives this grace to his
own humanity, so that as man he may receive it on our behalf. The same
person, God the Son, both gives salvation to humanity and accepts salvation on behalf of humanity, so that our salvation might be secure in him.

The implication of what these church fathers are saying is that it is
not sufficient simply to say Christ is one person who possesses two natures. This is true, but the church fathers said much more than this and
believed they *had* to say more than this. The crucial question is not
whether Christ is one person and whether he has two natures. Rather,
the crucial question is who the one person is. At the center of Christ's
being, is he a man who is indwelt by God the Son, or is he God the Son
living on earth as a man? While a handful of people affirmed the first
of these, they were condemned by the church,[4] and the Fathers in gen-

---

[4]These were Diodore of Tarsus in the fourth century, Theodore of Mopsuestia in the fourth
and fifth centuries, and Nestorius in the fifth century. Nestorius was condemned during his
lifetime at the Council of Ephesus (the Third Ecumenical Council) in 431, and Diodore and
Theodore were condemned posthumously at the Second Council of Constantinople (the Fifth
Ecumenical Council) in 553.

Athanasius on Christ "as God" and "as Man" (ca. 358):

> The grace which the Son gives from the Father, that the Son him-
> self is said to receive; and the exaltation, which the Son bestows
> from the Father, with that the Son is himself exalted. For he who
> is the Son of God became himself the Son of man; and, as Word,
> he gives from the Father, for all things which the Father does and
> gives, he does and supplies through him; and as the Son of man,
> he himself is said after the manner of men to receive what pro-
> ceeds from him, because his body is none other than his.

Ag. Arian., bk. 1, chap. 45 (NPNF[2], vol. 4, 333)

eral insisted on the second. The person of Christ was and is God the
Son. The baby who was born from Mary was the same person who had
eternally been the only Son of God the Father. Christ is not simply a
man in whom God dwells, a man who has been especially graced by
God. Notice in the sidebar from Athanasius at the top of the next page
that there would be nothing unusual about God's dwelling within a
person, since God has dwelt within all the just throughout history. This
would not constitute an incarnation.

Instead of a man in whom God dwells, Christ is God the Son living
personally on earth as one of us. This is what the church insisted, and
this is what the church *had to* insist, because only if Christ, as a person,
is the true, natural Son of God can he grant us to share by adoption in
his eternal relationship to the Father. Only the Son by nature could
make us sons and daughters by grace, so in order for us to be saved, the
natural Son had to come personally from heaven to earth through the
incarnation. He did this, the church proclaimed, by taking a human
nature into himself, that is, by assuming a human set of characteristics
and components into his own divine person to go along with the divine
characteristics (that is, the divine nature) he had eternally possessed. In
the sidebar at the bottom of the next page, notice that Cyril unequivo-
cally links our adoption to the fact that Christ was the natural Son of
God. He was God the Son who became man while remaining God.

The preceding paragraphs may have come as a surprise to you, be-

---

Athanasius on God's Becoming a Man (ca. 358):

> He became man and did not come into man; for this it is neces-
> sary to know, lest perchance these irreligious men fall into this
> notion also and beguile any into thinking, that, as in former times
> the Word was used to come into each of the Saints, so now he
> sojourned in a man, hallowing him also and manifesting himself
> as in the others. For if it were so, and he only appeared in a man,
> it were nothing strange. . . . But now, since the Word of God, by
> whom all things came to be, endured to become also Son of man
> and humbled himself, taking a servant's form, therefore to the
> Jews the cross of Christ is a scandal, but to us Christ is "God's
> power" and "God's wisdom."

Ag. Arian., bk. 3, chap. 30 (NPNF[2], vol. 4, 410)

---

cause we often hear today that the early church's central teaching about
Christ was that he is one person who possesses two natures. This was
part of what the early church affirmed, but it was not the only thing.
Rather, the fundamental assertion of the early church was that the one
person who is Jesus Christ is God the Son. It was God the Son as a
person (not just the divine nature) who came down from heaven. It was

---

*Cyril of Alexandria on the Claim That Jesus Made Himself Out to Be
God's Son (ca. 436):*

> He did not [simply] make himself out to be God's Son, but he truly
> was so. For he possessed the quality of sonship not from the out-
> side, nor as something added, but because he was the Son by na-
> ture, for this is what we must believe. For we are sons of God by
> adoption as we are conformed to the Son who has been begotten
> of him [the Father] by nature. For if there were no true Son, who
> would remain to whom we could be conformed by adoption?
> Whose resemblance would we bear? Where indeed would the re-
> semblance be, if we were to say that the original did not exist?

Pasch. Let., 24, par. 3 (Fairbairn's translation)

God the Son as a person who united humanity to himself (not two natures being united to make a new person). In fact, a careful reading of the Chalcedonian Definition (the church's central pronouncement about Christ, written and approved at the Fourth Ecumenical Council in 451) shows that this is the case.

The sidebar just below contains the Chalcedonian Definition, with two different kinds of highlighting. The italicized portion highlights the part of the definition that most Protestants consider to be its central affirmation. Here we see clearly the insistence that two natures are

---

The Chalcedonian Definition of Faith (451):

Therefore, following the holy fathers, we all unite in teaching that we should confess <u>one and the same Son, our Lord Jesus Christ.</u> <u>This same one</u> is perfect in deity, and <u>the same one</u> is perfect in humanity; <u>the same one</u> is true God and true man, comprising a rational soul and a body. He is of the same substance as the Father according to his deity, and <u>the same one</u> is of the same substance with us according to his humanity, like us in all things except sin. He was begotten before the ages from the Father according to his deity, but in the last days for us and our salvation, <u>the same one</u> was born of the virgin Mary, the bearer of God, according to his humanity.

He is <u>one and the same Christ, Son, Lord, and Only-Begotten,</u> *who is made known in two natures [united] unconfusedly, un-changeably, indivisibly, inseparably. The distinction between the natures is not at all destroyed because of the union, but rather the property of each nature is preserved and concurs together in one prosōpon and hypostasis.* He is not separated or divided into two *prosōpa* but is <u>one and the same Son, the Only-Begotten, God the Word, the Lord Jesus Christ.</u>

This is the way the prophets spoke of him from the beginning, and Jesus Christ himself instructed us and the council of the fathers has handed [the faith] down to us.

(Fairbairn's translation)

---

united in one person.[5] However, notice the text that is underlined—
the phrases "the same one" and "one and the same." These two phrases
occur a combined eight times in the definition, and clearly the dominant affirmation of the definition is not that Christ consists of two
natures but that Christ is one and the same. The one who is consubstantial with the Father is the same one who is consubstantial with us.
But to whom, to what person, do these statements refer? Notice that
the definition is structured around three parallel framing statements,
each of which begins with the affirmation "one and the same." (In the
sidebar, the framing statements are underlined along with the phrase
"one and the same" that marks them.) Notice also that these statements
become more explicit as the definition goes along. The first reads "one
and the same Son, our Lord Jesus Christ," the second "one and the
same Christ, Son, Lord, and Only-Begotten," and the third "one and
the same Son, the Only-Begotten, God the Logos, the Lord Jesus
Christ." The increasing specificity of the statements makes clear that
the person who is one and the same is the Word, the Only-Begotten.
Neither the early church as a whole nor the Chalcedonian Definition
in particular is affirming merely that Christ has two natures united into
one person. Both the church and Chalcedon affirm that the person
who possesses both divine and human natures is the eternal second
person of the Trinity, the Son of God.[6] And once again, as we have
seen from Athanasius and Cyril, this is what the church needed to say
about Christ, since only if Christ was God the Son as a person could he
give us a share in his eternal, personal relationship to God the Father.

GRAPPLING WITH THE DIFFICULTIES OF THE INCARNATION

There are several objections to this way of describing Christ that come
readily to mind, and I would like to deal with two such problems now.

---

[5]In the translation, I have left the Greek words *prosōpon* and *hypostasis* untranslated. These
are two different words that both correspond to "person" in Latin or English. Furthermore, it
is worth pointing out that the word *united* does not occur. The definition claims that the one
Christ "is made known" in two unconfused natures, not that those two natures are united per
se. The union is implied, not stated.

[6]For a fuller explanation of this claim, see Donald Fairbairn, "The One Person Who Is Jesus
Christ: The Patristic Perspective," in *Jesus in Trinitarian Perspective: An Introductory Christology,*
edited by Fred Sanders and Klaus Issler (Nashville: Broadman and Holman, 2007), pp. 80-113.

Perhaps the most common objection is that if Christ's person was divine, then he could not have been truly and completely human. People often argue that to be human, one must not merely have a human nature but must be a genuine, independent human person. A human nature living in a divine person is not truly human, or so we say. However, notice the assumption that undergirds this insistence. People who raise this objection are assuming that to be fully human, one must be independent of God. But none of us is meant to be independent of God; all of us are meant to share in the fellowship of the Trinity. To be independent of God is to be less human, not more human. If each human person is meant to be dependent on God, then it does not denigrate the full humanity of Christ whatsoever to say that his humanity dwells in the person of God the Son. This is human life in complete and obvious dependence on God, human life as God meant it to be. Our objection here is based on a skewed perception of humanity. All we ever see is the sinful, distorted version of humanity—human beings alienated from God after the Fall. We do not see humanity as God truly intended it to be. And so our working intuition about what it means to be human concerns what it means to be fallen, not necessarily what it means to be completely human.

A second objection that one might raise is closely connected to this first one. One might well argue that divine nature and human nature are incompatible and thus irreconcilable. Therefore, we might insist, it is not possible for both of these to coexist in a single person. If God were to become a man, we would think he would have to stop being God. But once again, we need to remember that what we think of as "human nature" is fallen human nature. If one considers human nature as God created it, human nature as Adam and Eve possessed it before the Fall, then it is much easier to believe that such a nature is consistent with the divine nature. Humanity was created in the image of God, and thus human beings are the most like God of any created beings. Surely the divine nature and animal nature are incompatible, or perhaps even the divine nature and angelic nature, but human beings bear the impress of God's nature in a way that is unique in the created universe. There is no reason for insisting that an unfallen, nonsinful human nature could not possibly coexist with the divine nature in the person of God the Son.

At this point, one might think that the argument in the preceding paragraph is valid for some aspects of the divine nature but not all of them. Since God is loving, just, and holy, and since nonsinful human nature can also exhibit these characteristics, then one can think of divine love and perfect human love, divine holiness and perfect human holiness, coexisting in the same person. But this argument seems not to be valid for other aspects of God's nature. God is present everywhere, supremely powerful and all knowing. Human beings, seemingly by definition, have finite power and knowledge, and they are unquestionably confined to a single place at any given time. One might well ask how God the Son could possibly become human unless he gave up these characteristics. And if he were to give up these attributes, then surely he would not be God any longer. To use the language of the early church, in such a case he would have turned into a man rather than becoming a man while remaining God. This is a strong objection, but it fails to recognize one thing about the incarnation—God the Son did not give up his divine attributes when he became human; he simply chose not to exercise all of them on most occasions. In order to live in keeping with the limits imposed by the human nature he had assumed, God the Son chose most of the time not to use all of his divine power, not to avail himself of his ability to do things in two places at once (that is, not to use his omnipresence). If he wanted to do something in Jerusalem, he usually walked there, because walking there in order to act there was consistent with the humanity he had assumed.

Significantly, however, he did not always do things this way. Sometimes he healed at a distance, and the fact that he did so is one of the indications that he did not relinquish his divine attribute of omnipresence. But most of the time, he chose not to use that power, in order that he could live as man. In fact, it is clear from the Gospels that Jesus knows he possesses abilities that he does not normally use. When Jesus is arrested and Peter draws a sword to try to defend Jesus from the soldiers, Jesus rebukes him and says, "Do you think I cannot call on my Father, and he will at once put at my disposal more than twelve legions of angels?" (Mt 26:53). Jesus could do this because he is God. But he consciously chooses not to do this. In this way, Christ's life on earth was somewhat akin to a World Cup soccer player playing a pick-up game with school children. In order to level the playing field somewhat, the player might agree never to touch the ball with his right foot but instead to dribble, pass and shoot only with his left. He still possesses all the ability he has ever had, but he is not using all of it, in order that he can genuinely experience some of the difficulty that inexperienced players encounter in the sport.

The incarnation, like the Trinity, is a profound mystery. It is virtually beyond our capacity to believe that God the Son could have stepped into human life by becoming one of us. It is perhaps even more beyond belief that he *would have* done this. But Scripture affirms that he has done so and that God's becoming a man is what set in motion the events that accomplished our salvation. With the help of the great thinkers of the early church, who spent untold years pondering and writing about the incarnation, we may perhaps get our minds around that wondrous event to the point that it moves from the unthinkable to the believable. But however poorly we grasp it, however incredible it seems to us, the Bible affirms that it had to happen and did happen. The Word became flesh and dwelt among us. The next issue to which we need to turn, then, is the life of the incarnate Word on earth and how that life affects each of us.

CHRIST'S LIFE:
DIVINE AND HUMAN LOVE IN THE SAME PERSON

Since God's purpose for humanity was that we share in his relationship between the Father and the Son, and since humanity lost this relationship through the Fall, then surely one of the great needs of the human race was and is to see anew what this kind of love looks like. In fact, as John describes the incarnation, he claims that through the earthly life of the incarnate Word, we have seen the glory of the One and Only from the Father (Jn 1:14). The glorious presence of the Son with the Father, the love that unites them, is made known to us through the Son's life on earth as a man. To state this differently, through Jesus' life, we see that he is the Son of God, and we see something of his eternal fellowship with God the Father. But this is not the only thing that we see through Jesus' life. In addition, we see in him perfect human life; we grasp something of what human sharing in the relationship between the persons of the Trinity was designed to look like before sin disrupted it. In other words, the life of Jesus shows us both what it looks like for God to share in the love of the Trinity—since Jesus is the second person of the Trinity—and what it looks like for a human being to share in that same love, since this second person of the Trinity has taken humanity upon himself and has become fully human. These parallel demonstrations of sharing in the love of the Trinity will be the subjects of this section.

At the end of his Gospel, John states his purpose for writing: "Jesus did many other miraculous signs in the presence of his disciples, which are not recorded in this book. But these are written that you may believe that Jesus is the Christ, the Son of God, and that by believing you may have life in his name" (Jn 20:30-31). Here we see that for us, life is connected to believing in Jesus, believing that he is the Son of God as the Gospel of John proclaims him to be. By "life," John does not mean mere physical existence. He means a certain kind of life, a life characteristic of the age at the end of history when God's purposes will be fulfilled. It is a kind of life in which we share in the fellowship between the Father and the Son, just as humanity did at creation before the Fall. John writes his Gospel so that we may believe that Jesus is that very Son and that by believing we may have a share in the Son's fellowship with his Father.

But notice what else John writes here. He refers to "miraculous signs," and he asserts that Jesus has done many of these. In fact, the other three Gospels—Matthew, Mark and Luke—record far more of these miraculous signs than John does. They are filled with accounts of the miracles Jesus performs, usually healings of people who were sick or demon possessed or even dead. In comparison to those Gospels, John records relatively few of Jesus' miracles, but the ones he chooses to include are particularly significant because they show most clearly that Jesus is the Son of God. In a nutshell, John records those miracles of

Jesus which are directly tied to Old Testament prophecies about the Messiah, the coming "seed" whom the Old Testament had promised and whom the people were expecting. By focusing on these messianic expectations, John is able to show how Jesus fulfilled and went beyond the Jews' expectations of the coming Messiah, and even in some cases how he corrected their mistaken expectations. Adequately describing the relation between the people's expectations and Jesus' actions would take a book in itself, but I will mention a few examples to give you a flavor of what John is doing in this Gospel.

One of the dominant Jewish expectations was that when the Messiah—the promised person who dominated the hope of Israel in the Old Testament—came, there would be a great banquet with unlimited food and wine (see Is 25:6 for the source of this expectation). Jesus' turning the water into wine at the wedding in Galilee (Jn 2:1-10) and his feeding the five thousand (Jn 6:1-15) are directed toward this expectation, and in both cases, John writes that the action was a "miraculous sign" (Jn 2:11; 6:14). In fact, in John 6:14, John records that the people specifically recognized the sign as a fulfillment of their messianic hope, and they believed that he was the Prophet who was to come into the world. Another expectation was that the Messiah would bring healing to the people, and specifically that he would heal the blind (see Is 35:5-6). Jesus' healing of the man born blind in John 9:1-41 addresses this expectation, and the public discussion that ensues from this healing deals with whether someone who was not from God could possibly do such "miraculous signs" (Jn 9:16). Furthermore, it was believed that the Messiah would bring an end to death and suffering (see Is 25:7; 26:19 in connection with this hope). Jesus' raising of Lazarus from the dead in John 11:1-44 addresses this belief, and even the Jewish leaders who opposed Jesus called this action a miraculous sign (Jn 11:47).

Because of these miraculous signs, Jesus' life generated an enormous amount of discussion among the Jews about whether he was the Messiah or the Prophet who was to come from God. What is noteworthy about these discussions swirling around Jesus is that the people understand the Messiah as a man sent from God, not as God. In this context,

Jesus patiently but repeatedly emphasizes that he is the one they were expecting, but he is not a mere man as they thought the Messiah would be. He is God the Son. In John 8:58, he stuns the Jews so much with his claim, "Before Abraham was born, I am," that they pick up stones to stone him to death.[7] In John 10:30, Jesus claims, "I and the Father are one," and again the Jews understand this correctly as a claim to be God, so they again try unsuccessfully to stone him to death. In John 14:9—in the midst of the upper room discourse—Jesus tells the apostle Philip, "Anyone who has seen me has seen the Father." By Jesus' actions he shows himself to be the promised Messiah, and in the midst of discussions about whether he is that Messiah, Jesus' words indicate that he is greater even than the sort of Messiah they are expecting. He is none other than God the Son, the one who has existed before Abraham and who is in union with the Father. This is the main point that John seeks to make in his Gospel, as his statement of the book's purpose shows.

Thus in watching Jesus the people have not merely seen the human Messiah they were expecting. They have seen the Son of God, the divine Messiah. As a result, they have glimpsed firsthand what the relationship within the Trinity looks like, because they have seen that relationship in Jesus' interaction with his Father while he was on earth. Jesus' striking claim to Philip, "Anyone who has seen me has seen the Father," comes in the midst of the upper room discourse, where Jesus explains his relationship with his Father at length. Earlier in the Gospel, John has claimed, "No one has ever seen God, but God the One and Only, who is at the Father's side, has made him known" (Jn 1:18). Jesus is God the One and Only—the unique, eternal Son of God. Through Jesus' life, his words, his actions, we see what the actual relationship between the Father and the Son looks like. Jesus has shown us what the love between the persons of the Trinity consists of.

But this is not all that we see when we look at Jesus' life. In addition, we see what it looks like for a human being to share in the fellowship

---

[7]In the Old Testament, the phrase "I am" was the name God applied to himself when speaking to Moses from the burning bush (Ex 3:14). No Jew would ever use this phrase of himself, and the Jews clearly understood Jesus' use of it here to be a claim that he was God. The penalty for blasphemy was stoning the blasphemer to death, as is made clear in Lev 24:10-16.

of the Trinity. Remember that the church fathers spoke of Jesus acting as God and as man. The Gospels show that even though Jesus is God the Son, during his time on earth he still lives as a human being, accepting the limitations that humanity imposes on him and living as we do. This aspect of Jesus' life shows up in all four Gospels, but it is perhaps clearer in the first three than it is in John. As an illustration, let us look briefly at Luke's Gospel, which gives us a picture of Jesus' perfect human life in three major ways.

First, Luke stresses the role of the Holy Spirit in Jesus' life and ministry. The Holy Spirit is involved in Jesus' divine conception (Lk 1:35), comes on Jesus at his baptism (Lk 3:22), leads him into the wilderness to be tempted (Lk 4:1), leads him into Galilee to begin his public ministry (Lk 4:14) and fills him with joy at the successful preaching of his disciples (Lk 10:21). Luke shows us that even though Jesus is God and thus that the Spirit is his own Spirit, Jesus still relies on the Holy Spirit for strength and comfort, just as any other human being should do. Luke also demonstrates the substantial place of prayer in Jesus' life. There are ten separate occasions where Luke mentions that Jesus prayed to his Father.[8] Again, even though Jesus is God and has from all eternity shared in fellowship with the Father, he lives on earth as a human being, turning to God in prayer as any other person should do. A third way in which we see Jesus illustrating perfect human life is in the astonishing degree of compassion he feels for the outcasts of his society. In Luke's Gospel, the long list of marginalized people for whom Jesus shows great compassion includes Samaritans (Lk 10:30-37; 17:11-19), Gentiles (Lk 13:28-30), "tax collectors and sinners" (Lk 5:30; 7:34; 15:1; 18:10-13), shepherds (Lk 2:8-20), women (Lk 8:2-3), children (Lk 9:47; 10:21; 17:2; 18:16) and the poor (Lk 1:53; 4:18; 6:30; 14:11-13; 16:19-31). Remember that one of the major characteristics of sinful human life is a concern to be associated with the people in power, so as to bolster one's own sense of significance. In contrast, nonsinful human life is marked by a concern for all people, especially those who are far from the corridors of power and influence. In the Gospels, we see Jesus

---

[8]See Lk 3:21; 5:16; 6:12; 9:18, 28-29; 11:1; 22:32, 41; 23:34, 46.

living perfectly as a man, and his human life shows us something of what it means for a human being to share in the love between the Father and the Son. Sharing in that love manifests itself in (among other things) our reliance on God, our obedience to God and our compassion for and service to other people.

If the Gospels of Matthew, Mark and Luke show us what Jesus' perfect human life looks like, the apostle Paul is the one who most clearly interprets the significance of that human life. In 1 Corinthians 15:45-49, Paul draws a contrast between Adam, the first man, and Christ, the second man. The first man is "earthly," the second man "spiritual," and thus spiritual life comes to us through the second man. Paul elaborates on this contrast in Romans 5, where he speaks of the transgression of Adam, which affected all people, and the obedience of Christ, which also affects the entire human race. Paul writes:

> For if, by the trespass of the one man, death reigned through that one man, how much more will those who receive God's abundant provision of grace and of the gift of righteousness reign in life through the one man, Jesus Christ.
>
> Consequently, just as the result of one trespass was condemnation for all men, so also the result of one act of righteousness was justification that brings life for all men. For just as through the disobedience of the one man the many were made sinners, so also through the obedience of the one man the many will be made righteous. (Rom 5:17-19)

This passage shows that Adam's sin brought condemnation upon himself and alienated the entire human race from God. However, notice the rest of what Paul writes here. For those who "receive God's abundant provision of grace," the death that came through Adam's sin will be replaced by life through the second man. The effects of Adam's disobedience are reversed by Christ's obedience. We who were dead in Adam are somehow made alive in Christ. And throughout this passage, Paul refers to Christ as "the one man." Somehow, it is not simply Christ's divine power that reverses the effects of the Fall. Rather, it is God the Son living as the second man (in contrast to the first man, Adam) who transforms death into life and condemnation into acceptance for those who receive his grace. Somehow the human life of Christ is the link that connects our sinful, fallen lives to God and reverses the effects of the Fall so that we may share in the fellowship of the Trinity. Perhaps this is why Paul writes in 1 Timothy 2:5 that the one mediator between God and humanity is "the man Christ Jesus." Christ is the eternal Son of God, but it is the mediatorial action of God's Son as a man that brings us back to God.

The writers of the early church, especially Irenaeus, explained the contrast between Adam and Christ using a word *(anakephalaiōsis)* that is translated "recapitulation." This word conveys two ideas. The first is a summing up or a review—human life is in a sense begun anew, reviewed and corrected. It is as if the DVD of early human history is stopped and played back from the beginning but corrected as it is played, rather than being allowed to be played with all its sins, mistakes and tragedies. In Christ, the DVD is played again, and fixed in the process. He obeys whereas Adam disobeyed, trusts whereas Adam failed to trust, resists temptation whereas Adam succumbed. The second idea of recapitulation is that humanity is given a new head, a new leader. Adam headed the human race as it went astray, but he is now replaced by Christ, whose obedience heads the human race and leads it back to God.[9]

We see clearly then that the incarnation was not simply a divine spectacle in which God came down to show us his greatness. Instead, God the Son came down so that he, God, might do a very *human* task, but a task which no other human being could do because all of us were and are tainted by sin. That human task was to rehead the human race, to replay the DVD and fix the story, to replace the devastating trespass of the first Adam with the liberating obedience that he, the second Adam, accomplished. Irenaeus makes this clear in the sidebar on the next page. Notice that in order for us to be saved, Christ had to be God the Son, since only God could grant us his own fellowship with the Father. But notice also that God the Son had to overcome our adversary as man, and indeed he had to pass through every phase of human existence in order for all aspects of human life to be restored to God.

[9]See also Eph 1:10, where Paul uses the verb form of this word to refer to God's action at the end of history to bring all things together under the headship of Christ.

Irenaeus on God the Son's Human Task (ca. 180):

> For unless man had overcome the enemy of man, the enemy would not have been legitimately vanquished. And again: unless it had been God who had freely given salvation, we could never have possessed it securely. And unless man had been joined to God, he could never have become a partaker of incorruptibility. . . . For in what way could we be partakers of the adoption as sons, unless we had received from him through the Son that fellowship which refers to himself, unless his Word, having been made flesh, had entered into communion with us? Wherefore also he passed through every stage of life, restoring to all communion with God.

Ag. Her., bk. 3, chap. 18, par. 7 (ANF, vol. 1, 448)

CONCLUSIONS

In this chapter, we have seen that the incarnation was an action of God, by which the Son took into his own person a full humanity, complete with a human mind and soul, human emotions, human attributes and so forth. The purpose of this was so that God the Son could himself live as a man, allowing the full range of human experience to happen to himself, and in so doing to heal humanity and restore us to God. The early church repeatedly insisted that Christ had to be none other than the natural Son of God in order to adopt us into God's family. The central feature of that adoption is that we share in the natural Son's fellowship with the Father and the Spirit, and only the natural Son could give us such fellowship. No graced man could have shared this relationship with us, even if he could have earned it for himself. Accordingly the church insisted correctly that the incarnation was not the exaltation of a man, the honoring of the man Jesus with greater grace than other people received. Rather, the incarnation was the personal, downward movement of God the Son to earth to live among us.

Furthermore, we have seen that both John (in Jn 20:31) and Paul (in Rom 5:17-19) link Christ's work in us to our ability to have life. John writes that we who believe that he is the Son of God have life in his name, and Paul writes that we who receive the grace he offers through his human obedience reign in life with him. Somehow, both Christ's divine relationship as Son to his Father and his human work are connected to us in such a way that when we believe/receive, we share in the life he has with his Father. It is not yet clear just how the obedience of Christ and the divine sonship of Christ are connected to us. But this connection becomes clear through the events that Christians regard as the centerpiece of human history, the death and resurrection of Christ. In the next chapter, I will turn to these events.

Chapter 8

Redemption

GOD'S GIFT OF HIS SON'S
RELATIONSHIP TO THE FATHER

In the last chapter, we saw that the incarnation was a personal movement of God the Son to earth so that he, God, could live among us as a man. Thus Jesus is God the Son, and he is also fully human because at the incarnation he took a full humanity into his own person. As a result, Christ's life demonstrates what perfect love looks like: he participates in the loving fellowship of the Trinity both as God (as he has from all eternity) and now also as man. But as dramatic as that demonstration of love is, the Bible does not speak of the life Jesus lived in nearly as dramatic a way as it speaks of the death he died and the resurrection that followed. This is the point where God's action most directly addresses our human problem. We have seen that all human beings since Adam and Eve have been born dead, that although we still bear the image of God, we are nevertheless marred by sin to such a degree that we can do nothing to escape our predicament. If the human life of God's Son is what reminds us what our human lives were meant to look like, it is the human death and resurrection of God's Son that undo our spiritual death and make us alive again. In this chapter, I will examine his death and resurrection in some detail.

CHRIST'S DEATH AND THE ATONEMENT

We have already seen that *redemption* means "buying back," and in connection with the death of Christ, this word is understood to mean God's action to bring us back to himself. A closely associated word is *atonement,* which usually refers specifically to the way the work of Christ brings people back to God. Modern treatments of the atonement typically speak of various views or theories of atonement, which are commonly put forth in three broad categories. Classic views, associated with the early church and common in Eastern Orthodoxy today, focus on Christ's life, death and resurrection as God's action to overcome the powers of sin, death and the devil that enslave fallen people. Through the incarnation, God the Son personally entered Satan's territory, and through the death of Christ, God overcame Satan's control over people, so that we are no longer bound by sin and death.[1] Substitutionary views of the atonement, associated with Anselm in the late eleventh century and common in conservative Western Christianity (Protestant and Catholic) today, focus on Christ's death as a payment of the debt we owe to God because of our guilt before him. On account of our sins, we were guilty before a holy God, but Christ took the penalty of our sin on himself, enabling our sins to be forgiven and us to be justified before God.[2] Various exemplary views focus on the way Christ's life and death motivate us to overcome our sinfulness and live selflessly in imitation of him. His life redeems us as we follow his example.[3]

As important as it is to consider various views of the atonement (both subdivisions within these three broad categories and other views that do not fit well into any of them), there was relatively little discussion of these issues during the patristic period, and there was no formal declaration by the church about which view was correct. The church affirmed that God the Son came down, suffered, died, was buried, rose and ascended, but it did not elaborate exactly what was involved in the death of Christ. Instead, the church was primarily concerned with the

---

[1]See, e.g., Col 2:13-15; 1 Cor 15:50-57; Heb 2:14-15; 1 Jn 3:8.
[2]See the four propitiation passages (Rom 3:25; Heb 2:17; 1 Jn 2:2; 4:10), which I will discuss in more detail later in this chapter. See also Is 53:3-6; Rom 5:8-11; 1 Pet 2:24; 3:18.
[3]See, e.g., Lk 7:47; 1 Pet 2:21.

question of who died on the cross. Nevertheless, the way the church answered this question had important implications for the way one relates various views of the atonement to the person of Christ and the life of the Trinity. So in this chapter, I will approach the subject of Christ's death and resurrection primarily with reference to patristic discussions of who died but also with the more modern concern to articulate what was accomplished when Christ died and was raised.

THE DEATH OF CHRIST AS THE DEFINITION OF LOVE

In one of the most famous passages from John's first letter, he writes:

> Dear friends, let us love one another, for love comes from God. Everyone who loves has been born of God and knows God. Whoever does not love does not know God, because God is love. This is how God showed his love among us: He sent his one and only Son into the world that we might live through him. This is love: not that we have loved God, but that he loved us and sent his Son as an atoning sacrifice for our sins. Dear friends, since God so loved us, we also ought to love one another. No one has ever seen God; but if we love one another, God lives in us and his love is made complete in us. (1 Jn 4:7-12)

One should instantly recognize how similar this passage is to Jesus' words in the upper room discourse. God is love, and if we are born of God, then our love for one another will grow directly out of God's love for us. In fact, the reason we may say that God is love is that the persons of the Trinity have eternally shared love with one another. Only in this way can God be eternally loving, because people have not always been here for him to love. So our love for one another reflects and derives from the love between the Father and the Son. Furthermore, John writes that God showed his love by sending his one and only Son into the world that we might live. So far this is a summary of what John has recorded for us in his Gospel.

However, pay attention to the rest of this quotation. John begins the next sentence by writing, "This is love." God's sending his Son as an atoning sacrifice is not merely an example of love, it is love itself. Another way to translate this clause would be, "This is what love consists of." In other words, this is the definition of love. Notice also the contrast between God's love and ours. We are able to love one another as a reflection of God's love for us, as John has just emphasized. But love in its definitive form is not something we are capable of (not even before the Fall). The defining essence of love is not that we have loved God; it is that God has loved us in a specific way at a particular time, by sending Christ to die for us.

So how does the sending of Christ constitute the definition of love itself? John writes that God "sent his Son as an atoning sacrifice for our sins." The word that the NIV translates "atoning sacrifice" *(hilasmos)* is one of the most important words in the Bible and requires a great deal of explanation.[4] In general, an atoning sacrifice—what older translations such as the King James Version call a propitiation—is something that is offered to God in place of people who are guilty of sin. The idea is that the sin of the guilty people is transferred somehow to this sacrifice, and the sacrifice (usually an animal) is killed in place of the people who deserve to die. God's wrath toward the people's sin is poured out on the sin-bearing sacrifice, which dies under that wrath in place of the guilty people. The idea of an atoning sacrifice is enshrined prominently in the central ceremonies of the Old Testament law.

This law instituted a number of ceremonial days each year, and the most solemn of these was called the Day of Atonement. (Jews still celebrate this today, and you may know it by its Hebrew name, Yom Kippur.) This was the day in the autumn of the year when the people were to remind themselves of their sinfulness and to offer sacrifices that would represent their hope that God would one day enact a greater sacrifice that would take away their sins. Leviticus 16 describes these sacrifices, and in this chapter, there are at least four details that indicate the sacrifices did not themselves take away sin but only symbolized the removal of sin. First, the ark was only the sym-

---

[4]This word occurs twice in the New Testament, in this passage and in 1 Jn 2:2. The verb form *hilaskomai* occurs in Heb 2:17 (where the NIV renders it "make atonement") and in Lk 18:13 (where it is translated "have mercy"). The closely related noun *hilastērion* refers to the cover of the ark of the covenant, the so-called mercy seat where the rituals of atonement take place. This noun occurs in Heb 9:5 and, strikingly, in Rom 3:25, about which I will write more in a subsequent note.

bol of God's presence; it was not the presence itself. But even so, only one person (the high priest) could ever enter the holy of holies where the ark was, and even he could enter it only once a year (Lev 16:2). If he tried to enter more often, he would die. Second, even after the high priest offered the bull as a sin offering for himself, he still had to use incense to hide the cover of the ark from his view, so that he would not die (Lev 16:11-13). This shows that the animal sacrifice did not qualify him to stand in the presence of God; it only symbolized forgiveness. Third, the fact that there were two goats to accomplish one purpose, that of removing Israel's sin (Lev 16:9-10, 15-16, 20-22), suggests that these goats did not accomplish this but only symbolized it. One goat as a substitute would have presumably been sufficient if this had been what brought atonement. The fact that another was needed to represent the sending away of sin indicates that this was symbolic and was done in two parts in order to make the symbolism more apparent. Fourth, the fact that these atonements could be carried out in only one place and had to be done again every year (Lev 16:34) suggests that they were symbolic rather than literally efficacious. This does not mean that the Old Testament people of God did not have genuine forgiveness. Rather, their forgiveness, like ours, was based on the atoning sacrifice of Christ. But since that foundational event had not yet happened when they lived, they needed an anticipatory symbol to assure them that they were then forgiven on the basis of an event that would happen later.

Thus we can see that the sacrifices of the law did not in and of themselves remove the people's sins; they pointed ahead to the sacrifice that would take sins away. This is why Paul writes in Romans 3:25-26 that "God presented him [Christ] as a sacrifice of atonement,[5] through faith in his blood. He did this to demonstrate his justice, because in his forbearance he had left the sins committed beforehand unpunished—he

---

[5]The word Paul uses here *(hilastērion)* is similar to the word John uses in 1 Jn 4:10. *Hilastērion* indicates the place where atonement happens, and *hilasmos* refers to the atonement itself. Although this is debated, I believe Paul is emphasizing that Christ, in his own person, is the place were atonement is made. Just as the mercy seat, the cover of the ark, was the place where atonement was symbolically made in the Old Testament, so also Christ is the place where atonement is actually made.

did it to demonstrate his justice at the present time, so as to be just and the one who justifies those who have faith in Jesus." Notice in this passage that if the sacrifices of the Old Testament law had actually brought about forgiveness themselves, then Paul could not have written that God left the previous sins unpunished. They would have been punished when the sacrificial animals bore the penalty for the people's sins. But Paul indicates that this is not what happened. Instead, God left sins unpunished then because he was planning to deal with them now, through the sacrifice of Christ. Therefore, the sacrifices of the Old Testament were prophetic and anticipatory; they did not bring about forgiveness of sins themselves. Similarly, the writer to the Hebrews points out that the sacrifices on the Day of Atonement provided an annual reminder of sins, which means that they did not once for all cleanse the worshipers from sin. In contrast, Christ's once-for-all sacrifice did bring forgiveness, and in the process, it meant that no further sacrifices needed to be offered. (See Heb 10 for this discussion.)

With this Old Testament background in mind, we can understand the word translated "atoning sacrifice" more precisely. The word includes the idea that our sins have estranged us from God, that God cannot approve of our sin and must oppose it. As terrible is this sounds, it is the reaction of a holy God toward people's disobedience. Remember that in Ephesians 2 Paul declares us to be not merely "dead in transgressions and sins" but also "by nature children of wrath." But the atoning sacrifice consists of God's transferring our sins to another and directing his wrath that we deserved toward the sin he had laid on that other. In doing so, he turns his wrath away from us so that we can be restored to fellowship with him. But who is the other? Throughout the Old Testament, the other consisted of sacrificial animals, usually bulls and goats. But as I have already claimed, these sacrifices did not take away sins or remove God's wrath; they merely anticipated that removal. An animal is not a suitable substitute for a human being. Only a human being can bear the sin of another human being. This is why the writer of Hebrews insists, "It is impossible for the blood of bulls and goats to take away sins" (Heb 10:4). Instead of an animal, the other is Christ.

THE DEATH OF CHRIST AS THE DEATH OF DEATH

In light of the Old Testament background that we have considered briefly, one should recognize that the primary thing preventing us from sharing in the fellowship of the Trinity was the fact that our sins had made us guilty before God, and as we have seen, Christ's death dealt directly and primarily with that problem. However, we have also seen that guilt was by no means the only aspect of our sin. Human sin did not just make us guilty before God, it made us die. Since the Fall, all people have been born dead, estranged from the Trinity and unable to do anything to reverse that alienation. If guilt were the only issue, then one might imagine that we could come up with an appropriate sacrifice to atone for our guilt. (In fact, we could not really come up with such a sacrifice, but one might easily *think* we would be able to.) However, when the Bible describes us as dead, it leaves no doubt about our inability to restore ourselves to God. Dead people cannot do anything to better their condition.

The early church recognized keenly that a major problem confronting humanity was its deadness, and thus many patristic writers wrote of the death of Christ in terms of its undoing our death. The words they used to describe this were *corruption* and *incorruption,* which correspond basically to *mortality* and *immortality.* After the Fall, we have been subject to death and corruption; we have been mortal. But we were created to live immortally, to share by grace in the natural immortality that characterizes the persons of the Trinity. So the death of Christ was intended to bring our corruption to an end.[6] In the sidebar (next page) by Athanasius, notice that he does not treat guilt as the primary problem. In fact, he asserts that if the guilt of transgression were the only issue, repentance would have been sufficient to restore us to God. But even if he is wrong on that point, Athanasius is surely correct that there is more to our predicament than just guilt stemming from our original transgression. The transgression has made us corruptible, and only the incorruptible Word of God can restore us to incorruption by his own death.

---

[6]Remember that part of the biblical basis for the patristic idea of *theōsis* is 2 Pet 1:4. In that passage, Peter equates participation in the divine nature with escaping the corruption that is in the world because of evil desires.

In fact, in several places Scripture specifically links the idea that Christ's death is a sacrifice with the idea that his death frees us from the power of death and corruption. Let us now take a look at two of these

---

Athanasius on the Necessity of Christ's Death (ca. 315):

What should God have done? Demand repentance from men for the transgression? For one might say that this was fitting for God, that as they had become subject to corruption by the transgression, so by repentance they might return to incorruption. But repentance would not have saved God's honour, for he would still have remained untruthful unless men were in the power of death. Repentance gives no exemption from the consequences of nature, but merely looses sins. If, therefore, there had been only sin and not its consequence of corruption, repentance would have been very well. But if, since transgression had overtaken them, men were now prisoners to natural corruption, and they had been deprived of the grace of being in the image, what else should have happened? Or who was needed for such grace and recalling except the Word of God, who also in the beginning had created the universe from nothing? . . . For since he is the Word of the Father and above everyone, consequently he alone was both able to recreate the universe and be worthy to suffer for all and to be an advocate on behalf of all before the Father.

On Incar., par. 7 (Thomson, 149-51)

---

passages. In Colossians 2:13-15, Paul writes: "When you were dead in your sins and in the uncircumcision of your sinful nature, God made you alive with Christ. He forgave us all our sins, having canceled the written code, with its regulations, that was against us and that stood opposed to us; he took it away, nailing it to the cross. And having disarmed the powers and authorities, he made a public spectacle of them, triumphing over them by the cross." Notice that the middle portion of this passage treats the crucifixion in terms of God's removal of guilt and bringing about forgiveness of sins, but the beginning and end of the passage treat the cross another way. At the beginning Paul speaks of death and life, and we should notice that this life comes "with Christ." We are somehow involved in the dying and rising of Christ, so that with Christ we are made alive. At the end of the passage, Paul speaks of the cross as the moment when God defeated the powers that oppose us. When Paul uses the phrase "powers and authorities," he is referring to demonic powers, to Satan and his minions.[7] Somehow our being dead is tied to the power of Satan and the demons over us, and Christ's death disarms those demonic powers that have held us captive.

This connection between our being born dead and the power of Satan becomes even clearer in Hebrews 2:14-17, which asserts of Christ:

> Since the children have flesh and blood, he too shared in their humanity so that by his death he might destroy him who holds the power of death—that is, the devil—and free those who all their lives were held in slavery by their fear of death. For surely it is not angels he helps, but Abraham's descendants. For this reason he had to be made like his brothers in every way, in order that he might become a merciful and faithful high priest in service to God, and that he might make atonement for the sins of the people.

Here we should notice that the devil is the one who held the power of death. That is, the reason the devil was allowed to put people to death was because we had alienated ourselves from God through our sinfulness. But the death of Christ destroyed Satan's power. Death died with the death of Christ, and we who were in slavery to death have now been set free. Furthermore, the passage goes on to use the verb form *(hilaskomai)* of the word for "atoning sacrifice" or propitiation. Just as in Colossians 2, so also here, the biblical writer describes Christ's death both as a sacrifice to remove wrath/guilt and as a victory over the demonic powers that hold us captive to death. Cyril of Alexandria describes both aspects of Christ's death in the sidebar on the next page.

With respect to the views of the atonement that I mentioned at the beginning of this chapter, it should be clear from these passages that

---

[7]See Rom 8:38; 1 Cor 15:24; Eph 3:10; 6:12; Col 2:10.

both classic and substitutionary emphases are part of the biblical depiction of the atonement. As Christ died, he was removing both our guilt before a holy God and our enslavement to the power of death and the devil. But at this point, we need to return to the question which dominated the thought of the early church: Who died on the cross? Of course, we say that Christ did. But as we saw in the previous

---

Cyril of Alexandria on the Sufferings of Christ (ca. 425):

He was scourged unjustly, that he might deliver us from merited chastisement; he was buffeted and smitten that we might buffet Satan, who had buffeted us, and that we might escape from the sin that cleaves to us through the original transgression. For if we think aright, we shall believe that all Christ's sufferings were for us and on our behalf and have power to release and deliver us from all those calamities we have deserved for our revolt from God. For as Christ, who knew not death, when he gave up his own body for our salvation, was able to loose the bonds of death for all mankind, for he, being One, died for all.

Com. Jn., bk. 12, intro. (Randell, 606)

---

chapter, Christ—as a person—is God the Son. And indeed, in 1 John 4:10, John affirms that the one whom God sent as the atoning sacrifice is the Son of God. Hebrews 1–2 also makes this clear, because the thrust of these two chapters is that the one who is "the radiance of God's glory and the exact representation of his being" (Heb 1:3) is the one who came down, shared in our humanity (Heb 2:14) and died to defeat the power of the devil over us (Heb 2:15) and to make an atoning sacrifice for our sins (Heb 2:17). What Scripture compels us to say, and what the early church recognized, is that somehow God the Son died for us.

Stop for a minute and allow this to soak in. We turned away from God. We lost the share in the fellowship between the Father and the Son that God had given us at creation. We are born spiritually dead, enslaved to death and the devil, and unable to return to God. How can

this terrible situation be remedied? By an atoning sacrifice. The consequence of sin is death, which implies both physical separation of the
soul from the body and, more significantly, alienation from God. So if
human beings are to be restored to life, then a substitute must be
brought forth who can take that alienation away from us by taking it
upon himself. The entire Old Testament sacrificial system testifies to
the necessity of such a sacrifice, and the repetition of the Old Testament
sacrifices shows that they do not provide that sacrifice; they merely
symbolize it. So who or what could be this sacrifice? It had to be a human being, since only a human would qualify to die in place of other
men and women. He had to be a sinless human being, one who had
never lost his share in the love between the Father and the Son, since a
sinful human being could die only for his own sin, not for someone
else's. And he had to be able to die not just for one other person's sin but
for the sin of many people at once, indeed for the sin of the world. Thus
he had to be somehow an infinite human being, whose life would be
of such infinite value that it could be laid down for the sin of the world
rather than just for the sin of one or two other people. Who then
qualifies to offer such a sacrifice? Who is fully human and utterly sinless and yet also infinite? Only the incarnate Word, God the Son after
he has become a man. And this, John says, is the one whom God sent
specifically to offer the atoning sacrifice.

With this assertion in mind, I need to supplement what I have written about the life of Christ. Not only was his perfect obedience to the
Father a demonstration to us of what sharing in the love between the
persons of the Trinity looks like. That obedience was also what qualified him to offer himself as the sacrifice that would turn God's wrath
away from us, reverse our spiritual deadness and restore us to the fellowship of the Trinity. In fact, as the church fathers pondered the description of Christ's life in the Gospels, they came to the conclusion
that his humanity, even though it was concrete and individual, still
somehow represented the humanity of each of us, and in this way his
obedience and his sacrifice could apply to each of us. Christ's humanity
is uniquely his own and yet still somehow stands for your humanity and
mine, as Cyril shows in the sidebar on the next page. Thus Christ's

---

Cyril of Alexandria on the Relation Between Christ, Believers and the Father (ca. 438):

> The Son came, or rather was made man, in order to reconstitute our condition within himself; first of all in his own holy, wonderful, and truly amazing birth and life. This was why he himself became the first one to be born of the Holy Spirit (I mean of course after the flesh) so that he could trace a path for grace to come to us. He wanted us to have this intellectual regeneration and spiritual assimilation to himself, who is the true and natural Son, so that we too might be able to call God our Father, and so remain free of corruption as no longer owning our first father, that is Adam, in whom we were corrupted.

Christ Is One (McGuckin, 62)

---

obedience undoes Adam's disobedience and ours, as Paul indicates in Romans 5. Furthermore, because Christ's humanity represents our humanity, he could truly stand in our place, bearing in his own person the penalty for our sin and undoing our death. The writers of the Bible affirm that this is what had to be done and was done to bring us back into the fellowship of the Trinity.

DID GOD REALLY DIE?

At this point, you might be marveling at the depths of God's love, by which he did precisely what was necessary to solve the problem we created for ourselves. Or you might be mentally revolting against the idea that God could die. If the latter, you are hardly alone, and here many Christians draw back from the assertions I have just made and say that it was not God who died. It was not the deity that died. Instead, it was the humanity of Christ that died.

Surely the notion that God the Son could die staggers the mind, even more so than the notion that God the Son could be born as a baby. In light of this, it is attractive to take refuge in the fact that Christ has two natures and to affirm that it was the humanity that died, not the deity of Christ. Many Christians, including many Christian theologians, do precisely this. However, as the great thinkers of the early church wrestled with this issue, most of them became convinced that one could not justifiably say this, and I firmly believe they were right. Their reasons for this grew directly out of the way they described the incarnation. Remember again that the incarnation was an action by which the eternal second person of the Trinity took upon himself a human nature so that he—God the Son—could live on earth as a human being. The humanity of Christ dwells in the person of God the Son, not in an independent person. Once the church fathers had thought through this, they were in a position to recognize a fundamental principle for talking about Christ: one may not treat a nature as if it were a person.[8] A nature, we have seen, is a complete set of characteristics or attributes, or even a set of components, like a mind, a will and so on. But as we have also seen, no nature exists in and of itself. Natures exist in persons. The divine nature exists in each of the three persons of the Trinity. The human nature each of us possesses exists in the specific human person each of us is. The divine nature of Christ exists, as it has from all eternity, in the person of God the Son. After the incarnation, the human nature of Christ also exists in the person of God the Son, not in an independent man Jesus.

Since this is the case, then we must say that the person who died on the cross was God the Son. We cannot say simply that the human nature died, because human natures do not die (or be born or do anything else). Persons die. We must grant that dying is not appropriate to the divine nature, and therefore that when the incarnate Son died, he did so according to his human nature, but nevertheless, the person who died was God the Son. Remember that the early church spoke of God the Son doing some things as God and others as man, so in this case they insisted that he died as man, but again, it was still God the Son who died. In fact, the church insisted on this point from the second century onward. In the ac-

---

[8]This was not originally the way the Fathers expressed this idea, because they did not make a clear distinction between the words we translate "nature" and "person" until the Council of Chalcedon in 451. Prior to this, the Fathers usually spoke of a single sonship and of predicating all the actions of Christ to that single sonship. But what they were saying at the time, expressed in post-Chalcedonian language, amounts to the statement I have used in the text: "one may not treat a nature as if it were a person."

Irenaeus on the Suffering of God the Son (ca. 180):

Their [the Gnostics'] doctrine departs from him who is truly God, being ignorant that his only-begotten Word, who is always present with the human race, united to and mingled with his own creation, according to the Father's pleasure, and who became flesh, is himself Jesus Christ our Lord, who did also suffer for us, and rose again on our behalf and who will come again in the glory of his Father, to raise up all flesh, and for the manifestation of salvation and to apply the rule of just judgment to all who were made by him.

Ag. Her., bk. 3, chap. 16, par. 6 (ANF, vol. 1, 442)

---

companying sidebar from Irenaeus, he argues against the Gnostic view of Christ that splits him into a fleshly Jesus and a divine Christ. In opposition to such a view, he insists that it was truly God the Word who became man, suffered, died and was raised. Similarly, in the sidebar just below from Tertullian, he ties the entire validity of the Christian faith to the fact that it was really God the Son who died. Tertullian recognizes that death is unbefitting of God, but he also sees clearly that in order for us

---

Tertullian on the Death of God the Son (ca. 210):

Was not God really crucified? And, having been crucified, did he not really die? And, having indeed really died, did he not really rise again? Falsely did Paul "determine to know nothing among us but Jesus and him crucified"; falsely has he impressed upon us that he was buried; falsely inculcated that he rose again. False, therefore, is our faith also. And all that we hope for from Christ will be a phantom. . . . For nothing did Christ suffer from them, if he really suffered nothing at all. Spare the whole world's one only hope, thou who art destroying the indispensable dishonor of our faith. Whatsoever is unworthy of God, is of gain to me. I am safe, if I am not ashamed of my Lord.

On Flesh, chap. 5 (ANF, vol. 3, 525)

Athanasius on the Death of the Word (ca. 315):

> Since the Word realized that the corruption of men would not be abolished in any other way except by everyone dying—but the Word was not able to die, being immortal and the Son of the Father—therefore he took to himself a body which could die. . . . Therefore as an offering and sacrifice free of all spot, he offered to death the body which he had taken to himself, and immediately abolished death from all who were like him by the offering of a like. For since the Word is above all, consequently by offering his temple and the instrument of his body as a substitute for all men, he fulfilled the debt by his death.

On Incar., par. 9 (Thomson, 153-55)

---

to be saved, it was necessary that God do something on our behalf that was "unworthy" of him. God the Son did this when he was crucified. Likewise, in the sidebar just above from Athanasius, he emphasizes not only that it was truly God the Word who died but even that the Word's purpose in taking a human body to himself was so that he would become capable of dying in our place.

Perhaps the church father who wrote most poignantly about the death of God the Son was Cyril of Alexandria. In the late fourth and early fifth centuries, a few prominent theologians rejected the church's prior teaching that it was God the Son who died, and this was their primary reason for arguing that Christ was not God the Word but a man indwelt by the Word. Cyril argued against these people primarily by insisting that God the Son truly took humanity into himself. At various points in his writings, Cyril likewise asserts that it was God the Son who died for us and that only the death of God the Son could be of any value for our salvation. For example, in the sidebar at the top of the next page, Cyril elucidates the significance of Paul's statement that God redeemed his church with his own blood. When one considers the Word in his own nature, the Word cannot suffer or die, but at the same time, fleshly suffering is ascribed to God the Word as a person, because the body that is capable of suffering is the Word's own body. God the

Cyril on Acts 20:28 (ca. 429):

> Do you hear the apostle openly proclaiming the crucified as God?
> For he says that they should lead like shepherds the Church of
> God, which he saved through his own blood. This is not to say
> that he suffered in the nature of the Godhead, but that the suffer-
> ings of the flesh are attributed to him, because this is not the flesh
> of a mere man but the Logos' own flesh. If, then, the blood is
> called God's blood, it is obvious that it was God, who was cov-
> ered with flesh.

Bearer of God, par. 22 (Dragas, 55)

Son suffered something by means of his humanity that he could not
have suffered prior to the incarnation. God the Son, who had been
incapable of death prior to taking a mortal human nature into himself,
did in fact die by virtue of that mortal human nature. Similarly, in the
sidebar just below, Cyril affirms that the Word is impassible—incapable
of suffering—in his own being, but nevertheless it was truly God the
Son who died for us.

Statements as bold as the ones I have been quoting in the sidebars to
this section have never been universally accepted, either in the early

Cyril of Alexandria on the Death of God the Word (ca. 431):

> Even though the Word of God is so [that is, impassible] by his own
> being, he made his own the flesh which is capable of death, so that
> by means of this which is accustomed to suffer he could assume suf-
> ferings for us and because of us, and so liberate us all from death and
> corruption by making his own body alive, as God, and by becoming
> the first fruits of those who have fallen asleep, and the first born from
> the dead. He who endured the noble cross for our sake and tasted
> of death was no ordinary man conceived of as separate and distinct
> from the Word of God the Father but it was the Lord of Glory himself
> who suffered in the flesh, according to the scriptures.

Expl. Anath., chap. 31 (McGuckin, 293)

church or subsequently. Nevertheless, I am convinced that they were the Fathers' consensus, in spite of a few loud dissenting voices.[9] And after much controversy in the fifth and sixth centuries, the church ultimately declared that God the Son personally died for our salvation. This was the conclusion of the Fifth Ecumenical Council, held in Constantinople in 553. In the sidebar just below, notice how forcefully the council proclaims the truth that all the events of Christ's life (suffering

---

The Fifth Ecumenical Council on the Death of God the Son (553):
If anyone says that God the Word who performed miracles is one and Christ who suffered is another, or says that God the Word was together with Christ who came from woman, or that [the Word] was in him as one [person] is in another, but is not one and the same, our Lord Jesus Christ, the Word of God, incarnate and become man, and that the wonders and the suffering which he voluntarily endured in flesh were [not] of the same [person], let him be anathema. . . . If anyone does not confess that our Lord Jesus Christ who was crucified in the flesh is true God and the Lord of Glory and one of the Holy Trinity; let him be anathema.

(Leith, 46-47, 50)

---

and death as well as birth and miracles) pertain to the same person, God the Word incarnate.[10]

With this careful reflection on the part of the church fathers in mind, let us look again at the common assertion that it was not the deity of Christ that died, it was the humanity. This statement is based on the assumption that a nature can do things and that things can happen to a

---

[9] I have already mentioned that Diodore, Theodore and Nestorius rejected this entire conception of Christ and that these three men were all condemned. Furthermore, the fifth-century bishop Theodoret of Cyrus also objected to the idea that God could suffer, and some of his writings were condemned as well.

[10] In this citation from the Fifth Ecumenical Council, the words in brackets have been added by the editor. The adjectives *one* and *same* preceding these bracketed words are masculine, indicating clearly to a Greek reader that the phrase in question refers to "one person" rather than "one thing." Adding the word *person* to the translation in brackets enables the English reader to understand the force of the masculine adjectives in Greek.

nature. In other words, it is treating a nature as if it were a person. But death is not something that can happen to a nature, just as birth and life are not things that can happen to a nature. All of these are things that happen to a person who bears a nature that enables that person to be capable of such things. In light of their reflection on the workings of natures and persons, the church fathers insisted that the person who died was God the Son. And as we have seen, this is what the Bible proclaims. According to John 1, who was the one who lived on earth? God the Word as a person. According to 1 John 4, who was the one who died as the atoning sacrifice? God the Son as a person. And Jesus cried out on the cross, "My God, my God, why have you forsaken me!" (Mt 27:46). Who said these anguished words? Was this the humanity crying out that the deity of Christ had abandoned it? No, because humanity cannot talk, or do anything else for that matter. Only persons can cry out. And the person who cried out was God the Son. He was expressing a very human emotion, an emotion that he experienced by virtue of the fact that he had a human nature and was living as a man, but the person who said this was God the Son.

HOW COULD GOD DIE?

If this is the case, then we now have a serious problem. If it is not accurate to say that only the humanity of Christ died on the cross, then we come back to the truly incredible assertion that God the Son died. How could God die? If there is any concept that our minds cannot accept, this must surely be it. If one takes the word *death* to mean "ceasing to exist," then it is definitely impossible for God to die. God is the only being who has indestructible life in himself; he has always lived, and he will always live. That life can never be taken from him.[11] If ceasing to exist is what one means, then God cannot die. But ceasing to exist is not what the Bible means by death. Instead, the sort of death that people are subject to after the Fall has two aspects to it—physical

---

[11]Scripture frequently refers to God as "the living God" (e.g., Deut 5:26; 1 Sam 17:26, 36; 2 Kings 19:4, 16; Ps 42:2; Jer 10:7-10; Acts 14:15; 1 Thess 1:9; Heb 9:14), and the fact that God is eternal (see, e.g., Ps 90:1-2; 102:25-27; Heb 1:12) indicates that he has always existed and will always exist. His life cannot be taken from him.

death and spiritual death. Physical death is the separation of the soul from the body as the body ceases to function, and spiritual death is alienation from God as a result of sin. If this is the human problem that God needs to solve by Christ's death, then to say that Christ has died is to say that he died in these ways—spiritually and physically.

So we need to get "ceasing to exist" out of our minds and instead to divide the question of how God could die into two parts. First, how could God the Son die physically? Certainly physical death is not something that is possible for God, because God is not physical in and of himself. To say it differently, physicality is not a characteristic (or attribute) of God. Therefore, it is clear that prior to the incarnation, when God the Son was nothing but divine and therefore exclusively spiritual rather than physical, he was not capable of physical death. But just as certainly, the human nature that he took upon himself at the incarnation included the characteristic of physicality. Indeed, such physicality is the most obvious idea conveyed by the word *flesh* in the statement "the Word became flesh." Since God the Son now had a human nature, and thus now had a physical component, it meant that he (not just the human nature) was now capable of physical death. And so it follows (as we saw in the sidebar by Athanasius on p. 171) that a large part of the reason for his taking a human nature on himself was so that he could die physically. To say this the way the church fathers did, God the Son did not physically die as God; he died as man. But still, the person who died physically was God the Son.

But what about spiritual death? Surely here we hit a brick wall of impossibility? Perhaps not, because we need to recognize that the early church's way of speaking of Christ as God and as man applies to his spiritual death as well as to his physical death. When one considers the Son of God in his eternal state as God, in terms of his eternal fellowship with the Father and the Spirit, then it is not possible for that relationship to be broken. As God, the Son cannot be alienated from the other persons of the Trinity. But when one considers this same eternal Son in his postincarnate state as man, then in terms of this human condition it is possible for him to be estranged from the trinitarian fellowship. To say this another way, one of the consequences of our sin is that we are estranged from God (this is what spiritual death means), and undoing this consequence requires that someone else must take upon himself that alienation from God, someone else must die spiritually in our place. That person can only be an infinite human being who is sinless and himself in fellowship with God. Therefore, in order for us to be restored, the Son in his human, postincarnate state must be alienated from God. This is what it means for God the Son to die spiritually. Again, let me emphasize that this does not mean he is alienated from the Father and the Spirit as God, but somehow the eternal Son is alienated as man, in the humanity that he took upon himself so as to accomplish our salvation.

At this point, if you are of a philosophical bent, you might be thinking, "Does Christianity not teach that impassibility—the complete inability to suffer—is one of God's attributes?" Indeed, many Christians have taught this, and the idea that God cannot suffer is so ingrained in most people's minds that we recoil at the suggestions I have made in the last couple of paragraphs. But there are two points I should make here. First, the Bible does not say directly that God cannot suffer. It says he does not change.[12] In ancient Greek philosophy, the inability to change (immutability) and the inability to suffer (impassibility) were regarded as two sides of the same coin. But we need to recognize that the god of Greek philosophy was very unlike the true God of the Bible. The Greek philosophers saw god as uninvolved with their world, unconcerned about them and utterly inactive. With that conception of god, the words *immutability* and *impassibility* made perfect sense. But the God of the Bible, the true God, is very involved with people and with the entire universe he has made. To say that he does not change must not mean the same thing it does when Greek philosophers talk about divine immutability. Instead, in the Bible, God's immutability means that his purposes do not change and that his love for his people is unchanging. (This is clear when one reads the biblical passages on God's immutability in their contexts.) He is constant in his love toward us, and this is a drastically different concept of immutability than that of Greek philosophy.

---

[12]See Num 23:19-20; Ps 102:25-27; Mal 3:6; Jas 1:17 for some illustrations of this.

The second point I need to make is that when the church fathers used the word *impassibility* to describe God (as they did in the passages I have quoted in sidebars earlier in this chapter), they did not mean this word in the same way the Greek philosophers did either. In the mind of the early church, impassibility implied that God could not be adversely affected or damaged by anything we might do. We cannot ruin the fellowship within the Trinity or disrupt the purposes of God or cause his will to fail. But this does not mean that God cannot choose to enter our world by becoming human, to live a fully human life and to suffer as man for our sakes.[13] In fact, the early church sometimes spoke of the death of Christ as God the Son's suffering impassibly.[14] This tantalizing paradox was an effort to hint at the mystery that God the Son, who is above all the effects of our sin and thus never suffers as God, has voluntarily chosen to stoop down to our level, to assume a human nature so that in that humanity he might suffer and even die, in order to bring us back to God. The idea that God is immutable and impassible, when properly understood, does not preclude what I am claiming here. God can and did suffer by means of the humanity that the Son took on himself at the incarnation. Furthermore, God did all of this voluntarily on our behalf, not because anything external to himself forced him to do this. He chose to have one of the persons, the Son, become human so that in that humanity the Son could suffer and die to bring us back to God. God chose to allow one person of the Trinity, the Son, to undergo alienation from the other two persons in terms of his humanity, even as the Son somehow remained united to the Father and the Spirit in terms of his deity.

With this in mind, let us return to Jesus' anguished cry from the cross, "My God, my God, why have you forsaken me!" At this moment, as he hangs on the cross, God the Son is suffering the full weight

---

[13]For an excellent treatment of the differences between the patristic understanding of impassibility and the Greek philosophical concept that went by the same word, see Paul L. Gavrilyuk, *The Suffering of the Impassible God: The Dialectics of Patristic Thought,* Oxford Early Christian Studies (Oxford: Oxford University Press, 2004).

[14]See, e.g., Cyril of Alexandria's statement that the Son "made his very own a body capable of tasting death and coming back to life again, so that he himself might remain impassible and yet be said to suffer in his own flesh" (*Christ Is One* [McGuckin, 128-29]).

of God's wrath toward our sin, yours and mine. The Father has loved his one and only Son from all eternity and still loves him now, considering the Son as God. Yet somehow, in this moment, the Father is also turning away from that Son, forsaking him because of the sin that the Son, considered as man, is bearing in place of us. The Son, considered as man, is alienated from the Father (and the Spirit as well, although Jesus does not mention him in this passage). Again, we must emphasize that this alienation comes about because God the Son has, in his humanity, been immersed in the consequences of our human sin. God the Son is not estranged from the Father as God. Instead God the Son is so alienated as man. But nevertheless the person who is alienated from the Father at this moment is God the Son. Why? Because this and only this could serve as an appropriate sacrifice to undo your estrangement from God, and mine.

Here the teaching of the Christian faith most seriously stretches the bounds of what we can possibly fathom. How could God the Son be at once both sharing in the eternal fellowship of the Trinity and estranged from that fellowship? We do not know how this could be possible, and the Fathers' expression "impassible suffering" was an attempt to convey the paradox of the cross. In fact, Cyril of Alexandria was fond of saying that here, when one reaches the limits of one's ability to understand, one should "adore the mystery in silence." This is the place where logic fades and reverent wonder replaces it. But if this moment is the most unfathomable moment in history, surely it is also the most terrible and yet at once the most wonderful moment in history. In the anguished days leading up to this event, Jesus tried to prepare his disciples for it by saying, "Now is the Son of Man glorified" (Jn 13:31). Of this moment the apostle John wrote, "This is love." Why glory? Why love? Why does the Bible use such wondrous words of such a terrible event? Because here we see God's presence with us. Here we see God's love for us.

We often say that true love is sacrificial, and it is. But what happened in that moment was beyond sacrificial. In order to bring us back into the fellowship between the persons of the Trinity, those very trinitarian persons agreed that God the Son would suffer as man under the wrath of God. That wrath should have fallen on us. That estrangement from God should have been ours—indeed it was ours, for we were already alienated from God. This was not just a great example of God's love or of his glorious presence with us. This is the definition of love, of glory. The Father and the Spirit were willing to be somehow distant from the incarnate Son (again, considered as man, not considered in his deity) in order to be gloriously present with us. They turned away from the Son in order to turn toward us in love. It was at this moment that God's love toward us was defined, not merely exemplified. This is the central moment in human history, and the proclamation of what happened in this moment is the central message the Christian faith has to offer to the world. It is a message that you have heard many times in the simple statement, "Christ died for you." But have you really heard it? Have you heard this message in all its terrible, majestic, glorious truth? If not, then now is the time to hear it anew, and in hearing this message anew, to peer into the depths of God's love for you.

CHRIST'S RESURRECTION AND US

The work of Christ did not stop with his death for us but rather continued to his resurrection and his ascension to the Father. After Jesus was crucified on a Friday afternoon, his tomb was empty on Sunday morning. Three women (Jesus' mother Mary, Mary Magdalene and Salome) came to the tomb and discovered two angels, one of whom greeted the women with the memorable words: "Do not be afraid, for I know that you are looking for Jesus, who was crucified. He is not here; he has risen, just as he said" (Mt 28:5-6). Looking back on this event later, the apostle Paul writes "that Christ died for our sins according to the Scriptures, that he was buried, that he was raised on the third day according to the Scriptures" (1 Cor 15:3-4).

Clearly, the resurrection of Christ is one of the most central truths of the Christian faith. Before his crucifixion Jesus predicted that he would die and rise,[15] and his resurrection and his subsequent appearances to

---

[15]See Mt 16:21; 17:9, 23; 20:19; 26:32; 27:63; 28:6; Mk 8:31; 9:9; 10:34; 14:28; Lk 9:22; 18:33; 24:7.

his followers are prominently described in all four Gospels.[16] Christ's resurrection was the central emphasis of the earliest Christian sermons, preached by the disciples in Jerusalem, beginning a bit more than seven weeks after Jesus died.[17] Christ's resurrection is explicitly affirmed in almost every book of the New Testament.[18] But what does it mean to say that Christ was raised from the dead? Clearly the biblical authors mean more than simply that his spirit somehow survived death or that his memory lived on in the minds of his disciples. The tomb was empty; there was no body there, so Christ was physically raised from the dead. In fact, in one of his appearances to the disciples after his resurrection, Jesus recognizes that they think he is a ghost, so he says: "Why are you troubled, and why do doubts rise in your minds? Look at my hands and my feet. It is I myself! Touch me and see; a ghost does not have flesh and bones, as you see I have" (Lk 24:38-39). He died physically, and he was raised physically, bodily. If his physical death took place instead of the physical death we deserve, then his physical resurrection undoes our physical death, serving as a seal that we too shall one day be physically resurrected from the dead as well.

But what about his spiritual death? If Jesus suffered alienation from the Father on the cross, then was this estrangement reversed with the resurrection? We find the answer to this question in Jesus' ascension to heaven after the resurrection. That ascension is described in Acts 1:9, and discussing the event later, the writer of Hebrews declares, "After he had provided purification for sins, he sat down at the right hand of the Majesty in heaven" (Heb 1:3; cf. Phil 2:10-11). The action of sitting down next to God the Father indicates both a kinship of authority and a close personal fellowship. Clearly, then, Christ (considered as man) has been fully restored to fellowship with his Father. In its creeds, the early church prominently enshrined the idea of Christ's sitting at the right hand of God, and once again Cyril of Alexandria best expresses these ideas. In the sidebar on the next page he comments on the exalta-

---

[16]See Mt 28; Mk 16; Lk 24; Jn 20–21.

[17]See Acts 1:22; 2:24, 32; 3:15.

[18]In addition to references in the four Gospels and the book of Acts listed just above, see, e.g., Rom 1:4; 1 Cor 15:3-4; 2 Cor 4:14; Gal 1:1; Eph 1:20; Phil 3:10; Col 2:12; 1 Thess 1:10; 1 Tim 3:16; 2 Tim 2:8; 1 Pet 1:3; Rev 1:18.

tion of Christ in Philippians 2:9-11, and he stresses that it is the same person who departed from his prior glory at the incarnation and takes it back up again with his ascension. But Cyril writes that the Son takes up his former glory "in a way that befits a man." He is united to the Father, he shares his Father's glorious presence, but now he does so not

---

Cyril of Alexandria on the Ascension of the Son (ca. 438):

Just as he is the Lord of Glory and then abases himself into the low status of the slave's form, so he asks to take up his eternally inherent glory again, and he does this in a way that befits a man. Since he is eternally God he ascends from the limitations of our condition to the pre-eminence and glory of his own Godhead so that every knee should bend before the one true and natural Son, albeit as I have said, one who is made flesh and has become as we are.

Christ Is One (McGuckin, 123-24)

---

just as God but also as man. In his humanity, he has been brought back to the Father.

Let us reflect on the significance of this. We know that Christ is the second person of the Trinity and that from the time of the incarnation, he has also been fully human. This means that since the time of the incarnation, one of the persons sharing in the fellowship of the Trinity has been a fully human person. In this way, Christ is the second Adam, the man who regains the human fellowship with God that Adam lost. But at the crucifixion, this person who had shared in that fellowship felt the full weight of human sin (not his own, but ours) and was crushed under the wrath of God toward that sin. He, considered as man, suffered utter alienation from God, and he died. And, as the church fathers recognized, the humanity of this person represents your humanity and mine, so his suffering could truly substitute for the suffering we deserve. With the resurrection and ascension, this person, considered as man, has been restored to the fellowship of the Trinity that had been his previously. This means that a person who has borne all human sin and suffered estrangement from God has been accepted back into the fellowship he had previously lost (again, through no sin of his own). Furthermore, precisely because the humanity of this person represents our humanity, we too can be restored to that fellowship as we are united to him. Just as God's action of alienating the Son from the Father substitutes for the alienation from God we deserve, so also God's action of receiving the Son back into fellowship with the Father provides the connection we need in order to be restored ourselves. The rejection and reacceptance of the divine Son in his human nature affect us because that person's human nature is linked to our humanity, and through our connection to that human nature we too can be brought into fellowship with God. If the death of Christ shows us the almost unimaginable depths of God's presence with us, so also the resurrection and ascension of Christ show us the wonder of our presence with God. God the Son was brought back into the fellowship of the Trinity, and through his humanity he brings us with him.

CONCLUSIONS

In this chapter, we have seen that the death and resurrection of Christ find their full significance in light of who it was that underwent them, and the early church insisted correctly that this person was God the Son. Since it was really God the Son who was born, it must have been and was really God the Son who died and rose for us. Accordingly, it is crucial for us to understand these events in light of the relationship between the Father and the Son. The first Adam participated in the Father-Son relationship as long as he remained obedient, but his relationship to God was unstable, could be lost and was in fact lost. With the Fall all humanity thus lost its participation in that relationship, and so in order to gain it back for us, God the Son assumed a humanity that enabled him, as man, to submit to death. That death estranged him (again, considered as a man) from his fellowship with the Father. Then as he was raised from the dead and ascended to heaven, he was reunited to the Father and the Spirit, in his humanity. (In his deity he had somehow remained united to the Father and Spirit even as he was alienated from them in his humanity.) This Son, the second Adam, not only accomplished our reunion with God through his death and resurrection but also received what he accomplished as a man, through his humanity. To state this another way, when God the Father received his Son back into fellowship after the crucifixion, he was receiving him as a man, and indeed, as a man who had borne the weight of God's wrath toward all human sin. As a result, the resurrection and ascension constitute the guarantee that just as God has taken Christ back, so he will receive us back as well. Thus, the restoration of fellowship with God is secure in a way that the initial gift at creation was not, because it is God who receives the gift as a man.

Now that we have looked in some detail at the way the Son participates in human life, we are in a position to understand more precisely how we in turn enter and participate in his divine life, his relationship to the Father. I will turn to this issue in the next chapter.

Chapter 9

Becoming Christian

ENTERING THE SON'S
RELATIONSHIP TO THE FATHER

I hope it is clear at this point that in the eyes of the early church, Christian salvation is not exclusively about forgiveness of sins. Sin is the barrier alienating people from God, and the death of Christ constituted God the Son's taking upon himself, in his humanity, the alienation from God that we deserve. This death then makes it possible for our sins to be forgiven, and forgiveness of sins is the indispensable prerequisite for Christian life, but it is not the sum total of Christian salvation. Therefore, as we turn in this chapter from the atonement to the topic of becoming Christian, we need to consider forgiveness of sins and other aspects of salvation in light of the heart of Christian faith, the love between the Father and the Son.

As we have seen, John writes of the way Christ's life is linked to ours in John 1:12 ("To all who received him, to those who believed in his name, he gave the right to become children of God") and in John 20:31 (he has written what he has about Christ "that you may believe that Jesus is the Christ, the Son of God, and that by believing you may have life in his name"). Both of these passages mention our believing in Christ, and the first one links such believing to receiving Christ. Furthermore, the passages indicate that our believing/receiving makes us children of God and gives us life in the name of the Son of God. The early church insisted that this life we receive by believing is divine life, and as we have seen, the Fathers used the word *theōsis* to describe our participation in divine life. Furthermore, according to the strand of patristic thought that I believe is most biblical and insightful, this divine life should be understood primarily in terms of the Son's relationship to the Father: our entering divine life involves our becoming by grace what Christ is by nature: a child of God. To be saved is not simply to be forgiven, although that is part of what it involves. More fundamentally, to be saved is to become an adopted child of God and therefore to share in the fellowship that God's only natural Son has eternally enjoyed with the Father.

Furthermore, what I wrote in chapter eight about Christ's resurrection implies that the way we become adopted children of God is through our link to Christ's humanity, a link which in turn ties us to him as the second person of the Trinity and thus to the loving relationship he has with the Father and the Spirit. We have also seen that Jesus said the Holy Spirit would come to dwell within the disciples. The Spirit enters into a person as that person begins to trust in Christ, and the Spirit unites that person to Christ in his humanity, so that the person begins to share in Christ's relationship as divine Son to his Father. Then, through one's share in that relationship and with the Holy Spirit's power, a person is able to begin living in a way that reflects the love between the Father and the Son. The kind of life we looked at in chapter four begins as the Holy Spirit unites a person to the Son who lived, suffered, died and was raised in order to bring us back to God.

With all of this in mind, this chapter will focus in more detail on four questions. First, what does it mean to believe in Christ or receive Christ? Second, what is the Holy Spirit's role in bringing us to faith? Third, what is the relation between God's action and our action in the process of turning to Christ? And finally, what are the specific changes that take place in us and in our relationship with God as we turn to him in faith?

DEATH, RESURRECTION AND FAITH

What is faith? What does it mean to entrust one's life to Christ? Perhaps the clearest biblical passage addressing this question comes in Romans 10. Paul affirms:

> If you confess with your mouth, "Jesus is Lord," and believe in your heart that God raised him from the dead, you will be saved. For it is with your heart that you believe and are justified, and it is with your mouth that you confess and are saved. As the Scripture says, "Anyone who trusts in him will never be put to shame." For there is no difference between Jew and Gentile—the same Lord is Lord of all and richly blesses all who call on him, for, "Everyone who calls on the name of the Lord will be saved."
>
> How, then, can they call on the one they have not believed in? And how can they believe in the one of whom they have not heard? And how can they hear without someone preaching to them? And how can they preach unless they are sent? As it is written, "How beautiful are the feet of those who bring good news!" (Rom 10:9-15)

In this passage Paul describes saving faith in various ways: confessing who Christ is (the Lord), believing that the saving events of his life (especially his resurrection) really happened, trusting in God/Christ and calling upon him. Furthermore, Paul discusses the mechanism by which faith is engendered: God sends preachers to proclaim the message of Christ, people hear this message, they believe in Christ, and so they call on him for salvation. Shortly later Paul declares, "Faith comes from hearing the message, and the message is heard through the word of Christ" (Rom 10:17). This is the pattern of proclamation and faith that God has used to bring people to Christ throughout Christian history.

However, in Protestantism, and especially in modern evangelicalism, we have rarely been content simply to affirm such a basic definition of faith and of the mechanism by which it is produced. Because of our insistence that justification is by faith alone, we have sought to delineate what constitutes faith and what constitutes a work, and anything that falls into the category of a work we deem not to be necessary for salvation. In light of our concern over this issue, it may come as a surprise that the early church was relatively unconcerned about defining faith or distinguishing it from works. That may lead some of us to charge that they believed in salvation by works, but this charge is misplaced. Far from denying justification by faith, they were, in my opinion, truer to that great biblical truth than we sometimes are, but they expressed their allegiance to this truth in a different way from the way we do.

Consider for a moment the way we evangelicals sometimes talk about faith and works. In keeping with our roots in the Protestant Reformation, we affirm that no human action is necessary for salvation; God does everything. This is what we mean when we contrast faith with works. Therefore, we label common expressions of devotion to God—prayer, Bible reading, receiving baptism and the Lord's Supper—as works, and we insist that these are an important part of Christian life but also that they are not necessary for salvation. At the same time, because of our roots in modern pietism and revivalism, many of us also want to affirm that there are clear signs accompanying the beginning of faith, and we have developed our own rituals for choreographing that beginning. A person goes through a confirmation class, or walks the aisle in response to an altar call, or prays the prayer in the back of the "Four Spiritual Laws" booklet, or even sits on the "anxious bench" at a tent meeting. We have established various patterns that we believe promote and accompany the inception of genuine faith. So we say that praying a sinner's prayer is not a work, but rather it expresses faith. In contrast, giving money to the poor is a work, and thus it is part of the continuation of Christian life, not the beginning. One should notice here that in the way we develop these patterns, our focus is on ourselves. We ask, "What do I have to do?" And we answer, perhaps oddly, both that I cannot do anything and that I have to do this or that ritual that we associate with the beginning of faith. Even the statement "we have to have faith" represents an unintentional focus on ourselves.

Contrast this way of speaking with the way the early church typically dealt with the same issue. The fathers of the church did not normally try to define what faith was, and they certainly did not try to delineate which religious activities belonged in the category of works and which belonged in the category of faith. Instead, they wrote of faith by writing about the one toward whom we are to direct our faith. They wrote endlessly about God the Trinity. They wrote endlessly about Christ. They wrote substantially (although not nearly as extensively) about the Holy Spirit. This is why the early church produced our great creedal statements about the Trinity and the person of Christ but did not produce any creedal statements about how faith begins or what it is. Just as they modeled submission to Scripture in the way they handled it but did not articulate a doctrine of Scripture (as we saw in chapter one of this book), so also they modeled faith in God the Trinity by directing everyone's gaze toward God but did not articulate what it meant to have faith.

On this point, I think the church fathers have a great deal to teach us, because when we today speak of what faith is or whether one has it, we are unwittingly obscuring the fact that everyone already has faith. Everyone trusts in someone or something. That is, all people in their efforts to achieve fulfillment or happiness or anything else of value entrust those efforts to someone or something. Many of us entrust our lives to ourselves. Some of us entrust them to a religion or a philosophical worldview. Some of us entrust them to another person. Some of us entrust them to an institution. Christianity insists that for this trust to be salvific, it must be directed only toward Christ. He holds what is truly valuable in life—his relationship with the Father. He has shown the uttermost depths of love for us. He is able through his Spirit to unite us to his Father, to make us adopted sons and daughters. Our lives are infinitely safer in his hands than in our own hands or in the hands of anyone else or any institution or philosophy. He is the one to whom we should look, the one in whom we should trust. Jesus says, "Come to me, all you who are weary and burdened, and I will give you rest" (Mt 11:28). In light of this, it is perhaps appropriate today for evangelicals to spend less time seeking to nail down exactly what faith is and instead to point other people to the only one who is truly worthy of their faith, Jesus Christ. Conversion to Christianity is not so much a process of gaining faith where one had none before as it is a process of transferring one's trust from whatever or whomever one was trusting previously to Christ alone.[1]

---

[1] An excellent example of this emphasis in the early church comes in Augustine's *City of God*. For much of bks. 1–10, Augustine emphasizes that the gods whom the Romans have trusted are not

If we are willing to grant that it is appropriate to focus more on the one whom we trust than on what faith is or how it is different from works, then we are in a better position to understand the link between our faith and Christ's death and resurrection. In the previous chapter, we saw that Christ's humanity represents ours, and so when he was estranged from the Father for our sins and then was accepted back by the Father (in terms of his humanity), he opened the way for us to be accepted back as we are united to him in his humanity. This is why the New Testament writers insist that the death and resurrection of Christ are more than just the means of our salvation. In Romans 3:25, Paul writes of Christ's person as the place where the atoning sacrifice is offered, the locus where salvation is accomplished. Later in the same letter, he writes:

> Don't you know that all of us who were baptized into Christ Jesus were baptized into his death? We were therefore buried with him through baptism into death in order that, just as Christ was raised from the dead through the glory of the Father, we too may live a new life.
>
> If we have been united with him like this in his death, we will certainly also be united with him in his resurrection. For we know that our old self was crucified with him so that the body of sin might be done away with, that we should no longer be slaves to sin—because anyone who has died has been freed from sin. (Rom 6:3-7)

Here Paul affirms that through baptism, and thus through the beginning of faith in Christ (since in the New Testament baptism was the sign associated with that beginning), believers have died with Christ, been buried and been raised. These central events of Christ's life do not merely pertain to us. Rather, we participate in them because the humanity of Christ represents and substitutes for our humanity, and thus we participate in God the Son who underwent death and resurrection for us in his own humanity.

Similarly, we have already seen that in Ephesians 2:1-3, Paul indicates that people after the Fall have all been born dead. Paul continues: "Because of his great love for us, God, who is rich in mercy, made us

---

able to bring them happiness, either in this world or in the next. Over and over again in these books, Augustine insists that the one who is truly worthy of the Romans' trust is Christ.

alive with Christ even when we were dead in transgressions—it is by grace you have been saved. And God raised us up with Christ and seated us with him in the heavenly realms in Christ Jesus" (Eph 2:4-6). Again we see that our being made alive is directly connected to Christ. We were made alive "with Christ," that is, through his being made alive again at the resurrection. We were raised up "with Christ" and

---

Cyril of Jerusalem on Believers' Participation in Christ's Death and Resurrection (ca. 385):

> You were naked in the eyes of all and felt no shame. In fact you were imitating the first man Adam, who was "naked" in Paradise "but not ashamed." Then, once you had removed your clothes, you were anointed with exorcised oil from the topmost hairs of your head to the lowest parts of your body, and became sharers in Jesus Christ, the true olive. You were cut from the wild olive and grafted on to the true olive, and began to share in the richness of the genuine olive. . . . After this you were led to the holy pool of sacred baptism, just as Christ was taken from the cross to the tomb which stands before you. . . . You made the saving profession of faith and three times you were immersed in the water and came up from it again. There in the font you symbolically re-enacted Christ's three-day burial. . . . At the same moment you both died and were born; that saving water became your tomb but also your mother.

Myst. Cat., 2, par. 2-4 (Yarnold, 173-74)

---

seated "with him" in heaven through his ascension to the Father. This is the context in which Paul makes his famous assertion, "It is by grace you have been saved, through faith—and this not from yourselves, it is the gift of God—not by works, so that no one can boast" (Eph 2:8-9). Our salvation does not simply come to us because of what Christ did. Instead, we are saved when by a gift of God's grace we trust in Christ and therefore go through his life, death and resurrection with him. He came down to earth to participate in human life, to bear human sin, to become our brother and be made sin on our behalf. We participate in his life, death and resurrection, and in so doing we participate in his eternal relationship to the Father.

One of the ways the early church impressed upon new Christians the direct link between their own lives and that of Christ was by delivering a series of sermons to candidates for baptism. These catechetical lectures typically included an extended discussion of the persons of the Trinity and an explanation of each rite in the baptismal ceremony. We possess such catechetical lectures from several early-church theologians, and the most celebrated ones come from Cyril of Jerusalem in the fourth century.[2] In the first of the two accompanying sidebars (previous page), Cyril is speaking to new believers who have just been baptized. Notice how strongly he makes the connections between the events of Christ's life and the believers' lives, while still pointing out that the believers are going through these events symbolically, whereas Christ went through them literally.[3] Notice also that he refers to the believer's profession of faith just prior to baptism as "the saving profession of faith," thus indicating that what unites the believer to Christ is faith rather than the simple act of baptism itself. Then in the second sidebar (next page), Cyril explains more fully the significance of this connection between the Christian and Christ. Once we direct our faith toward Christ (and thus are baptized to express this faith in him), we participate with him in his crucifixion, death and resurrection, so that we may receive in him the salvation that consists of sharing his fellowship with his Father.[4]

---

[2]One should not confuse this Cyril with Cyril of Alexandria, who was born about a dozen years before Cyril of Jerusalem died.

[3]It is worth mentioning that the various rites of the baptismal ceremony were rather elaborate in comparison with ours and that Cyril points out the connection between each action and relevant scriptural passages that link us to Christ. For example, the anointing with oil connects us to Christ as the true olive tree, and the threefold immersion reminds us of the three-day period during which Christ was dead.

[4]Some readers may find these sidebars unnerving because they attach so much importance to baptism. One should remember that the New Testament connects baptism and faith in Christ very closely, even to the point of saying that baptism saves us (see 1 Pet 3:21). The church fathers maintained this close connection as well. They saw no need to make the sharp distinction between faith and baptism that we sometimes do, although Cyril's words here show that he (and they) did see a distinction. Faith in Christ is the channel through which we are united to the Trinity, but because baptism is the means Christ has ordained to express the beginning of faith, it is often spoken of in the same breath as faith itself.

Cyril of Jerusalem on the Significance of Believers' Participation in Christ (ca. 385):

> What a strange and wonderful thing! We did not literally die, we were not literally buried, we did not literally rise again after being crucified. We experienced these things only in symbols and representations; but salvation we experienced literally. Christ was really crucified and really buried and literally rose again, and all of this he did for our sake, so that by sharing in his sufferings in imitation, we might gain salvation in truth. . . . No one should imagine that baptism only confers the forgiveness of sins and the grace of adoption, just as John's baptism only conferred the forgiveness of sins. We should be clear about this, that just as baptism cleans away our sins and conveys the gift of the Holy Spirit, so too it represents Christ's sufferings. . . . It was truly to teach us what Christ suffered "for us and our salvation" truly and not in make-believe, and that we have become sharers in his sufferings.

Myst. Cat., 2, par. 5-7 (Yarnold, 174-75)

THE HOLY SPIRIT AND OUR PARTICIPATION IN THE SON

If a faith that is directed at Christ is the link uniting us to God the Son in his humanity and enabling us to participate in his relationship to the Father, then it is appropriate to probe more deeply into the process by which God leads people to transfer their faith to Christ alone. Of course, the human mechanism is preaching and hearing the Word, but these human actions alone do not bring about faith in Christ. Rather, Christian faith comes about as the Holy Spirit works to unite believers to Christ in his humanity, therefore bringing us by grace into the Father-Son relationship. We have already seen that some patristic writers, especially Cyril of Alexandria, understand God's breathing the breath of life into Adam (Gen 2:7) as God's giving him the Holy Spirit, thus causing prefallen humanity to participate in fellowship of the Trinity. Humanity lost this participation with the Fall, but during the upper room discourse, Jesus shows his disciples that the Spirit will soon begin to dwell in human beings anew. It is appropriate to look at part of this passage (Jn 14:15-21) again. Jesus says, "I will ask the Father, and he will give you another Counselor to be with you forever—the Spirit of truth. The world cannot accept him, because it neither sees him nor knows him. But you know him, for he lives with you and will be in you. . . . Because I live, you also will live. On that day, you will realize that I am in my Father, and you are in me, and I am in you" (Jn 14:16-17, 19-20). Notice that the Spirit's dwelling within believers is the key that enables us to know that the Son is in the Father, that believers are in the Son and that the Son is in believers. The mutual sharing of relationship between Father and Son and between Son and believers depends on the Holy Spirit. The Spirit is the one who links us to that relationship by uniting us to the Son.

Later in the upper room discourse, Jesus talks in more detail about the ministry of the Holy Spirit, and here he deals with the Spirit's work in the world (convicting the world of its guilt with respect to sin, righteousness and judgment—Jn 16:7-11) as well as his work in the lives of the disciples (Jn 16:12-15). In the latter discussion, Jesus says: "When he, the Spirit of truth, comes, he will guide you into all truth. He will not speak on his own; he will speak only what he hears, and he will tell you what is yet to come. He will bring glory to me by taking from what is mine and making it known to you. All that belongs to the Father is mine. That is why I said the Spirit will take from what is mine and make it known to you" (Jn 16:13-15). As we consider this passage, we need to keep in mind Jesus' famous statement earlier in the discourse, "I am the way and the truth and the life" (Jn 14:6). In light of that prior identification of truth with Jesus himself, it seems that what Jesus means here is not only that the Spirit will show the disciples what is true but also that the Spirit will guide them to Christ, to the one who is the truth. Furthermore, we need to read Jesus' statements about what is his and what belongs to the Father in light of what Jesus has said about the love between the Father and himself. If it is correct to make these connections, then Jesus is saying here that the Holy Spirit, by coming to dwell in believers, will bring us to Christ, who is the truth, and will cause us to share in that which Christ possesses, namely, his eternal fellowship with the Father. This action of the Spirit will bring glory to Christ because it will share the glorious presence of God the Son with us. As in John 14, so also here in John 16, Jesus implies that the Holy Spirit brings believers into the fellowship that characterizes the Trinity.

For people who began to trust Christ after the day of Pentecost (Acts 2), this indwelling of the Spirit has coincided with conversion. The entrance of the Holy Spirit into a person is what leads one to transfer one's trust to Christ and therefore what unites one to the fellowship of

---

Cyril of Jerusalem on the Holy Spirit's Presence in Believers (ca. 385):
Just as Christ was truly crucified and buried and rose again, while you are privileged in baptism to be crucified, to be buried and to rise again with him in likeness, so it is with the anointing with chrism. He was anointed with the spiritual "oil of gladness," that is, with the Holy Spirit, which is called the oil of gladness because it causes spiritual gladness; you were anointed with *muron* and became partners with Christ and began to share with him. . . . This holy *muron* is no longer ordinary or, so to say, common ointment, but Christ's grace which imparts to us his own divinity through the presence of the Holy Spirit. To symbolize this truth you are anointed on your forehead and on your other senses. Your body is anointed with visible *muron,* while your soul is sanctified by the life-giving Spirit.

Myst. Cat., 3, par. 2-3 (Yarnold, 177)

---

the Trinity. In the early church, this indwelling of the Holy Spirit was celebrated through the ceremony of chrismation (anointing with oil), and this ceremony was closely associated with baptism, the rite that signified the beginning of faith. In the sidebar just above, Cyril of Jerusalem stresses that receiving the Holy Spirit is what makes us "part-ners with Christ," people who "share with him." He argues further that through the presence of the Spirit in believers, Christ "imparts to us his own divinity." As we have seen earlier, this cannot mean that Christ gives us his union with the Father in the sense that we become equal to him. Such unity by nature cannot be shared with us, and Cyril of Jerusalem makes this just as clear as other church fathers do.[5] Instead, Cyril means that through the Holy Spirit, Christ imparts to us a share in his relationship with his Father.

Accordingly, the key to our sharing in the Father-Son relationship is the work of the Holy Spirit, who enters us personally in order to bring us to trust in Christ and thereby to unite us through Christ to his Father. Thus, the salvation that becomes possible through the incarnation, life, death and resurrection of Christ, and is announced as being available through preaching, becomes actual through the work of the Holy Spirit.

GOD'S ACTION AND OURS IN THE PROCESS OF CONVERSION

This focus on the Holy Spirit's work in bringing people into a relationship with the Trinity raises an issue that has been a source of controversy (mainly in the Western church) for nearly sixteen hundred years. This is the question of how God's action of sending the Holy Spirit into a person relates to that person's action of placing trust in Christ. Does God's work follow the human will to trust Christ or precede it? Does God act in conjunction with our free choices, or does he override them? These questions are related to one of the Bible's more infamous teachings: that God has "elected" or "predestined" those who are to be saved.[6] In this section, I do not intend to address even briefly the many controversial issues that have surrounded election and human free will. Instead, my purpose is to point out a way in which the themes of this book could recast the debate about election in a helpful way.

Throughout the long history of this debate, the assumption seems to have been that God's predestination of certain people to be saved and the human action of believing in Christ must be related in a logically sequential way. We argue about which logically comes first, God's choosing a

---

[5]See, e.g., Cyril's clear distinction between Christ as Son by nature and Christians as sons by adoption in *Cat.,* 3, par. 14 (Yarnold, 95); *Cat.,* 11, par. 1, 4, 9 (Yarnold, 129-32).

[6]Among the many biblical passages discussing election, the most extended are Rom 9 and Eph 1:3-14. See also Mt 24:22, 24, 31 (and the parallel Mk 13:20, 22, 27); Lk 18:7; Jn 13:18; 15:16-19; Acts 13:48; Rom 8:28-33; 11:7; 2 Thess 2:13; 2 Tim 2:10; Tit 1:1; 1 Pet 1:1; 2:9; 5:13.

person for salvation (in which case God then causes that person to trust Christ) or God's knowing that a person will trust Christ (in which case God's choosing is a matter of knowing the future, not causing it per se). Either God has simply chosen whom to save, and then everything that happens on earth in time is the means of carrying out his salvific will, or God has sought to save everyone, and the question of who does and does not come to Christ is ultimately determined by who accepts his universal saving will and who refuses it. In the first case, the will of God is primary and cannot be thwarted, and the human actions of praying, preaching, trusting Christ and so on are the means of carrying out that will. In the second case, the will of God is more general and can be thwarted, and the human actions are much more independent. Both of these ways of understanding election have been present at many periods in Christian history, but the idea that predestination was logically prior to foreknowledge dominated Augustine's later thought and has been taken up at various points in medieval and modern Roman Catholicism, as well as in much of Protestantism. In contrast, most of the early church, the medieval Western church, the Eastern church throughout its history and some of modern Protestantism and Roman Catholicism have favored the idea that God's knowing who would believe was logically prior to his electing that person. Among those who have seen foreknowledge as logically prior to election, there has been a stronger emphasis on the freedom of human action than there has been among those who have seen election as being logically prior.

I suggest that both of these frameworks are inherently problematic. One could argue that the first model (in which God chooses people and then ordains the means by which his chosen people will believe) implies that not only our actions of preaching, praying and believing, but even the incarnation and work of Christ, are merely necessary formalities that have to be carried out in order to achieve a preordained purpose. Of course, no one intends to speak of these things as mere formalities, but the more one stresses the independence of God's election and places that logically prior to everything else, the more one runs the risk of sounding like the whole plan of redemption is just a formality. This would lead one unwittingly to denigrate both our human actions and God's actions in the incarnation and the work of Christ. On the other hand, one could argue that the second model (in which human action ultimately determines who will be saved) also unwittingly denigrates human action by making it too independent of God's purposes and his person. Action that we take apart from God is less significant than action that ties us to God, and this second model seems to sever human action too severely from God. Thus it seems to me that both models unintentionally denigrate the actions that are played out in history, one model by giving election too independent a status, and the other by giving human decisions too independent a status. In contrast, Scripture ties both election and human action directly to Christ. God has chosen believers in Christ (see especially Eph 1:3-14), and he has decided that human action is to be action in Christ, action that reflects and participates in Christ's relationship to his Father.

Contrary to the assumption apparently underlying both of these models, I suggest that it is inappropriate to think in sequential terms about concepts that do not pertain to time. Even when one grants that "before" and "after" have to do with logical order rather than strict chronology, is there any sense in speaking of one concept (election or foreknowledge) coming "before" or "after" another when one is speaking of God? Is there perhaps a nonsequential way of relating predestination, foreknowledge and free human actions to one another? I suggest that there is. If one may dare to contemplate God's action in eternity past of establishing his will for the world, perhaps what he did was neither simply to decide whom to save and then ordain the means by which those people would believe in Christ nor simply to seek to save all but then to know who would trust Christ and who would not. Perhaps what God did was to incorporate all human action (proclaiming the gospel, praying that unbelievers would come to Christ, choosing to trust in Christ) into the very determination of his will. If something like this is what happened, then it seems to me that our human actions bear more significance than they would in either of the sequential understandings with which we normally approach this issue.

To spell this idea out a bit more, I suggest that in our discussions of election/predestination, we should not place such priority on God's choosing particular people that we imply he has nothing to do with those he will not ultimately save. Conversely, I suggest that we not place such priority on God's universal desire to save that we imply that he deals exactly equally with everyone and all differences between people are due to their own responses to God (responses that God foreknows). Rather, I suggest that we place the priority on God's eternal decision to honor his own relationship with his beloved Son and his Spirit by bringing people into that relationship. God's eternal will was, first and foremost, a will to accomplish human redemption through the person and work of his Son and his Spirit. That eternal will included within its determination all that God ordained to happen, all that he knew would happen, all that both he and we would do. This means that when a person begins to trust in Christ or a believer prays for the salvation of others or someone proclaims the gospel, these people are privileged to share in what God has from all eternity determined that he would do. We are not merely the means by which he achieves his purpose, we are somehow privileged to be a part of the determination of that purpose, the establishment of the will of God in connection with his Son Jesus Christ. Such a way of looking at the relation between election and human action may help to ease the logjam that Western discussions of this issue have created for a millennium and a half. But even if it does not succeed in doing that, such a way of looking at the issue does place the emphasis where Scripture indicates it should lie—not on a seemingly arbitrary decree or on allegedly independent, free human action but instead on Christ the beloved Son of the Father, the one in whom we are chosen to participate.

WHAT IS DIFFERENT NOW?
UNDERSTANDING OUR NEW RELATIONSHIP TO GOD

Now that we have examined the process of becoming a Christian, it is time to consider what is different once a person has entered this new relationship to God. Protestant treatments of this issue often focus on the question of a person's status before God and use various biblical/ theological terms to describe the changes that take place in that status when a person becomes a Christian. In this section, I will briefly address several of the major concepts Protestants use to describe the changes at the beginning of Christian life, but my primary purpose will be to show how all of them relate to and depend on the truths around which I have organized this book.

The first of these concepts, and to Protestant evangelicals the most important, is justification. The Greek word translated "justification" *(dikaiosynē)* can also be rendered "righteousness," and some Christians insist that it should always be translated this way. But in keeping with the Reformers, Protestants argue correctly that in a number of crucial New Testament passages, the word refers not to righteousness in general but specifically to a righteousness that is credited to believers or imputed to them. This idea, based on Old Testament passages such as Genesis 15:6 and Psalm 32:1-2, is that God does not credit our actual righteousness to our account, since if he were to do so we would all stand condemned for our sinfulness. Instead, God credits Christ's righteousness to our account as we trust Christ for our salvation. Just as Christ bears the weight of God's wrath toward our sin, so we bear the benefit of God's favor for his righteousness. Justification, then, is the act by which God declares a person to be righteous in his sight and imputes Christ's righteousness to that person even though in actuality that person is still sinful and would still be guilty before God if he had to stand on his own. (The most extended discussions of this idea come in Romans 3:21–5:11 and Galatians 2:11–3:25.) This is the central truth whose rediscovery by Luther in the 1510s sparked the Protestant Reformation. Closely associated with justification is the forgiveness of sins, or more properly, the remission *(aphesis* in Greek) of sins, the sending of sins away from a person. This concept is based on part of the ritual for the Day of Atonement in Leviticus 16. The priest takes a goat—referred to as the scapegoat—and confesses over its head all the sins of the people. The goat is then released into the desert in order to demonstrate symbolically that God has taken the sins of the people far away from them (Lev 16:20-22). The New Testament writers announce that the remission of sins that was dramatically represented by the Old Testament scapegoat has now been realized by and in Christ.[7] Taken together, justification and remission

---

[7]Remission of sins is the theme of John the Baptist's preaching (Mk 1:4; Lk 3:3), it is the purpose Christ gives for his death as he institutes the Lord's Supper (Mt 26:28), and it is a major theme of the apostles' preaching (see Acts 2:38; 5:31; 10:43; 13:38; 26:18). During his ministry, Jesus repeatedly announces to various people that their sins are forgiven (e.g., Mt 9:2-5; 12:32; Mk 2:5-9; 3:28; Lk 5:20-23; 7:47-48; 12:10; Jn 20:23). See also Eph 1:7; Col 1:14; Heb 9:22;

of sins comprise the legal or juridical side of salvation. We were guilty before God, but because Christ bore our guilt on the cross, his righteousness is now imputed to us and we receive a new legal status before God—a status of "not guilty."

However, these legal images of salvation are not the only ones the New Testament uses. Other images of salvation are intensely personal, and some of the major words for describing these personal aspects of salvation are redemption, reconciliation and adoption. The word "redemption" (*apolytrōsis* in Greek) means "buying back," and the idea is one of personal ownership and dominion. We originally belonged to God, but our sin has placed us under the ownership of Satan (in fact, if not by right). Through the incarnation and work of Christ, God has made it possible for us to be restored to our rightful owner—himself. This is why we refer to the work of Christ generally as redemption. Furthermore, through the work of the Holy Spirit in bringing us to faith in Christ, God has transferred us from Satan's ownership back to his ownership. For example, in Colossians 1:13-14, Paul writes that God "has rescued us from the dominion of darkness and brought us into the kingdom of the Son he loves, in whom we have redemption, the forgiveness of sins."[8] Closely related to redemption is the concept of reconciliation (*katallagē* in Greek), which implies that two sides which were enemies have been made friends; the gap of hostility between opposing parties has been bridged, enabling peace to replace hostility. Paul writes in Romans 5:10-11 that while we were God's enemies, God reconciled us to himself through the death of his Son. And in 2 Corinthians 5:18-21, he asserts that in Christ, God has reconciled the world to himself by not counting our trespasses against us.[9] Both redemption and reconciliation are personal images, but more personal than either of them is the image of adoption (*huiothesia* in Greek). In Christ, we have been brought into God's family by becoming his adopted sons and daughters. We have already seen that this is a major image in John's writings, and it is common in

---

10:18. In the Old Testament, forgiveness of sins is such a major concern that one could scarcely list the references; virtually every chapter would be included.

[8]For other New Testament references to redemption, see, e.g., Lk 1:68; 2:38; 21:28; Rom 3:24; 8:23; 1 Cor 1:30; Eph 1:7, 14; 4:30; Heb 9:12-15.

[9]See also Rom 11:15; Col 1:22.

Paul as well. In Romans 8:15-16, Paul writes, "You did not receive a spirit that makes you a slave again to fear, but you received the Spirit of sonship. And by him we cry, '*Abba*, Father.' The Spirit himself testifies with our spirit that we are God's children."[10]

From this brief look at some of these key New Testament words, it is clear that the changes God brings about in the believer's relationship with himself involve both legal and personal dimensions. However, my primary point in discussing these concepts is to point out that justification, remission of sins, redemption, reconciliation and adoption are not separate things that happen when one begins to trust Christ. Rather, all of these derive from and revolve around the same reality, the believer's union with Christ through the Holy Spirit, and thus the believer's sharing in the trinitarian relationship. The New Testament descriptions of these aspects repeatedly use phrases like "in Christ" to describe them. We are adopted in Christ; we are justified in Christ; we are reconciled in Christ. In other words, justification and the other concepts I have been discussing are results of the fact that believers share in the Father-Son relationship. Protestant theology is correct in mentioning various aspects of salvation, but if that theology tries to understand those results independently of one another, or worse yet, independently of union with Christ, then it becomes problematic.

Consider the doctrine of justification, which affirms that we are not actually righteous but rather that the righteousness of Christ is imputed to us. On what basis is it imputed to us? On the basis of our union with Christ. One receives Christ's righteousness by participating in Christ, the righteous one. When we are united with Christ and participate in his death and resurrection, then and only then is his righteousness credited to us. Or consider the concept of adoption, which affirms that we have become sons and daughters of God. God has only one Son, Jesus Christ. How then can we be sons and daughters of God? Only by participating in the true Son, by being united to Christ who is the one and only Son. Similarly, we are the enemies of God, not his friends. Only when we are united to his true Friend, his Son, do we become his

---

[10]See also Rom 9:4; Gal 4:5; Eph 1:5.

friends. The central reality of Christian life is that believers are united to Christ, and the reason this is so central is because it links us to the central relationship that there is, Christ's relationship to his Father. Once we understand this properly, and once we notice just how often

---

Cyril of Alexandria on Salvation in Christ (ca. 432):

Since sin reigned over all people on account of the transgression committed in Adam, the Holy Spirit departed from humanity, and humanity was established in all evil because of this. But it was necessary for humanity to be raised up again through God's mercy to that worthiness that came from the Holy Spirit, so the only-begotten Word of God became man and appeared to those on earth in an earthly body. He was free from sin, so that in him and in him alone human nature might be crowned with the glories of sinlessness and might be enriched with the Holy Spirit and might be re-formed to God through holiness. In this way also, the grace that took as its beginning Christ, the firstborn among us, passes on to us.

Schol., chap. 1 (Fairbairn's translation)

---

the New Testament links the other concepts of salvation to our being in Christ, then we are able to see justification, reconciliation and so on as what they are—results of that central reality.

The early church recognized this, and so they wrote of salvation by writing of the God in whom we participate when we are saved. They did not normally parcel out different aspects of salvation, discussing them individually as if one could possess one or another of them in isolation. Instead, whenever they wrote of salvation, the context for the discussion was a treatment of God, of Christ, of the Holy Spirit. And whenever they did write of different aspects of salvation, they made clear that these aspects hinged on and revolved around participation in Christ. The sidebar just above contains one of Cyril of Alexandria's most comprehensive statements about the Fall and salvation. He ties the sinfulness of humanity to the departure of the Holy Spirit after the Fall, and he links the possession of holiness to our being enriched with the Holy Spirit. Furthermore, the Holy Spirit is the one through whom the sinlessness of Christ passes to us. The Holy Spirit unites us to Christ, causing us to participate in his sinlessness and holiness.

CONCLUSIONS

This chapter has focused on four major questions related to the process of becoming a Christian. First, we have looked at the human mechanism for coming to faith in Christ, and in the process, we have seen the close connection between our participation in Christ and his death and resurrection. We are united to Christ in his humanity, and thus we die with him and are raised with him. Second, we have seen the role of the Holy Spirit in uniting a person to Christ and thus bringing that person into the Father-Son relationship. Third, I have dealt briefly with controversies over the relation between divine and human action in the process of conversion. I have suggested that a nonsequential way of relating election and human action may be fruitful in considering this complicated and controversial issue. Finally, we have seen that all aspects of salvation revolve around and derive from the believer's participation in Christ through the Holy Spirit. It is through sharing in the Father-Son relationship that we receive other benefits of salvation such as justification and reconciliation. One should not treat these aspects as either independent of one another or as primary in salvation, since they are derivatives of our participation in Christ. In this way, I have sought to tie various biblical images of salvation that Protestants normally emphasize to the emphases I have learned from the early church and stressed throughout this book.

With this look at becoming Christian in mind, we are now in a position to consider Christian life. What does it look like, and what does it involve, for us to share in the Father-Son relationship? To some degree, I have already examined this question in chapter four, but in the final chapter, I would like to consider the question again, not from the perspective of human life as it was meant to be before the Fall but specifically from the vantage point of Christian life now.

Chapter 10

Being Christian

ANOTHER LOOK AT REFLECTING
THE FATHER-SON RELATIONSHIP

In chapter 4 of this book, we saw several aspects of reflecting the Father-Son relationship in everyday life: recognizing that all people are inherently significant because we have been created in the image of God, sharing in the peace that Christ has as a result of his relationship with his Father, understanding the value of work that is done "in the Lord," and transforming human relationships through the concept of willing giving and receiving, leading and following—modeled on the way the Father and the Son act toward each other. At that point we were concerned about human life in general, as God meant it to be. But it should be obvious that in the post-Fall world in which we live, the kind of transformed attitudes and relationships I discussed in that chapter are ultimately possible only for Christians. Those who trust in Christ are the ones who not only should but also can live in a way that reflects the Father-Son relationship. Christians are the ones into whom the Spirit has come, and through his presence in us, we are able to live in a way comparable to the way God meant humanity to live originally. The same Spirit who unites us to Christ also enables us and leads us to live in a way that reflects the Father-Son fellowship of which the Spirit has given us a share.

To go into adequate detail on the many facets of Christian life would far exceed the scope of a chapter or even this whole book, and I do not intend to try to cover or even to summarize these facets with any comprehensiveness. Instead, I would like to devote this chapter to four aspects of being Christian, aspects on which I think the modern evangelical church can learn from the early church. The first of these is the relation between what Protestants call justification and sanctification (an issue which the early church did not regard as crucial, but modern Protestantism does). The second is the task of cultivating one's direct relationship to the Trinity. As any Christian can attest, there is nothing automatic about our reflecting the life of the Trinity once we become believers. The presence of the Spirit in one's life does not mean that person will always and necessarily live in a new way. Instead, the new relationships we have entered and the new life we have begun must be fostered. The third aspect I would like to consider in this chapter is reflecting the Father-Son relationship in the fallen world in which we live, and the fourth is the way our Christian lives anticipate the culmination of human history.

JUSTIFICATION, SANCTIFICATION AND PARTICIPATION

One of the common ideas in the New Testament is that of imitating God or Christ. Paul writes in 1 Corinthians 11:1, "Follow my example, as I follow the example of Christ." In Ephesians 5:1-2, he writes, "Be imitators of God, therefore, as dearly loved children and live a life of love, just as Christ loved us and gave himself up for us, as a fragrant offering and sacrifice to God." First Peter 2:21 affirms, "Christ suffered for you, leaving you an example, that you should follow in his steps."[1] This idea of imitation is linked to the fact that Christ is the unique, uncreated image of God and we are the created images of God. Paul writes in Romans 8:29 that "those God foreknew he also predestined to be conformed to the likeness of his Son," and in Colossians 3:10 he affirms that believers "have put on the new self, which is being re-

---

[1]See also passages that speak of believers imitating the apostles and other mature Christians or of mature Christians being examples to other believers: 1 Cor 4:16; Phil 3:17; 1 Thess 1:6; 2:14; 2 Thess 3:7, 9; 1 Tim 4:12; Heb 6:12.

newed in knowledge in the image of its Creator." Equally significant, Jesus implies that we are to imitate God when he affirms during the Sermon on the Mount, "Be perfect, therefore, as your heavenly Father is perfect" (Mt 5:48).

Clearly the imitation of Christ is an important part of living the Christian life. However, the concept of imitation can be dangerous, because it might imply that our following the example of Christ is the basis for our salvation. Protestants normally combat this danger by making a sharp distinction between justification (our being declared righteous in God's sight) and sanctification (our being made actually righteous). Justification in the Protestant sense of the word comes at the beginning of faith and is purely an act of God, but sanctification is an ongoing process throughout Christian life, and at least the way some Protestants describe it, sanctification is primarily a matter of our efforts to follow Christ's example. While it is correct and useful to make a distinction between justification and sanctification, there are two potential problems to which it might lead.

First, one might unwittingly minimize the centrality of the Holy Spirit's work in sanctification. In the New Testament, our becoming holy is repeatedly tied to the Holy Spirit's action, just as a person's initial turning to Christ in faith is tied to the work of the Holy Spirit. For example, Paul affirms that as we are led by the Spirit, we put to death the misdeeds of the body by the Spirit (Rom 8:12-14), that just as Christians have begun our Christian lives by the Spirit, so we should also continue them by the Spirit (Gal 3:1-5), and thus that we are to "live by the Spirit" (Gal 5:16). Furthermore, Peter prefaces a long list of character qualities that Christians are to develop (2 Pet 1:5-9) by affirming, "His divine power has given us everything we need for life and godliness" (2 Pet 1:3), and this divine power is the power of the Holy Spirit. Clearly human action is involved in the process of becoming more like Christ, but it would be a great mistake to assert that Christians could achieve our sanctification through our own efforts. Instead, just as the Holy Spirit is the one who has brought us to faith in Christ, so the Holy Spirit is the one who leads us to sanctification. And just as the relation between the Holy Spirit's action and ours in coming to faith is a mysterious one, so also the relation between divine and human action in sanctification is also mysterious. Paul hints at this mystery in Philippians 2:12-13, when he writes: "Continue to work out your salvation with fear and trembling, for it is God who works in you to will and to act according to his good purpose."

Relatively few Protestants fall into the trap of thinking that sanctification is wholly our work, but there is a second, more subtle problem to which our justification/sanctification distinction might lead. It might cause one to omit or underemphasize the direct connection between the holiness or righteousness a believer gains through sanctification and the person of Christ. Unfortunately this problem is one to which Protestants are much more prone. Remember that justification is the result of union with Christ. The reason God imputes or credits the righteousness of Christ to us is that we have become united to Christ who is the righteous one. Since we are in him, his righteousness is counted as our righteousness. But what is true of justification is also true of sanctification. As we remain in Christ (remember Jesus' "vine and branches" speech in John 15), as our union to Christ is deepened by our continued adherence to him, then our lives begin more and more to reflect his righteousness. To say this a different way, in Christ we are righteous (that is, we have been justified through union with Christ), and in Christ we become more and more who we already are (that is, by remaining in Christ we begin more and more to reflect his character and thus to be more and more sanctified). Thus neither the righteousness of justification nor the righteousness of sanctification is ours in the sense that we could possess it on our own. In both cases, righteousness belongs to Christ, the righteous one, and we participate in that righteousness as we are initially united to him (justification), and we reflect and grow in that righteousness as we continue to remain in him. All aspects of Christian life, from beginning to end, revolve around our union with the Son and our reflection of his relationship to his Father. In a corresponding way, all aspects of Christian life involve our trust in Christ—we trust him to share his righteousness with us in sanctification just as much as we initially trusted him to share his righteousness with us in justification. This is why Paul can begin a discussion of Christian living in Colossians 3 by writing: "Since, then, you have been raised with Christ, set your hearts on things above, where Christ is seated at the right hand of God. Set your minds on things above, not on earthly things. For you died, and your life is now hidden with Christ in God. When Christ, who is your life, appears, then you also will appear with him in glory. Put to death, therefore, whatever belongs to your earthly nature" (Col 3:1-5). In this passage, notice that we have participated with Christ in his death, and now our life is intimately linked to Christ and God. Christ is our life, and because he is our life, we are to put to death the earthly nature.

This recognition that both justification and sanctification are linked to Christ's righteousness was one of the fundamental insights of the early church, although the church fathers rarely expressed it using the words we use. Instead, they spoke of salvation as *theōsis,* a word that emphasizes the believer's participation in the life of God. Believers are given this participation at the onset of faith and grow in it through what we call sanctification. Therefore, one may not speak of the righteousness that comes from sanctification as being our own any more than one may speak of initial justification as being our own. Instead, we come to life by union with Christ, and we grow in Christian life by remaining united with Christ, by fostering our relationship with him through the action of the Holy Spirit. Accordingly, we may not take the credit for our sanctification (although our effort is involved) any more than we may take the credit for our initial justification. In the sidebar on the next page, Cyril of Alexandria makes clear that no creatures possess holiness on our own, but instead all borrow that holiness from Christ who is holy by nature. In fact, even the humanity of Christ (if one were to consider that humanity on its own) could not be said to be holy in its own nature, but rather God the Son sanctified his own humanity as he assumed it into his person. If one cannot speak of even Christ's humanity as being holy on its own, then we certainly should not speak of ourselves as being holy on our own. We receive holiness from Christ when we are united to him.

Since both the initial holiness (justification) of believers and our continued, progressive growth in holiness (sanctification) are Christ's holi-

---

Cyril of Alexandria on the Holiness of Christ and of Believers (ca. 425):
For he came among us and became man, not for his own sake, but rather he prepared the way, through himself and in himself, for human nature to escape from death and to return to its original incorruption. . . . And if it be true to say that all rational creatures, and in general everything that has been called into being and ranks among created things, do not enjoy holiness as the fruit of their own nature but, as it were, borrow grace from the One who is by nature holy, would it not be the height of absurdity to think that the flesh had no need of God, who is able to sanctify all things? Since, then, the flesh is not of itself holy, it was therefore sanctified, even in the case of Christ—the Word that dwelt therein sanctifying his own temple through the Holy Spirit and changing it into a living instrument of his own nature.

Com. Jn., bk. 11, chap. 10 (Randell, 541-42, translation slightly modified)

---

ness, we recognize that sanctification is by participation in Christ just as completely as justification is. Furthermore, the language of righteousness is by no means the only way to describe this transformation. As we have seen, the New Testament also uses profoundly personal language to describe the same thing: we have become sons and daughters of God through Christ and the Holy Spirit, and now we are to act like the children of God that we are. Accordingly it is important to speak of Christian life not just as growth in holiness but as cultivating and reflecting the share in the Father-Son relationship that we have been given at the beginning of Christian life. This is the angle on Christian life that I would like to explore in the subsequent sections of this chapter.

CULTIVATING BELIEVERS'
DIRECT RELATIONSHIPS TO THE TRINITY

In John 15, Jesus urges the disciples to remain in him, just as the branches remain in the grape vine and bear fruit. Earlier in John's Gospel, Jesus has given us some rather startling images describing the way Christians are to remain in him, images that revolve around eating and drinking. The day after Jesus feeds the five thousand, as the crowds clamor around him looking for another free lunch, Jesus twice asserts that he is the bread of life (Jn 6:35, 48), and then he says:

> I tell you the truth, unless you eat the flesh of the Son of Man and drink his blood, you have no life in you. Whoever feeds on my flesh and drinks my blood has eternal life, and I will raise him up at the last day. For my flesh is real food and my blood is real drink. Whoever feeds on my flesh and drinks my blood remains in me, and I in him. Just as the living Father sent me and I live because of the Father, so the one who feeds on me will live because of me. This is the bread that came down from heaven. Your forefathers ate manna and died, but he who feeds on this bread will live forever. (Jn 6:53-58, translation slightly modified)

In this striking passage, three things are especially noteworthy. First, notice that Jesus connects eating and drinking to remaining in him, and thus we should understand this passage in relation to his vine-and-branches talk later. Part of the way we remain in the vine/Christ, part of the way we cultivate our direct relationship to the Trinity, is by somehow eating and drinking the body and blood of Christ. And not surprisingly, as Jesus links eating and drinking to remaining in him, he also connects the believer's life to that of the Trinity. The Father is "living," the Son lives "because of the Father," and the believer lives because of Christ. Somehow, eating and drinking are connected to sharing in the Father's relationship to the Son.

Second, notice that eating and drinking are metaphors about continued action, not once-for-all action. The dramatic changes that take place in individuals when they begin to trust in Christ are represented by baptism, and as we have seen, the New Testament writers speak in the past tense when discussing those changes—we have died with

Christ, we have been buried with him, we have risen with him through baptism. But the language in this passage is not once-for-all but continual. In order to sustain life, one must eat and drink regularly, and likewise, in order to sustain spiritual life by remaining in Christ, one must spiritually eat and drink regularly. Once one has been made alive by Christ, that person must continually eat and drink of Christ in order to remain alive. To be made alive is to begin sharing in the Father-Son relationship, and once one has begun to do this, one remains in this relationship by eating and drinking of Christ.

Third, notice that Jesus uses two different words for eating in this passage: the regular word *(esthiō)* translated "eat" and another word *(trōgō)* translated "feed on."[2] In Greek, as in English, the second word was normally used for animals' eating, and it was often considered a bit too coarse a word to apply to human beings. But in later Greek, the word began to be more commonly applied to human eating as well, and modern commentators typically argue that there is no significance to the switch from one word to another here. However, it is also possible that the use of a rather coarse word here implies that Jesus is making a point of speaking of literal eating, not just of something purely symbolic. If this is correct, then Jesus is saying that in order to remain alive spiritually, we somehow actually feed on his body and blood. This is the way the early church understood this passage, and I will return to the significance of their interpretation momentarily. In the meantime, let us look at another closely related image that Jesus uses in the next chapter of John's Gospel.

In ancient Israel, one of the major festivals of the year was called the Feast of Tabernacles, which was held in September or October and which constituted both a celebration of the recently gathered harvest and a prayer that God would provide the rain needed for the next season's crops. One of the ceremonies of that feast consisted of the priests' bringing water from the Pool of Siloam up to the altar outside the temple, pouring the water on the altar and praying for

---

[2]The NIV is not consistent in the way it translates *trōgō* in this passage. In the text above, I have modified the translation simply by rendering *trōgō* with "feed on" in all four cases it occurs in this passage.

rain. In the midst of that ceremony one autumn, presumably with water sloshing all around him, Jesus stood up and said: "If anyone is thirsty, let him come to me and drink. Whoever believes in me, as the Scripture has said, streams of living water will flow from within him" (Jn 7:37-38). John explains Jesus' words by adding, "By this he meant the Spirit, whom those who believed in him were later to receive. Up

---

John Chrysostom on the Holy Spirit as Living Water (ca. 395):

He calleth that "living" which ever worketh; for the grace of the Spirit, when it hath entered into the mind and hath been established, springeth up more than any fountain, faileth not, becometh not empty, stayeth not. To signify therefore at once its unfailing supply and unlimited operation, He hath called it "a well" and "rivers," not one river but numberless; and in the former case he hath represented its abundance by the expression "springing."

Hom. Jn., 51, chap. 1 (NPNF[1], vol. 14, 184)

---

to that time the Spirit had not been given, since Jesus had not yet been glorified" (Jn 7:39). In these words, as in John 6, we see Jesus moving from a literal event to a spiritual one. There Jesus fed the five thousand, and then he turned their attention from literal food to spiritually feeding on himself. Here, in the presence of a great deal of water and in the context of prayers for literal water that will be needed to grow food to sustain life, Jesus speaks of himself as the source of living water and of the Holy Spirit as that living water itself. Furthermore, like eating, the image of drinking is once again a metaphor for continued action. Drinking is something we must do repeatedly, regularly, and Jesus says that he is the one from whom we should drink and that the Holy Spirit brings forth living water as we drink from Christ.[3] As the church fathers commented on this passage, they correctly likened the Spirit to an unquenchable spring who could give

---

[3]Compare Jesus' discussion with the woman at the well in Sychar (Jn 4:4-15). The woman misunderstands both what Jesus means (water for spiritual life rather than water for literal life) and the continual nature of drinking spiritual water.

water endlessly without ever running dry. As an example, see the sidebar (previous page) from John Chrysostom, the late-fourth-century bishop of Antioch and then Constantinople who was regarded as the patristic era's greatest preacher.

Furthermore, the early church recognized that only if the Son and the Spirit were fully God, equal to the Father, could they give such

---

Athanasius on Christ as the Source of Life (ca. 360):

> By partaking of him [Christ], we partake of the Father; because that the Word is the Father's own. Whence, if he was himself too from participation, and not from the Father his essential Godhead and Image, he would not deify, being deified himself. For it is not possible that he, who merely possesses from participation, should impart of that partaking to others, since what he has is not his own but the Giver's; and what he has received is barely the grace sufficient for himself.

On Syn., chap. 51 (NPNF^2, vol. 4, 477)

---

abundant grace. No mere creature could receive grace or living water from God and then pass it on to others. Such a person would quickly run dry, because the grace/water would not be that person's own but borrowed from another. Only one who is truly God (and thus the source of living water) can give spiritual life continually to those who come to drink. In the sidebar just above from Athanasius, notice that what we receive through Christ (and thus also through the Holy Spirit) is participation in Christ himself and participation in his Father. Such personal participation cannot be received and then passed on to another; only the source, the giver, can give this to someone else.

We see that in John 6 and John 7, Jesus links our remaining in him to the ideas of eating and drinking. He is the only one who can truly satisfy our thirst/hunger, and continuing in Christian life involves continual eating and drinking from him through the Holy Spirit. In 1989, I heard a remarkable message from the (then) well-known Christian

youth speaker Dave Busby,[4] a message that boiled down to a single
sentence: "Full people give; empty people take." The reason we so
often act manipulatively, the reason we use family and work relationships for our own benefit rather than for the good of others, is because
somewhere deep within our souls we are empty, and we are trying to
fill up from other people. Only when we are full are we able to be self-
less and use these relationships for the benefit of others. Only when we
are full can these relationships reflect the love between God the Father
and God the Son. Furthermore, trying to get full from other empty
people does not work. The only way we can get full is from someone
who is an inexhaustible source of true food, true drink and living water. That someone is Christ and Christ alone, and through his Spirit he
grants us to eat and drink from him.

But what is involved in eating and drinking from Christ? In a nutshell, eating and drinking involve cultivating one's direct relationship to
Christ so as to be fulfilled from that relationship, so that one can in turn
give selflessly to other people as a reflection of that relationship. When
contemporary evangelicals speak of this direct relationship, we normally
discuss it in terms of learning from him and communicating with him.
The first of these, we correctly argue, takes place primarily through
learning the Bible, the book which taken as a whole, shows us as much
as we need to know about the character, relationships and purposes of
God. We have already looked at the teaching of the Bible closely enough
that you should be able to sense how utterly indispensable it is to the
Christian understanding of what life is meant to be. The Bible is God's
communication with us, and regular, lifelong attention to its pages is a
necessary part of getting spiritually full and remaining spiritually full.
Evangelicals correctly argue that the second part of one's direct relationship with God takes place primarily through prayer, the practice of
speaking to and even listening to God, the practice of being in his presence. "Being in his presence" is a funny phrase, because all of us are
always in God's presence, whether we admit it or not. (See Ps 139 for a
poignant statement of this truth.) But prayer is our way of reminding

---

[4]Busby suffered from cystic fibrosis, liver and heart disease and diabetes, yet he was perhaps the
most dynamic Christian speaker I have ever heard. He died in December 1997.

ourselves that we are in God's presence, repeatedly turning our attention to him throughout our daily lives, rejoicing in his presence with us and asking him for the things we need or want. Many books have been written about these two central aspects of life, and I do not intend to discuss Bible study and prayer here. Suffice it to say that these two continual activities are a large part of the way God intends people to share directly in fellowship with the persons of the Trinity. Therefore, these disciplines provide our connection to the source of living water, to Christ, and this connection in turn produces the transformed attitudes and actions that characterize Christian living.

However, as central as Bible reading and prayer are to the cultivation of one's relationship to Christ, neither of these practices fits the images Jesus uses in John 6–7 as well as another common Christian practice, the Lord's Supper or the Eucharist. Jesus is speaking here of eating and drinking, and while it is true that Bible reading, prayer and other Christian disciplines are ways of eating and drinking from Christ, the one rite of the church that involves literal eating and drinking is the Lord's Supper. Furthermore, we should remember that unlike Matthew, Mark and Luke, John does not record Jesus' institution of the Lord's Supper, even though he gives us the longest description of the disciples' time with Jesus in the upper room. The reason John omits the institution of the Lord's Supper is perhaps that he conveys the teaching about the Lord's Supper by recording Jesus' words in John 6, which the Synoptic Gospels do not include. Jesus' discussion of eating his flesh and drinking his blood may function within John's Gospel in the same way that the institution of the Lord's Supper functions in the Synoptic Gospels. In fact, many church fathers understood John 6 as referring to the Eucharist, and they all saw the Eucharist as being central to the lifelong process of abiding in Christ.

Cyril of Alexandria offers perhaps the best explanation of the way faith, the Eucharist and the Holy Spirit are all related in our sharing in the life of the Trinity. In the sidebar at the top of the next page, he explains why Jesus does not mention the Eucharist in John 6: those who do not yet believe cannot grasp the means by which they are to eat his body and blood, so he speaks here of the benefit that comes from

Cyril of Alexandria on the Relation Between Faith and the Eucharist (ca. 425):

> How he will give them his flesh to eat, he tells them not as yet, for he knew that they were in darkness and could never avail to understand the ineffable: but how great good will result from the eating he shows to their profit, that haply inciting them to a desire of living in greater preparation for unfading pleasures, he may teach them faith. . . . For this cause (I suppose) did the Lord with reason refrain from telling them how he would give them his flesh to eat and calls them to the duty of believing before seeking. For to them that had at length believed he broke bread and gave to them, saying, Take, eat, this is my body. Likewise handing round the cup to them all, he saith, "Drink of it all of you, for this is my blood of the New Testament, which is being shed for many for the remission of sins." Seest thou how to those who were yet senseless and thrust from them faith without investigation he explaineth not the mode of the mystery, but to those who had now believed, he is found to declare it most clearly?

Com. Jn., bk. 5, chap. 2 (Pusey, 417-18)

such eating (having life in the Father and the Son); and only later, when he institutes the Lord's Supper, does he describe the Eucharist as the actual means to that continued life. In the sidebar on the next page, Cyril stresses that Christ continues to live in believers in two ways. In terms of his divinity, he dwells in us through the Holy Spirit, who is also God and who lives in us. But bodily, he dwells in us as we continually eat his body and blood through the Eucharist.

If Cyril and the early church are correct here, then repeated, lifelong participation in the Lord's Supper is central to one's growing relationship to the Trinity, just as lifelong devotion to God's Word, to prayer and to the indwelling of the Holy Spirit are central. This may come as a surprise to many evangelicals, and we may be tempted to reject such an understanding on the grounds that it is too sacramentalist. However, several points are worth making here. First, even though the Reformers rejected certain aspects of the eucharistic practice prevalent in late medieval Roman Catholicism, most of them did not diminish their emphasis on the Lord's Supper. But it is probably fair to say that in contrast to the Reformers, most traditions within contemporary evangelicalism seriously underemphasize the Lord's Supper. Taking our cue from Paul's summary of the institution of the Lord's Supper, we argue that its purpose is to "proclaim the Lord's death until he comes" (see

---

Cyril of Alexandria on the Relation Between the Eucharist and the Holy Spirit (ca. 430):

> Which do we eat, the Godhead or the flesh? . . . But we eat, not consuming the Godhead (away with the folly) but the very flesh of the Word which has been made lifegiving, because it has been made his who liveth "because of the Father." And we do not say that by a participation from without and adventitious is the Word quickened by the Father, but rather we maintain that he is life by nature, for he has been begotten out of the Father who is life. . . . And as the body of the Word himself is life-giving, he having made it his own by a true union passing understanding and language; so we too, who partake of his holy flesh and blood, are quickened in all respects and wholly, the Word dwelling in us divinely through the Holy Ghost, humanly again through his holy flesh and precious blood.

Ag. Nes., bk. 4, chap. 5 (Pusey, 145)

---

1 Cor 11:26), but we seem to assume subconsciously that it is better for us to proclaim Christ's death through preaching than through the Eucharist, because in most of our churches we celebrate the Lord's Supper relatively rarely. In contrast to our comparative lack of attention to the Supper, the early church made the Eucharist the central aspect of worship and celebrated it regularly (at least once a week, and in some churches several times a week or even every day). Paying attention to the early church's attitude can perhaps call us back to the centrality of the Lord's Supper in cultivating our relationship to the Trinity.

A second noteworthy point is that one should not take Cyril's language (and that of the early church as a whole) to support one position or another on what we call "the presence of Christ in the Lord's Supper." At the time of the Reformation and afterward, there were intense debates about just how literally one was supposed to understand Christ's presence. Are the bread and wine actually the body and blood of Christ? If so, how and when do they become such? If not, are they symbols of his body and blood, or are they somehow more than symbols but less than literally his body and blood? As important as these questions are, I believe that the early church does not help us answer them. During the patristic period, the focus was not on whether Christ was literally, really, figuratively or symbolically present in the elements of the Lord's Supper. Instead, the focus was on Christ himself. Just as the early church submitted to Scripture without articulating a doctrine of Scripture, and just as the Fathers directed their faith toward Christ without explaining clearly what was and was not faith, so also here, the Fathers insisted that the Eucharist points us to Christ and enables us to feed on him, without seeing the need to define with any specificity how that can be possible. And here again, I believe the Fathers have much to teach us on this point. The Greek fathers' word for what we call "sacraments" or "ordinances" was "mysteries," and perhaps because of this word choice, they did not believe it was necessary or profitable to explain the mysteries. Instead, they affirmed that when we partake of the Lord's Supper, we participate in Christ's body, and thus that we remain in him and in his Father as well.

Thus we see that in addition to the spiritual disciplines evangelicals emphasize (prayer, Bible study, perhaps fasting and others), the early church saw its regular celebration of the Eucharist as crucial to believers' continuation in Christian life. In fact, to say that the Eucharist is central is also to imply that communal worship in general is central to the cultivation of people's relationship to the Father and the Son. In the early church, copies of the books of the Bible were barely available to individuals—only the wealthiest of Christians would have been able to afford copies, and even they would likely have had only some books of the Bible. For the vast majority of Christians, their main contact with the Word of God came through the reading and preaching of the Bible in public worship. Prayer as well was as much a public, communal activity as a private one. And the Eucharist was always a public activity; it was never carried out privately, although it sometimes is today.

Thus we see that in the mind of the early church, cultivating a direct relationship to Christ was not by any means an individual task. It involved the entire community of faith, as well as the devotion of each individual. In contrast, many (perhaps most) evangelicals today see the cultivation of their relationship to Christ as almost exclusively an individual task, something that is not really related to what goes on in church on Sundays. If the early church can teach us to make the Eucharist more central to our understanding of being Christian, perhaps the church fathers can also help us to recognize that in general, even the most fundamental element of being Christian—cultivating a relationship to God—is as much a communal process as an individual one. Life in the Trinity is life in the church and involves regular participation in the worship and the mysteries Christ has entrusted to the church.

REFLECTING THE FATHER-SON RELATIONSHIP IN A FALLEN WORLD

If the seemingly individual task of cultivating one's share in the communion of the Trinity is a communal activity as well as an individual one, then it should also be clear that reflecting the Father-Son relationship is necessarily a communal activity. Remember that early in the upper room discourse, Jesus emphasizes that the love between believers is the way people outside the church will know that we are his disciples (see Jn 13:35). Remember also that human beings as God originally created them were intended to reflect the life of the Trinity through their relationships with one another. If we apply these truths to the present situation of believers, we recognize that both among Christians, and between Christians and non-Christians, we are called to reflect the Father-Son relationship. The vast corpus of Christianity's moral and ethical teaching (in the Old Testament, the New Testament, sermons, books, treatises) is at heart a commentary on the central truth that Christian life is to reflect both the character of God and the rela-

tionship that characterizes the Trinity. As I mentioned at the beginning
of this chapter, it is not my purpose here to go into any detail on the
myriad ways in which Christians do this. Instead, I would like to focus
on two ways in which Christians are called to reflect the Father-Son
relationship in the fallen, sinful world in which we live. These two
ways are through our own suffering and through our servant ministry
to those who suffer, and on both of these issues, the early church has
much to teach us.

Suffering and union with Christ. One of questions that arises most
commonly in our world is that of suffering. Many people suffer as a
result of their own actions, but people in staggering numbers suffer
apart from their own actions. Illnesses, disease, accidents, natural disas-
ters and many other events bring unwanted, unexpected and seemingly
undeserved suffering upon people. And as everyone knows, such suffering befalls believers as well as unbelievers. Ultimately all suffering
derives from the Fall, because the Fall affected not only Adam and Eve,
and not only all people born from them, but even the physical universe
as well. In Genesis 3, God curses the natural processes of life (childbearing and working the ground for food), bringing pain and suffering
to those processes that would have been joyful and painless apart from
the Fall. And in Romans 8:22, Paul declares that the physical world
itself groans as if it were a woman in childbirth. Suffering—as a direct
result of our own sins, as a direct result of other people's sins and as an
indirect result of the Fall—is all around us, and this suffering makes the
fallen world in which Christians are called to reflect the Father-Son
relationship stand out in stark contrast from the world as God originally
meant it to be.

Christians have written many books and preached many sermons
about suffering, and one of the major themes of that Christian proclamation has been that believers will not suffer God's wrath. God the
Son, our representative and substitute, took upon himself the wrath of
God toward us, so as to turn that wrath away from us. Thus, Paul can
confidently declare, "Since we have now been justified by his blood,
how much more shall we be saved from God's wrath through him!"
(Rom 5:9). Elsewhere, he claims, "God did not appoint us to suffer

wrath but to receive salvation through our Lord Jesus Christ. He died for us so that, whether we are awake or asleep, we may live together with him" (1 Thess 5:9-10). Believers undergo God's discipline that we may grow in faith,[5] but we do not and will not suffer his wrath.

Unfortunately, in evangelical circles this biblical truth has often been generalized into the mistaken belief that since Christ has suffered in our place, believers do not have to suffer at all. This idea is clearly unbiblical, because the Scriptures assume that Christians will suffer and focus on the attitude with which we should approach suffering, not on how to avoid it. Two passages are especially pertinent to this issue. Early in his letter, James writes, "Consider it pure joy, my brothers, whenever you face trials of many kinds, because you know that the testing of your faith develops perseverance. Perseverance must finish its work so that you may be mature and complete, not lacking in anything" (Jas 1:2-4). Similarly Paul affirms that Christians rejoice not only in our justification but even in suffering: "We also rejoice in our sufferings, because we know that suffering produces perseverance; perseverance, character; and character, hope. And hope does not disappoint us, because God has poured out his love into our hearts by the Holy Spirit, whom he has given us" (Rom 5:3-5). In both of these passages, the reason suffering can be a source of rejoicing is that God uses it to bring about perseverance in faith and maturation of our Christian character.

To connect this discussion to the previous section, suffering is part of the way we remain in Christ, and Paul elsewhere links our suffering directly to our union with Christ. In Romans 8:17, just after stating that we receive the Spirit of sonship and are thus adopted into Christ's relationship to the Father, Paul writes, "The Spirit himself testifies with our spirit that we are God's children. Now if we are children, then we are heirs—heirs of God and co-heirs with Christ, if indeed we share in his sufferings in order that we may also share in his glory" (Rom 8:16-17). Likewise, in Philippians 3, Paul writes that he considers anything by which he might have profited to be lost for the sake of Christ, so that he may be found to have a righteousness that comes

---

[5]God's discipline is a major theme in both the Old and New Testaments. See, e.g., Deut 8:5; Ps 118:18; Prov 3:11-12; 13:18; 19:20; 1 Cor 11:32; Heb 12:6, 11; Rev 3:19.

through faith. After this stirring affirmation, he continues, "I want to know Christ and the power of his resurrection and the fellowship of sharing in his sufferings, becoming like him in his death, and so, somehow, to attain to the resurrection from the dead" (Phil 3:10-11). In these and similar passages, Paul connects our sharing in Christ's glory (the resurrection) with our sharing in his sufferings.

If we think about this idea in connection with the major themes of this book, we can recognize that suffering is a way of both deepening our participation in the Son's relationship to the Father and reflecting that relationship in a broken world. Suffering was not a part of God's original plan, but from the moment of the Fall, the Son's entrance into our fallen world and his suffering the effects of our sin became necessary. God the Son even suffered the consequences of our sin in our place, in order to bring us into the fellowship of the Trinity. God's action in a fallen world centers around the Son's suffering through the humanity he assumed at the incarnation, and similarly, our task of being Christian in a fallen world involves suffering. Just as our obedience reflects the Son's obedience to the Father, so also our suffering reflects the Son's coming into and suffering in this world. When we suffer, we have the privilege of reflecting not the way the Father-Son relationship has been carried out in eternity but the way that relationship has been acted out on the stage of our world.

This is why, when Jesus tells Peter that he will die a martyr's death, John adds, "Jesus said this to indicate the kind of death by which Peter would glorify God" (Jn 21:19). This is why the disciples, after they were rebuked by the Sanhedrin for proclaiming Christ, rejoiced "because they had been counted worthy of suffering disgrace for the Name" (Acts 5:41). Like the original disciples, the church fathers regarded suffering as a badge of honor, a way of linking them more closely with the Lord who had suffered for them in his humanity. The sidebar on the next page gives a famous statement by Ignatius of Antioch, the early second-century martyr who wrote letters to various churches while he was being escorted from Antioch to Rome to be executed for his faith. Notice that he is so intent on sharing in Christ's sufferings that he begs other Christians not to try to obtain an imperial pardon for him. Notice also his longing to imitate the suffering of his Lord and his reference to eating and drinking Christ's body and blood

---

Ignatius of Antioch on His Coming Suffering (ca. 107):

Allow me to be an imitator of the suffering of my God. If anyone has Him within himself, let him understand what I long for and sympathize with me, knowing what constrains me. The ruler of this age wants to take me captive and corrupt my godly intentions. Therefore none of you who are present must help him. Instead take my side, that is, God's. Do not talk about Jesus Christ while you desire the world. . . . I take no pleasure in corruptible food or the pleasures of this life. I want the bread of God, which is the flesh of Christ who is of the seed of David; and for drink I want his blood, which is incorruptible love.

Let. Rom., par. 6-7 (Holmes, 173-75)

---

in connection with his impending death. Suffering, for Ignatius, is a way of participating in God the Son.

One can argue that the eagerness with which the early church courted suffering was inappropriate. It is also true that not all Christian suffering is the direct result of unbelievers' persecution of believers. But whether our suffering comes directly because of our Christian faith or because we suffer from the consequences of other people's actions or from the natural consequences of living in a cursed world, all suffering can be a cause of joy for Christians. The Father's plan by which the Son would bring us into fellowship with the Trinity involved the Son's suffering all the consequences of living in a fallen world. When we face some of those consequences, God is giving us the privilege of sharing in and reflecting the Son's obedient mission into our world. With this perspective, we can indeed rejoice in our sufferings.

Ministry to those who suffer. As I have emphasized, much human suffering is the consequence either of other people's actions or of sin in general. One of the primary ways that Christians are called to reflect the Son's entrance into our fallen world is through our ministry to those in the world who suffer greatly. Jesus showed compassion to the poor, the outcasts of society, the sick, and others, and he calls us to do the same. Perhaps Jesus' most haunting words on this subject come in Matthew 25, as he tells the parable of the sheep and the goats. Listen again to these familiar words, which come just after Jesus commends the sheep on his right: "Then the righteous will answer him, 'Lord, when did we see you hungry and feed you, or thirsty and give you something to drink? When did we see you a stranger and invite you in, or needing clothes and clothe you? When did we see you sick or in prison and go to visit you?' The King will reply, 'I tell you the truth, whatever you did for one of the least of these brothers of mine, you did for me'" (Mt 25:37-40).

There is disagreement on whether the phrase "the least of these brothers of mine" refers to all people or to believers, but my purpose here is neither to address that issue nor to describe the many ways we should and do serve others. Rather, my purpose is to call attention to the link between the "least" and Christ. We should not interpret this connection as implying that in some sense, the least are Christ. Jesus is not identifying himself with the persons per se; he is identifying an action done for those persons with an action done directly for him. Why does he make this identification? In light of the issues we have considered in this book, one may say that our service to others (whether believers or the people in general) is a reflection of Christ's service of the world and thus a reflection of Christ's relationship to the Father as that relationship is manifested to this fallen world. Remember that Jesus began the upper room discourse by claiming that the way the world would know that we are his disciples is by the love we have for one another (Jn 13:35) and that as the discourse continued, Jesus tied that love directly to the eternal love between the Father and himself. If this passage in Matthew 25 is talking about serving believers, then it directly ties to that discussion in John's Gospel. We are called to reflect the Father's love for the Son, and part of the way we do that is by serving the least of the believers—the neediest, the ones who are loneliest, the ones who suffer the most in this fallen world. If this passage is referring to service to all people (not just believers), then the major point still holds. We share in and reflect the Son's love for the world by the way we serve the neediest of the world's people.

From this brief discussion, we see that for Christians, suffering represents a privilege and an opportunity. Our suffering strengthens the bond between Christ and ourselves, because our suffering mirrors Christ's willingness to enter into and suffer for this world. Our ministry to others who suffer reflects Christ's ministry to the world, as that ministry grows out of his relationship to the Father. We remain in and reflect the Father-Son relationship by the ways we respond to the suffering that characterizes this fallen world.

ANTICIPATING THE CULMINATION OF HISTORY

If human life was originally meant to reflect the eternal relationship between the Father and the Son, and if Christian life today (especially Christian suffering) reflects the manifestation of the Father-Son relationship in time and in a fallen world, then Christian life is also called to anticipate the future reality when this world will be transformed. The study of the last things (called "eschatology," from the Greek word *eschaton*, meaning "the end") is one of the most controversial parts of Christian theology. I do not intend to discuss any of the great controversies here, but instead I would like to call attention to what is not controversial but rather is clear in Scripture: In the great drama of redemption, all the arrows point down, not up. To say this more plainly, at no point in the biblical panorama is redemption a matter of our rising up to achieve a higher condition ourselves. Instead, at every point, God comes down to us, and at every point, this world is the focus of God's gracious activity. God initially created this world for humanity and gave the first human beings a share in the communion of the Trinity in this world. After the Fall, God gave his promise that in this world he would act to bring about redemption. That redemptive action began as the Son personally came down to this world to live, die and be raised so as to give us a share in his own relationship to his Father. When the Son returned to the Father, he sent the Spirit to this world to dwell personally within believers, thus uniting us to the Trinity. Thus far the redemptive arrows have pointed downward, as God has acted in this world, and the Son and Spirit have personally come to this world to unite us to the Trinity.

Scripture also clearly teaches that in the next great redemptive event (yet to happen), the Son will come down a second time to this world. Of the twenty-seven New Testament books, twenty-three (all except Galatians, Philemon, 2 John and 3 John) explicitly mention the return of Christ. See in particular Jesus' statement that he will return in glory with his holy angels during his discussion of the costs of discipleship (Mt 16:27; Mk 8:38; Lk 9:26), his lengthy discussion of his return during his discourse on the Mount of Olives outside Jerusalem three days before his crucifixion (Mt 24; Mk 13; Lk 21) and his affirmation to the high priest during his trial that he will return (Mt 26:64; Mk 14:62).[6] Clearly the Bible indicates that Jesus the Messiah will come to earth again. Just as the arrow has pointed down at the incarnation, so the arrow will point down again as the Son returns to this world.

Finally, Scripture indicates that at the close of history God the Father will bring his dwelling place, heaven itself, down to this world. The closing words of Isaiah's prophecy (Is 65:17–66:24) indicate this, and the closing words of the whole Bible (Rev 21–22) echo the words of Isaiah. Just after John sees the vision of judgment in Revelation 20:11-15, he writes:

> Then I saw a new heaven and a new earth, for the first heaven and the first earth had passed away, and there was no longer any sea. I saw the Holy City, the new Jerusalem, coming down out of heaven from God, prepared as a bride beautifully dressed for her husband. And I heard a loud voice from the throne saying, "Now the dwelling of God is with men, and he will live with them. They will be his people, and God himself will be with them and be their God. He will wipe every tear from their eyes. There will be no more death or mourning or crying or pain, for the old order of things has passed away." He who was seated on the throne said, "I am making everything new!" Then he said, "Write this down, for these words are trustworthy and true." He said to me: "It is done. I am the Alpha and the Omega, the Beginning and the End. To

---

[6]See also Acts 1:11; Col 3:4; 1 Thess 4:13–5:11; 2 Thess 1:5–2:12; Tit 2:13; Jas 5:8; 2 Pet 3:1-13; 1 Jn 3:2; Rev 1:7.

him who is thirsty I will give to drink without cost from the spring of the water of life. He who overcomes will inherit all this, and I will be his God and he will be my son." (Rev 21:1-7)

We should notice that several of the themes I have considered in this book figure prominently in this passage. Each believer will be God's son/child, and God will be with his people to live among them and be their God. He will give us the water of life freely and without cost. In addition, we see here a striking assertion of the radical newness of heaven and earth—the old order will have passed away and all things will have been transformed.

But most striking of all is the fact that God will not bring us up to himself in heaven; he will bring heaven itself down to the renewed earth to complete his redemptive work of dwelling with us. First the Father sent the Son down; then the Father and Son sent the Spirit down. Later God will send the Son again. And finally, stunningly, the Father will come down, bringing heaven and all the heavenly host with him. From beginning to end, this world is the focus of God's activity, and God comes down to accomplish his redemptive work among us. As stunning as it is to think that God chooses to give us a share in his own intratrinitarian fellowship, it is equally stunning to recognize that God's final act will be to change his address in order to dwell with us in the world he created for us originally, a world that he will re-create for us at the end of history.

These truths are clear in Scripture and were clear to the early church. In fact, in the sidebar on the next page, Irenaeus argues that one cannot assign the blessings Scripture describes to a merely heavenly paradise; one must understand them as pertaining to the reconstituted earth, to this world. Nevertheless, the fact that ultimately the dwelling place of believers will be in this world is surprisingly underemphasized in contemporary evangelical preaching. We tend to focus a great deal on our being taken up to heaven rather than on heaven's being brought down to us. And there are biblical reasons why we do this. For example, in the upper room discourse that has played such an important part in this book, Jesus says that he is going to the Father and will prepare a place for the disciples there (Jn 14:1-3). In the parable of the rich man and Lazarus, Jesus implies that departed believers reside outside this world (Lk 16:22). Jesus promises the repentant thief on the cross that he will be with him in paradise (Lk 23:43). But although it is true that believers who die during the current age will go to heaven (as a different place) to be with God, we need to recognize that such a condition will be temporary, not just for us but even for God. As Revelation 21–22 show, this world is where God and his people will ultimately dwell together.

We need to recognize two major implications of this truth for the task of being Christians in this world now. First, Christianity is not world-rejecting but ultimately world-affirming. Popular presentations of the Christian faith often give us the impression that the material realm is ultimately temporary and unimportant, that life in this physical world is merely a means to a purely spiritual, ethereal existence in heaven later.

Irenaeus on the Earthly Dwelling of Believers in Eternity (ca. 180):

For as it is God who raises up man, so also does man truly rise from the dead, and not allegorically, as I have shown repeatedly. And as he rises actually, so also shall he be actually disciplined beforehand for incorruption, and shall go forwards and flourish in the times of the kingdom, in order that he may be capable of receiving the glory of the Father. Then, when all things are made new, he shall truly dwell in the city of God. . . . For neither is the substance nor the essence of the creation annihilated (for faithful and true is he who has established it), but "the fashion of the world passeth away"; that is, those things among which transgression has occurred, since man has grown old in them. And therefore this [present] fashion has been formed temporary, God foreknowing all things. . . . But when this [present] fashion [of things] passes away, and man has been renewed and flourishes in an incorruptible state, so as to preclude the possibility of becoming old, [then] there shall be the new heaven and the new earth, in which man shall remain [continually], always holding fresh converse with God.

Ag. Her., bk. 5, chap. 35, par. 3; chap. 36, par. 1 (ANF, vol. 1, 566-67)

But such presentations do not do justice to the way the Bible closes, and they do not do justice to the Christian teaching on the goodness of the created world, the reality of the incarnation or the resurrection of the body. It is a serious distortion of the Christian faith to reduce it to pie in the sky, to treat the believer's life as a flight from this world or to deny that God is at work transforming this world to prepare it for the day when he will bring heaven down to this world eternally.

The second implication of what I am considering here—closely related to the first—is that in Christianity, the believer's life in this world has direct continuity with the life we will live eternally. Some religions call their adherents to give up x, y and z now in order to get x, y and z in another world later. But Christianity is not like this. Instead, when our faith calls us to give up x, it is because y is better not only in a future world but in this one as well. Christian life is the task of beginning to live now in the way we will live perfectly later, in the new heavens and new earth that God will bring about at the end of history. One of the movements from the early church that can help us to learn this lesson is, ironically, monasticism. Protestants are often critical of monasticism because we believe that the monks and nuns were abandoning both the church and the world in order to aspire to a better world themselves, without much concern for the people they were leaving behind. And while it is true that there was a world-rejecting element in monasticism, I think monasticism at its best has followed a different pattern. Rather than being a group of elitists who sought to rise up to God on their own and who cared little for the rest of humanity, the monks (at least some of the monks) understood their lives as a particular kind of calling—not the only way to serve God but one of the important ways. This particular calling was that of anticipating the direct communion with God and with other believers that all Christians would share in eternity.

One of the best illustrations of this comes from John Cassian, an early fifth-century monastic leader in southern France. In the sidebar on the next page, Cassian discusses how one can most fully deepen the union with God which will characterize the age to come. He says that the monk has already been designated a member of Christ and already possesses the pledge of union which joins him to the body of Christ.

The monk's desire for perfection grows out of the fact that he has already been given this seal, and his goal is to anticipate in the present time the blessed way of life that the saints will have in the future age. In that age, all believers will be fully dedicated to the contemplation of God and will be perfected in their communion with him. The monk's special role is to dedicate himself completely in the present to the task

---

John Cassian on the Present and Future Life of Believers (ca. 425):
No one will arrive at the fullness of this measure in the world to come except the person who has reflected on it and been initiated into it in the present and who has tasted it while still living in this world; who, having been designated a most precious member of Christ, possesses in this flesh the pledge of that union through which he is able to be joined to Christ's body; who desires only one thing, thirsts for one thing, and always directs not only every deed but even every thought to this one thing, so that he may already possess in the present what has been pledged him and what is spoken of with regard to the blessed way of life of the holy in the future—that is, that "God may be all in all" to him.

Confer., bk. 7, chap. 6 (ACW, vol. 57, 253-54)

---

that will belong to all Christians in eternity, and in this way, the monastery serves as an emblem of the coming age.

What is true of monasteries is also true in different ways of all Christian communities. All of us are called to anticipate the future age in which the entire church will gather to worship God and to share in the fellowship of the Trinity. There are many different ways we do this in the present, many different callings, and one should not imagine that one particular kind of Christian life is normative for all Christians. To live a life of intense concentration on the persons of the Trinity, such as that which Cassian followed, is one way to reflect the coming age. To live a life of active dedication to justice, to the transformation of societies according to Christian principles is another way, because transformed, just societies are also reflections of the life of the Trinity. To live a life of dedication to missions and the extension of the church is obviously another way to anticipate the time when people from every nation will worship the true God. In these and other varied ways, Christians reflect the life of the Trinity and anticipate the ultimate transformation of this world that God will bring about at the end of history.

CONCLUSIONS

This chapter has dealt with only a few aspects of Christian life. We have seen that one may fruitfully understand the distinction between justification and sanctification in the context of the patristic understanding of participation. The righteousness that believers gain through sanctification is no more our own than the righteousness we have been given through justification. In both cases the righteousness belongs to Christ, and we participate in and reflect that righteousness when we participate in him and reflect his relationship to his Father. Furthermore, we have seen that Christian life involves the direct cultivation of believers' relationships to Christ. The Bible's primary imagery for the cultivation of these relationships is that of eating and drinking, and we saw that the early church placed as much emphasis on feeding on Christ through the Eucharist as it did on reading the Bible and prayer. Furthermore, we saw that reflection of the intratrinitarian relationship in this fallen world involves suffering for us as well as for Christ and that we can rejoice in this suffering because of the way it deepens our union with Christ. Finally, we saw that sharing in the life of the Trinity involves anticipating the transformation God will bring about in this world at the end of history, when the Father will come down to a renewed earth to complete his work.

★ ★ ★

With this chapter I also bring the book as a whole to a close. As I stated in the preface, I have made no attempt to be comprehensive, and I ask you again to remember that my silence in this book about a given theo-

logical point does not at all imply that it is unimportant. But under the
tutelage of the church fathers, I have sought to lay out the big picture
of Christian theology, the scarlet thread running through what sometimes seems to be a labyrinth of confusing ideas. The Fathers expressed
this scarlet thread using the Greek word *theōsis,* a word that is so easy
to misunderstand that we today should probably not use it, but nevertheless a word that, properly understood, conveys to us a profound
truth—the fact that human life is intimately connected to the life of
God. We have seen that different patristic theologians drew the connections between divine life and human life in somewhat different
ways, and I have argued that the most fruitful and biblical way to link
the two is to understand divine life primarily in terms of the eternal
relationship between the Father, Son and Spirit. The strand of thought
that understood *theōsis* in this way was represented by many church
fathers (I believe it was the consensus, at least in the fourth and fifth
centuries), among whom Irenaeus of Lyons, Athanasius of Alexandria,
Augustine of Hippo and Cyril of Alexandria have influenced me the
most.

With the help of these four and other Fathers as well, I have argued
that we can understand and appreciate the various aspects of Christian
teaching and Christian life in relation to the fundamental relationship
between the Father and the Son. God created us to share in this relationship and gave us a share in the communion of the Trinity at creation. This is the primary thing that we lost through the Fall. God's
promise after the Fall, around which one may organize the entire history and teaching of the Old Testament, was ultimately a promise that
the Son of God would come to bring human beings back into a share
in the communion of the Trinity. In fulfillment of this promise, God
the Son personally entered human life by becoming man while remaining God, and in his human life he showed us both God's love and
perfect human love. At his crucifixion, God the Son bore in his own
person our estrangement from God; as man he was crushed by our sin,
and as man he was forsaken in our place by his own Father. Through
his resurrection and ascension, he was restored as man to the fellowship
of the Trinity which he had always shared as God, and in the process

he opened the way for people who are united to him by faith to be restored to fellowship with the Trinity as well. The Holy Spirit, whom the Father and the Son sent to earth, dwells in believers, uniting us to the Son and thus granting us the participation in the Father-Son relationship that became possible through Christ's life, death and resurrection. Through the Spirit, Christians are called to live—both individually and as the church—so as to anticipate the time when God will transform the entire created world and bring his dwelling here to be with his people for eternity.

All of this implies that fundamentally, our task as Christians is not to aspire to some higher or better world, either through our own efforts or with God's help. The effort we put into Christian life is not our attempt to achieve something we do not already have, because God has already given us a share in the Son's relationship to the Father. We are already daughters and sons of God, and we are called to live like sons and daughters by reflecting the relationship of the true Son to his Father. Furthermore, the better world is not some other world than this, but it will be this world itself once God transforms it by removing the effects of sin, restoring it to its pristine glory and even bringing his own dwelling place down into it. As a result, this is where human life ultimately finds its significance. The way life is meant to be is tied to four great realities: who God is as a Trinity of loving persons, how God created the world and humanity within it, how God has redeemed fallen humanity, and how God will transform the world and the lives of his adopted children in eternity. Christian life looks up to the Father-Son relationship, back to both creation and redemption and ahead to the culmination of history, and this web of participation, reflection and anticipation provides the context in which we understand the details of Christian life and recognize their significance. Life as God has always had it, and life as it was meant to be for people, will one day become life as it is for believers. We are called to participate in, reflect and anticipate that life.

Appendix

SUGGESTIONS FOR READING
FOUR CHURCH FATHERS

As I indicated in the preface to this book, my thinking has been most strongly influenced by four major patristic thinkers: Irenaeus, Athanasius, Augustine and Cyril of Alexandria. In the front matter, I have listed the translations from which I quote in the sidebars, but in many cases these translations are inaccessible, prohibitively expensive or difficult to read, and in a few cases, no translations are available. Accordingly, in this appendix I would like to offer some explanation of the writings by these four church fathers and some suggestions for students interested in reading them directly for themselves, in English. Students with the ability and the desire to consult these writings in Greek or Latin may find information about the best available original-language texts of the works in the introductions to the translations I mention below.

IRENAEUS OF LYONS

Today we possess only two of Irenaeus's works, his mammoth refutation of Gnosticism titled *Against Heresies,* and his much shorter instructional manual *Demonstration of the Apostolic Preaching. Against Heresies* survives completely only in a Latin version (Irenaeus wrote in Greek), but there are also substantial fragments of the work extant in Greek. The nineteenth-century English translation of the Latin version found in ANF, vol. 1, 315-567 is still the only complete translation available, although book 1 of the work is available in a more recent translation in ACW, vol. 55. The *Demonstration of the Apostolic Preaching* is extant only in a single Armenian manuscript discovered in 1904. This short work is a much easier entry point into Irenaeus's thought than the longer *Against Heresies*. The translation from which I quote in the book is the most recent and best one:

Irenaeus of Lyons. *On the Apostolic Preaching.* Trans. John Behr. Popular Patristics Series. Crestwood, N.Y.: St. Vladimir's Seminary Press, 1997.

ATHANASIUS OF ALEXANDRIA

Many of Athanasius's works survive, and the most readily accessible place to find English translations of them is in NPNF[2], vol. 4. These are nineteenth-century translations and are difficult to read, but in the case of most writings, nothing newer is available. Interested readers may want to read his festal letters and other personal writings as well as his longer dogmatic treatises. Of the latter, the most important is his *Orations Against the Arians* (NPNF[2], vol. 4, 306-431). Athanasius's most famous work (and the easiest entry point into his thought) is *On the Incarnation of the Word.* The translation from which I quote in the book is the best one, but it is not very affordable. A good, inexpensive translation is the following:

Athanasius. *On the Incarnation.* Popular Patristics Series. Crestwood, N.Y.: St. Vladimir's Seminary Press, 1993.

AUGUSTINE OF HIPPO

We possess more from the pen of Augustine than from any other patristic writer, and there have also been more recent translations of Augustine than of any other theologian from the early church. All of the translations from which I quote in this book are readily available and reasonably priced. Students new to Augustine should probably begin with either the *Confessions* (an autobiographical account of Augustine's conversion, with a great deal of reflection on the Christian life, human psychology and the thought world of his time), the *Enchiridion on Faith, Hope and Love* (a short handbook on Christian theology) or *On Christian Doctrine* (a short work on biblical interpretation and preaching). Interested students may also want to consult his longest works, *On the Trinity* (which also deals with the human mind as an image of the Trinity) and *City of God* (a sweeping view of human history as a conflict between two cities, the city of man and the City of God). Among the many good translations of these works are the following:

Augustine. *Confessions.* Trans. R. S. Pine-Coffin. London: Penguin, 1961.

Augustine. *The Enchiridion on Faith, Hope and Love.* Trans. J. F. Shaw. Ed. Henry Paolucci. Chicago: Gateway, 1996.

Augustine. *On Christian Doctrine.* Trans. D. W. Robertson Jr. The Library of Liberal Arts. New York: Macmillan, 1958.

Augustine. *The Trinity.* Trans. Edmund Hill. The Works of Saint Augustine: A Translation for the Twenty-first Century, vol. 5. New York: New City Press, 1991.

Augustine. *Concerning the City of God Against the Pagans.* Trans. Henry Bettenson. London: Penguin, 1972.

CYRIL OF ALEXANDRIA

Of the four patristic writers on whom I rely most in this book, by far the least accessible is Cyril of Alexandria. His exclusion from the standard series NPNF led to his being neglected for most of the twentieth century. But more recently, as patristics scholars have recognized his importance, more translations of his work have become available. Good places to begin reading Cyril are the following works, all three of which include extended and helpful introductions, as well as translations of several important texts:

McGuckin, John A. *St. Cyril of Alexandria: The Christological Controversy.* Supplements to *Vigiliae Christianae* 23. Leiden: E. J. Brill, 1994.

Russell, Norman, ed. *Cyril of Alexandria.* The Early Church Fathers. London: Routledge, 2000.

Wickham, Lionel R., ed. *St. Cyril of Alexandria: Select Letters*. Oxford Early Christian Texts. Oxford: Oxford University Press, 1983.

Two shorter works by Cyril from the time of the christological controversy are available in paperback editions:

Cyril of Alexandria. *On the Unity of Christ*. Trans. John A. McGuckin. Popular Patristics Series. Crestwood, N.Y.: St. Vladimir's Seminary Press, 1995.

Cyril of Alexandria. *Against Those Who Are Unwilling to Confess That the Holy Virgin Is Theotokos*. Trans. George Dion Dragas. Patristic and Ecclesiastical Texts and Translations. Rollingsford, N.H.: Orthodox Research Institute, 2004.

Cyril's most important work, and surely one of the greatest theological commentaries ever written, is his mammoth *Commentary on John*. However, it is currently available in English only in an extremely archaic nineteenth-century translation. Studying this work is not for the faint of heart, but the rewards are great. Until recently, the translation was not only hard to read but even harder to locate, but it has now been reprinted (but alas, not revised!) as part of the Oriental Orthodox Library.

Cyril, Archbishop of Alexandria. *Commentary on the Gospel According to S. John. Vol. 1: S. John 1-8*. Trans. P. E. Pusey. Library of the Fathers of the Holy Catholic Church, vol. 43. Oxford: James Parker & Co., 1874.

Cyril, Archbishop of Alexandria. *Commentary on the Gospel According to S. John. Vol. 2: S. John 9-21*. Trans. Thomas Randell. Library of the Fathers of the Holy Catholic Church, vol. 48. London: Walter Smith, 1885.

Index of Names and Subjects

Scripture Index

Adam + H.S - Jn 20:20 22 + Gen 2:7 p62
Peace   p 66
SIN   p 99

P190 Cyril on Baptism
192 Baptism + H.S

192 Breathed breath of life = H.S
195-6 Election - Predestination